Lecture Notes in Computer Science 15190

The series Lecture Notes in Computer Science (LNCS), including its subseries Lecture Notes in Artificial Intelligence (LNAI) and Lecture Notes in Bioinformatics (LNBI), has established itself as a medium for the publication of new developments in computer science and information technology research, teaching, and education.

LNCS enjoys close cooperation with the computer science R & D community, the series counts many renowned academics among its volume editors and paper authors, and collaborates with prestigious societies. Its mission is to serve this international community by providing an invaluable service, mainly focused on the publication of conference and workshop proceedings and postproceedings. LNCS commenced publication in 1973.

Marinos Ioannides · Drew Baker ·
Athos Agapiou · Petros Siegkas
Editors

3D Research Challenges in Cultural Heritage V

Paradata, Metadata and Data in Digitisation

 Springer

Editors
Marinos Ioannides ⓘ
Cyprus University of Technology
Limassol, Cyprus

Drew Baker ⓘ
Cyprus University of Technology
Limassol, Cyprus

Athos Agapiou ⓘ
Cyprus University of Technology
Limassol, Cyprus

Petros Siegkas ⓘ
Cyprus University of Technology
Limassol, Cyprus

ISSN 0302-9743   ISSN 1611-3349 (electronic)
Lecture Notes in Computer Science
ISBN 978-3-031-78589-4   ISBN 978-3-031-78590-0 (eBook)
https://doi.org/10.1007/978-3-031-78590-0

This Springer imprint is published by the registered company Springer Nature Switzerland AG
The registered company address is: Gewerbestrasse 11, 6330 Cham, Switzerland

If disposing of this product, please recycle the paper.

Preface

The use of digital technologies especially in the area of three-dimensional (3D) data acquisition is a major step in the documentation, analysis and presentation of cultural heritage. In this book, this technological evolution is well captured by the works of several researchers who have discussed the benefits and risks of 3D digitisation. It is important to note that one of the most crucial elements that contribute to efficiency and credibility of these digital representations is documentation of the workflow. This documentation, known as paradata along with metadata, is critical to the scientific rigour, replicability and sustainability of digital heritage resources. The findings of Luengo et al. (2024) offer a comprehensive analysis of how paradata can be methodologically integrated into the process of digitising-built heritage and how the resulting 3D models can be trusted as reliable sources for further study.

As many authors including Ioannides et al. (2024) have pointed out, paradata is used to document the different decisions, conditions and processes that were involved in the development of models. Contrary to metadata that often refers to the characteristics of the digital object per se, such as size, resolution or format of a file, paradata represents the context of creating the object. This may involve such factors as the conditions under which data was captured, the settings that were used in the software and even the interventions done by the technicians. The significance of such information cannot be overemphasised in Baker (2024) where he postulated that the lack of such documentation undermines the scientific validity of 3D models. Reproducibility and replicability of results are fundamental to scientific inquiry, and paradata offers the necessary openness to accomplish this in the field of digital heritage.

Nevertheless, as numerous researchers have pointed out, the use of paradata in 3D digitisation initiatives is still rather variable. This is well illustrated by the fact that different platforms and researchers have adopted different measures. For instance, although sources such as SketchFab and OpenHeritage offer some information on the 3D models they host, there is a lack of sufficient paradata. As noted by Luengo et al. (2024), there are many aspects that are usually not reported, including the environmental conditions under which data was captured or the specific difficulties that were experienced while converting the data. Such gaps in documentation can lead to important discrepancies that reduce the practical and theoretical value of these digital models for further studies and applications.

One of the major issues that have been noted to affect the use of paradata is the lack of certified procedures for its documentation. This is because each project or platform is likely to have its own approach, and so the whole area is fragmented and it becomes hard to make comparisons and linkages, or even to advance them. This is well described by Cassar (2024) in his research where he stresses the importance of standardisation in the digitalisation of national collections. The absence of such standards not only impacts the quality and accuracy of the digital models but also makes difficult their integration into larger databases or repositories, which is crucial for the large-scale preservation of cultural heritage. While the technical aspects of digitisation, for example the number of polygons or the software used, are usually emphasised, attention to the human factors involved in the process is lacking, as is also pointed out by Huvila (2024) in his reflections on the role of paradata in the process of guaranteeing the credibility and usefulness of digital heritage resources.

In order to overcome these challenges, various suggestions have been made by researchers, including Luengo et al. (2024), which is the development of a general and unified guideline for paradata documentation. This is a framework which can embrace all the methods used in 3D digitisation, including photogrammetry, 3D scanning and Computer-Aided Design (CAD), and at the same time it offers a clear structure that can be used in different platforms and for different projects.

Fieldwork is the backbone of any 3D digitisation project, and therefore strong documentation is crucial. This documentation should comprise a list of all the technicians and researchers and the roles they played. Taking such detailed records means that there would be some level of accountability and it would also be easier to determine where errors might originate from. Furthermore, other factors that surround data capture including temperatures, lighting and other conditions should also be described. These conditions can considerably affect the quality of the data and, therefore, their registration is essential to evaluate the accuracy of the obtained digital models. Furthermore, the equipment that was used during field work, and the actual methods that were used should also be described in detail. Such information is crucial for assessing the strengths and weaknesses of the digital models generated, as Brumana et al. (2024) pointed out in the case of the digitalisation of built heritage through the use of technologies such as LiDAR and photogrammetry.

Even the laboratory phase, in which data gathered during field research is analysed and refined, must be documented meticulously. This should also involve a description of the software that was used in the data processing stage as well as the functions that each program served. Such documentation is important in order to understand the changes that have been made to the data and to make sure that the digital models are correct and can be replicated. In addition, all the changes that are made to the files including conversion to different formats, resizing and other alterations should be recorded to help in evaluating the quality of the final digital models. Another important aspect pointed out by these researchers is error control; it is important to record any errors that are found in the data processing phase and how they were corrected so that the user can know the weaknesses of the digital models and areas that may be recommended for enhancement in other projects.

Beyond the digitisation and creation of 3D heritage assets is the important factor of rights management, which deals with the legal and ethical use of the models. The framework suggested by Luengo et al. (2024) also involves the definition of ownership rights concerning the digital models and indicating the institutions or individuals who are to be considered as authors of the models. This information is important in order to be able to use and distribute the models legally. Any other conditions that may be put in place regarding the use or distribution of the models should also be recorded. Such documentation guarantees that the models are implemented as intended by the creators and the law, which is especially relevant to public heritage institutions, as pointed out by Cassar (2024) in his work on the digitisation of national collections. Furthermore, the DOI number related to the models must be also provided, as well as the information on where they can be found, to guarantee their further availability and reusability.

The suggested guidelines for paradata documentation present a valuable contribution to the development of 3D CH digitisation, the systematic application of which will entail a consistent framework implementation, which increases the scientific credibility of the digital models by making the process of digitisation clear, easily understandable and reproducible. Also, it enables the future reuse of such models in research, education and outreach by offering a record of the context and choices in their development. The work of Luengo et al. (2024), Ioannides et al. (2024) and other scholars in this field is crucial in preparing for such a framework that if adopted can go a long way in enhancing the quality and usefulness of digital heritage assets.

Nevertheless, the creation and implementation of this framework are not without challenges. As highlighted by Huvila et al. (2024), there is a constant need to modify and develop the framework to cope with emerging issues in the field including the incorporation of new digitisation technologies as well as the complexity of the models. Furthermore, there is a need to invest more in rights management and accurate documentation so that in the future digital models can be used both ethically and efficiently. Institutional, research and platform stakeholders must work together to develop and agree on the paradata documentation framework, as well as on the sharing of best practices and experiences.

Finally, it can be stated that the use of 3D data acquisition technologies in digitising cultural heritage provides great potential for preserving and disseminating the history of mankind. However, to achieve these opportunities in full, it is necessary to create and apply the guidelines for documenting the process of digitisation. When paradata is comprehensive and when it is integrated with metadata, the long-term usefulness of digital models is guaranteed, thus increasing their worth to the research, educational and outreach communities. The approach to digital documentation presented in this work is based on the framework developed by the scientific community and the EU Study VIGIE2020/654 on quality in 3D digitisation of tangible cultural heritage and builds upon the work of other scholars in this field, thus providing a solid structure and flexibility for this type of work across various digitisation projects in cultural heritage.

The papers included in this State-of-the-Art Survey were originally submitted to one of two webinars organized by the UNESCO Chair on Digital Cultural Heritage. The double-blind review of the 36 papers originally submitted was carried out by 33 experts in the domain of Digital Cultural Heritage.

Further cooperation and research will remain critical to the development of 3D CH digitisation practice and guaranteeing that digital assets are credible and useful to future generations.

Marinos Ioannides
Drew Baker
Athos Agapiou
Petros Siegkas

Contents

Imperative of Paradata 1
   Isto Huvila

Paradata: The Digital Prometheus 12
   Drew Baker

Integrating Paradata, Metadata, and Data for an Effective Memory Twin
in the Field of Digital Cultural Heritage 24
   Marinos Ioannides, Elena Karittevli, Panayiotis Panayiotou,
   and Drew Baker

Dive into Heritage: Paradata and Metadata in an Immersive Digital
Heritage Experience 36
   Luisa Ammirati, Bethany Watrous, Amira Ftaita, Thomas Rigauts,
   and Michelle de Gruchy

Digital Representations of Cultural Heritage: Enabling the Quality
to Speak for Itself 52
   Mark Mudge and Carla Schroer

Making the Europeana Data Model a Better Fit for Documentation of 3D
Objects 63
   Antoine Isaac, Kate Fernie, Valentina Bachi, Eleftheria Tsoupra,
   Marco Medici, Henk Alkemade, Sander Münster, Valentine Charles,
   and Lianne Heslinga

Publishing and Long-Term Archiving 3D Data in Humanities 75
   Matthieu Quantin, Sarah Tournon, Mehdi Chayani, Xavier Granier,
   and Florent Laroche

Virtual Access to Fossil & Archival Material from the German Tendaguru
Expedition (1909–1913): More Than 100 years of Data-Meta-paradata
Management for Improved Standardisation 89
   Marin Depraetere, Sara Akhlaq, Verónica Díez Díaz, Ina Heumann,
   and Daniela Schwarz

IDOVIR – A New Infrastructure for Documenting Paradata and Metadata
of Virtual Reconstructions 103
   Marc Grellert, Markus Wacker, Jonas Bruschke, Daniel Beck,
   and Wolfgang Stille

Documentation and Publication of Hypothetical Virtual 3D
Reconstructions in the CoVHer Project 115
    Igor Piotr Bajena, Fabrizio Ivan Apollonio, Karol Argasiński,
    Federico Fallavollita, Riccardo Foschi, Jakub Franczuk,
    Krzysztof Koszewski, Piotr Kuroczyński, and Jan Lutteroth

A Metadata/Paradata Design Framework for Historic BIM 127
    Maurice Murphy, Petra Krajacic, Eimear Meegan, Rebecca O. Reilly,
    Garrett Keenaghan, Alain Chenaux, Rafael Fernandes Dionizio,
    and Eloisa DezenKempter

Toward a Trustable Digitisation of Built Heritage: The Role of Paradata 139
    Pedro Luengo, Gerardo Boto Varela, Sergio Coll Pla,
    Agustí Costa Jover, Albert Samper Sosa, and David Vivó Codina

Paradata to Reuse Holistic HBIM Quality Models
in the SCAN-to-HBIM-to-VR Process. The Mausoleum of Cecilia Metella
and the Castrum Caetani 151
    Raffaella Brumana, Stefano Roascio, Dario Attico,
    Maria Radoslavova Gerganova, and Nicola Genzano

Three-Dimensional Reconstruction of an Egyptian *Sāqia*: A Computational
Approach to Preserving Cultural Heritage and Water Management Systems 164
    Jean-Baptiste Barreau

Usable, Useful, Reviewable and Reusable Metadata: From Metadata
and Paradata to UXdata and Back 176
    Erik Champion

Digitising the National Collection 184
    Anthony Cassar

Author Index 197

Imperative of Paradata

Isto Huvila$^{(\boxtimes)}$ 🆔

Department of ALM, Uppsala University, Thunbergsvägen 3H, 75238 Uppsala, Sweden
isto.huvila@abm.uu.se

Abstract. Heritage visualisation has been one of the pioneers in acknowledging the imperative of paradata i.e. that of documenting not only the outputs of knowledge making but also the practices and processes, including decisions and intellectual work underpinning of how they came into being. However, even if the need and technical means to represent such information exist, the practical understanding of how to capture such information remain underdeveloped. The aim of this chapter is to delve into the imperative of paradata as a theoretical and practical challenge and to outline how to get grips with it: what is possible and how, and what is probably unachievable and why. A model of a process for identifying and acquiring usable paradata is outlined and major pitfalls of paradata generation, relating to non-actionable standards and exceeding data cleaning are discussed.

Keywords: paradata · processes · practices · heritage · visualisations · documentation · metadata

1 Introduction

In recent decades, digital research and curation of visual cultural records have advanced significantly, making the past more accessible for research, education, and societal benefit. We have standards and knowledge how to describe assets to make them findable and usable. However, documenting the practices and processes involved in creating, managing, and using these assets has received less attention. Despite early recognition of this need, as highlighted by the London Charter [43], the crucial task of producing and retaining paradata remains unresolved. While we have the means to represent this information, practical approaches for capturing it are still underdeveloped.

This chapter explores the imperative of paradata: the challenges and possibilities of paradata, focusing on its theoretical and practical aspects. It builds on the European Research Council-funded CAPTURE project, which investigates the necessary information about the creation, processing, and use of research data to ensure future reusability [20]. Drawing on research on research data—in broad sense, diverse materials and ingredients of research—the outlook in this chapter is inherently both narrower and broader than that of its specific focus on heritage visualisation. It aligns with views that emphasise the use of visualisation in scholarship rather than just public communication (e.g., [13, 40]) and has implications for this chapter and its scope especially in how visualisations—understood here broadly as visual (re)presentations of *referents* (incl. e.g.,

© The Author(s) 2025
M. Ioannides et al. (Eds.): 3D Research Challenges in Cultural Heritage V, LNCS 15190, pp. 1–11, 2025.
https://doi.org/10.1007/978-3-031-78590-0_1

tangible or intangible things, processes and practices the visualisations visualise) of any kind—are considered as part of an ongoing continuum rather than the final product of a process.

2 Problem: Documenting Practices and Processes

The main issue with heritage visualisations is that while descriptive metadata indicates what the visualisation and its underpinning data are about, it does not explain their underpinning creation processes, data handling, or decision-making. A lack of thorough understanding of these aspects hinders the assessment of their utility for research, education, or public display. A spectator can recognise that a visualisation depicts a tangible object, ritual practice, or archaeological process without paradata. Paradata is needed, however, to understand how a visualisation relates to its *referents* i.e. what it depicts. Without paradata it is impossible to know, for example, how detailed or accurate a visualisation is in relation to what it visualises, whose decisions led to the particular kind of visualisation, how the decisions were premised, and consequently, how and to what purposes the visualisation can be used.

The problem itself, similarly to the general conundrum of the reuse of research documentation [12], can be framed in from multiple perspectives. A predominant critique is to call attention to the inadequacy of documentation and how a visualisation should be completed with sufficient metadata *and* paradata (e.g., [10, 14]). Another perspective to framing the problem is to ascribe it to suboptimal infrastructures and technologies used to communicate the visualisations, or to explain it as a competence or literacy problem [32]. Further, at least a part of the problem can also be traced back to the medium itself. Visualisations and especially highly realistic three-dimensional images can be intuitive for conveying information in time and space but at the same time, they might be less intuitive for communicating other types of information such as abstract concepts [4]. Also the interpretative ambiguity of visualisations has raised concerns [21].

The core issue with practice and process documentation in visualisations is a mismatch of knowledge between creators and users. Often, it is assumed that once a visualisation is handed off from creators to its users, it conveys all necessary information. In reality, this handoff is rarely complete and the disconnects in the continuum require substantial efforts to bridge them (e.g., [17]). Much like the concept of a "discontinuum" [8] used to describe the use of museum collections, the similarly patchy chain of 'making and taking' [23] visualisations mean that they are rarely ready-to-use assets [21]. A more apt metaphor could be, besides discontinuum and handoffs [8], to compare the process to sowing a plant. We can imagine a creator of visualisation leaving behind a seed for future knowledge making. Any secondary users need to find it and have some experience and documentation often far from adequate to directly understand how to grow it. The visualisation has to be sown, watered and grown for the purposes of reuse with a lot of care and consideration.

3 Paradata as a Solution

The nature of the problem of (in)adequate information on practices and processes underpinning heritage visualisations affects potential solutions. Paradata itself is a volatile concept with various definitions [41]. Broadly, it refers to data or information about processes and practices. Such a framing aligns with the undoubtedly most cited definition of paradata in the heritage visualisation field in the London Charter for the Computer-based Visualisation of Cultural Heritage [43]. The baseline of these and comparable definitions is to devise paradata as an informational concept that in turn imply that related solutions are similarly informational.

The informational and documentary nature of paradata can be contrasted to the concept of digital twin. Even if digital twin can be conceptualised in informational, paradata-like terms, for example how Niccolucci and colleagues define it as "the complex of information about digital counterparts of real-world heritage objects, both material and immaterial ones" [37], the two concepts operate on different assumptions. Paradata is a documentary concept focused on capturing processes and practices, while digital twins aim to create functional replicas that replicate entire systems. (cf. [16, 37]. Although paradata can underpin digital twins (e.g., [37, 44]) and vice versa. At the same time, however, they represent distinct approaches to engaging with their referents. Digital twins seek to *encode complete system explanations*, while paradata is oriented through *explaining* providing varying levels of transparency and understanding of practices and processes. Consequently, paradata's narrower explanatory ambition allows for more flexibility and diverse opportunities in addressing different aspects and elements of the problem of the adequacy of documenting practices and processes.

Another, however, doubtfully useful distinction to articulate understanding paradata is between paradata and metadata. In the literature, it has a become almost a trope to refer to metadata *and* paradata (e.g., [3, 7, 12]) as two, at least outwardly, distinct forms of second-order data, respectively about data (metadata) and practices and processes (paradata) (e.g., [34, 42]). This dichotomy highlights the importance of documenting both data and its related processes. However, it oversimplifies the broader landscape of information relevant to practices and processes, especially in creating heritage visualisations. Additionally, this distinction struggles to capture the continuous and evolving nature of information, knowledge, and artifacts, which are always in the process of being made rather than being static [23].

A key question about paradata concerns its implications. Literature suggests that paradata is essential for the reusability, reproducibility, and understandability of research and assets, and for assessing their reliability and trustworthiness [9, 12, 22]. In heritage visualisation, paradata is promoted for ensuring the reusability and reproducibility of 3D visualisations and for drawing reliable conclusions. It also helps assess the reliability and suitability of visualisations for their intended purposes [2, 43]. The growing collections of 3D visualisations [33, 36] of tangible heritage objects highlight the need for adequate paradata to avoid documentation that may appear self-explanatory [21] but risk remaining insufficient.

While paradata literature often links it to the quality of its referents—such as reliability, trust, and reproducibility (cf. [1, 39])—it may be more fruitful to view paradata through different lenses. Instead of being a straightforward measure of quality, paradata reveals both more and less: Less in that it might not clearly indicate whether a heritage visualisation is "good" or trustworthy, but more in how it provides deeper insights into the visualisation, its creation process, and beyond, offering more than just evidence of adequacy.

Instead of focusing solely on quality, the fundamental aspect of good paradata is its ability to make the practices and processes behind its referent *transparent* to diverse stakeholders. While paradata should ideally make these processes understandable, achieving full understandability is often impractical, especially with complex technologies like artificial intelligence [9] but also with a much broader variety of algorithmic processes and human practices often extremely difficult to explain in detail to outsiders [22]. The key question is not whether paradata is (an indication) of good or bad quality, but how complete it is for specific purposes and stakeholders. The same applies naturally to its referents. Similarly, the quality of a visualisation is tied to its intended use, making it better or worse rather than absolutely good or bad.

Finally, the complexity, incompleteness and situated nature of paradata means also that to be useful for everyone, it clearly needs to be everyone's concern and responsibility that there is relevant paradata for all of its key stakeholders. All means literally all from researchers developing visualisations to those who are using them, data managers, funders, policy makers, and everyone else who is engaging with heritage visualisations in the society.

4   Paradata in Practice

After delving into the problem paradata is envisioned to solve and what can be expected of paradata as a solution, the next step is to proceed into probing what it takes to make paradata work in practice. In the following, this chapter will review recent findings on paradata needs, types, and how user requirements align with available information.

4.1   Matching Needs and Paradata Types

The diversity, complexity, and situatedness of paradata mean that effectively operationalising it requires understanding the creators' and users' ideas about what types of paradata are helpful, what information is available, and how it supports users' goals. The same caveats that apply to the notion of information need [38] are relevant also to the concept of 'paradata need'. Although people may express clear needs for paradata-like information, these needs are subjective and situational, often reflecting deeper human needs beyond just being informed about specific practices or processes. Acknowledging this, the CAPTURE project has explored what people say they need to know when they are referring to paradata-like information [5, 18] and what types of paradata (or paradata-like information) is included in research data (e.g., [6]), standards [7], guidelines [29] and documentation [6, 24, 26, 27, 29–31].

As per desiderata, we have identified four major categories of paradata needs relating to research data including scope paradata, provenance paradata, methods paradata, and knowledge organisation and representation paradata [5]. When collated with the literature on heritage visualisations, the expectations of problems paradata has been suggested to solve (incl. [43]) have many similarities with the identified categories. Transposed to heritage visualisation context, the four categories of paradata needs [5] can be deduced to include at least following information:

- *Scope of visualisation*: how the visualised entity was selected and framed, what it covers, what methods were used in collecting initial data);
- *Provenance*: the disciplinary origins of data collection and making of the visualisation, its epistemological premises, and underpinning rationales;
- *Methods*: used in creating the visualisation, what decisions were made;
- *Knowledge representation and organisation*: how the visualisation represents and organises the knowledge it aims to convey, what standards and formats were used to represent and structure knowledge and information, what semantics were used for representation, and for example, how different pieces of information were linked to each other.

Similarly to how the research on research data related paradata needs can help to understand basic needs related to heritage visualisation paradata, earlier studies of paradata types illustrate what types of information can inform of practices and processes in the same context. Beyond narrative descriptions and annotations (e.g., [15, 35]) useful paradata includes literature on the visualisation, photographs, diagrams, methods, tools, actors, and even the visualisations themselves, which can reveal traces of their creation processes [6, 30, 31].

Although much paradata exists within current documentation and visualisations, the main challenge lies in its fragmentation, making it hard to identify, locate, and grasp. The complexity and diversity of the documentation, while enriching, complicate its management [22] and integration within formal data management systems and infra infrastructures.

4.2 Documenting Enough, Not Too Much

Another key conundrum of working with paradata is the lack of clear limits on perspectives and how meticulously practices can be documented. However, there are practical limits on resources for meta-level documentation. The informativeness of documentation does not increase linearly with its amount. The key is to document enough, not too much, and focus on useful information.

Documenting "useful" information may sound obvious, but it is challenging in practice. Often, information is documented based on documenters' assumptions without considering its actual usefulness for others. Another common mistake is assuming that what is useful to one person will be useful to others. The CAPTURE project survey indicates that while data creators and users may agree on general documentation aspects, their ideas of useful documentation can differ significantly [25]. Documenting is time-consuming, expensive, and often boring, and excessive demands of the extent of documentation can reduce its quality. Lack of time and resources can result in insufficient detail. Therefore, it is critical to decide at the outset what to document and focus efforts on supporting specific scenarios, identifying likely users, and determining necessary paradata [19]. For the same reason, as stipulated in the London Charter [43], it is essential that documentation is planned in advance with adequate resources.

To facilitate the *reuse* of visualisations through paradata, it is crucial to determine what paradata is needed in formal search metadata for *findability* and what information is needed when users start interacting with the visualizations. Planning what to document is essential, but it is also vital to reflect on the usefulness of the generated paradata and identify missing critical aspects. The process of generating paradata and determining necessary documentation should be iterative, without a definite, predetermined end.

4.3 A Paradata Documentation Process

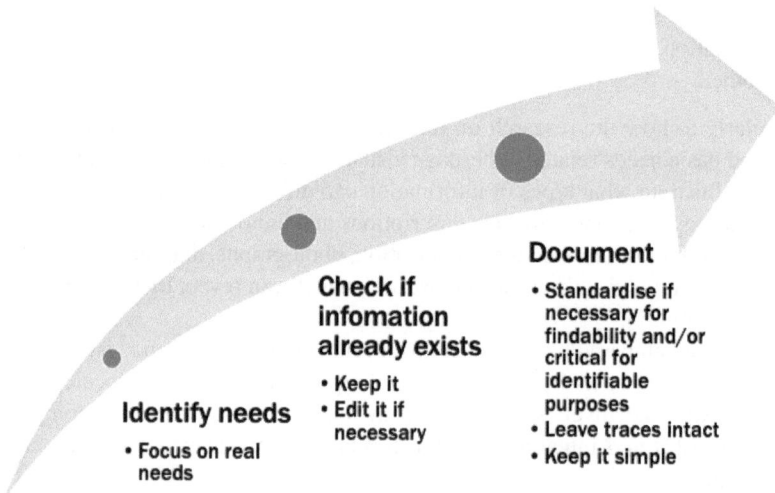

Fig. 1. A model for paradata documentation process.

Even if many of the key considerations regarding paradata are specific to individual contexts and domains, it is possible to formulate certain general recommendations on the basis of the research so far. The most crucial steps and critical considerations in the process of generating paradata can be modelled in terms of a three-step process model (Fig. 1).

The first step is to identify specific facets of the practices and processes underpinning a visualisation, focusing on well-documented or foreseeable needs linked to detailed and real, or at least realistic, scenarios rather than assumptions. Second, to avoid redundancy, it is crucial to verify if necessary information already exists in some form already exists or can be deduced from the visualisation or its data. If the necessary information is available, it should not be generated again unless it is important to capture and record for additional viewpoints or interpretations. It might be enough to link the existing information to the visualisation itself and other documentation, or if necessary for the sake of making the information searchable, to produce a corresponding standardised (metadata) description and incorporate it in formal repository information structures. The final step is to document remaining necessary aspects not covered elsewhere, using appropriate formats and level of detail. Formal standards should be used to improve findability and machine operability, while other documentation can be tailored to individual workflows and perspectives.

5   Avoiding Pitfalls

When outlining a workflow for identifying paradata needs and matching them with relevant formats, there are multiple pitfalls. When outlining a workflow for identifying paradata needs and matching them with relevant formats, there are multiple pitfalls. Beyond the inherent difficulty of dealing with the contextuality and complexity of paradata, and determining what is needed and feasible, two major pitfalls are related to solutions rather than the problem itself. First, while paradata standards are needed, the nature of paradata makes it hard to standardise, and difficult-to-use standards risk undermining the generation of relevant paradata. Second, the complexity and multimodality of paradata suggest that instead of focusing solely on well-formed documentation, there is lot to win by making use of the informativeness of the complexity itself.

5.1   Actionable Standards are Crucial

While paradata is acknowledged and incorporated to some degree in several documentation standards, the mechanisms of how it is proposed to be represented vary between being extremely complex and highly simple and schematic. The major conceptual reference model in cultural heritage context, the CIDOC-CRM with accompanying extensions provide highly advanced technical means to represent comprehensive information on practices and processes [11]. At the opposite end of the spectrum, some standards, for example the CARARE metadata schema, incorporate a single free-text field called paradata [15]. While there is nothing inherently wrong with either of the approaches, both the complexity and simplicity of approaches limit their usability for an average maker or user of heritage visualisations. Both complexity and unspecificity can make a standard difficult to use [7] with a risk of leading to inconsistencies and over-documentation of such aspects of processes that are self-evident and easily documentable according to the standards, and under-documentation of others.

Moreover, current standards and specifications lack clear guidelines on what should be documented. On-going efforts to develop and test means to incorporate paradata in project-specific documentation schemes and the basic research comparable to that in the CAPTURE project are important steps to be taken but there is also a dire need for concerted work across domains to bring together the emerging general and project specific knowledge of paradata and make it actionable in within and across domains for shared understanding, collaboration and interoperability. This applies also to heritage visualisation where despite long engagement with paradata, there is no shared understanding of what needs to be documented to make visualisations transparent. Making paradata work requires substantial, case-based efforts where standards development is integrated with ongoing visualisation work rather than top-down approaches focused on individual stakeholders. Without such a cross-cutting approach, there is a major risk that the standards may support individual stakeholders, for example, visualisers, management or long-term preservation, but fail to support the others and paradata chain as a whole.

5.2 Data Cleaning Impoverishes Paradata

The complexity and multimodality of paradata mean that standardisation can lead to simplification and information loss. Cleaning data by normalising and standardising expressions and values, or for example, omitting working documents and earlier versions from preservation can hinder the ability to trace the processes behind heritage visualisations. Redundancy is crucial in paradata, as unruly secondary material often holds significant information value [22]. Despite the cost and burden of maintaining large amounts of material, the great advantage of tapping into redundancy rather than generation of new paradata is that the existing data is already there and does not need to be generated anew.

A parallel advantage of exploiting trace data [30] is that the residues and redundancy are generated during the visualisation process instead of being a retrospective reconstruction of past practices and processes. Traces can also mediate unconscious working knowledge that is embedded in the practice or process itself not included in formal *post hoc* documentation. There might also be traces of such phenomenon that are largely intangible and different to describe in a comprehensive manner. Thus, traces are a crucial complement to formal schematic paradata (cf. [28]). Incidentally, even much of the formal paradata paradata often straddles the line between tangible and intangible, relying on abstractions and simplifications. Even standardised verbal descriptions require a good command of terminology and the connotations of terms similarly to how a text or video recording is best understood by someone with first-hand knowledge of described practices or processes.

Finally, the redundancy, complexity and dirtiness of the abundance of artefacts including formal documentation and diverse traces of practices and processes that form an assemblage of resources approachable as paradata unfold as a critique and a reminder of the limits of practice and process documentation. Documentation and paradata are always partial and incomplete renderings of their referents. Nevertheless, even if practices or processes cannot be fully stabilised, approximations can make them more intelligible for for current and future use.

6   Conclusion

We have an imperative to deal with paradata. If we fail, we end up having piles and piles of heritage visualisations that are only marginally useful if usable at all. This is especially true with visualisations that are not meant to be end-products but means, starting points or material—data—for future knowledge making. What makes dealing with the conundrum of paradata exceedingly difficult is that with paradata, we are not dealing with a clearly delimited and easily solvable problem. While there are technical standards that could be used to represent paradata, there is a lack of social and cultural standards—lines of appropriate action and strategies—of what is required for the transparency of many of the predominant cultural artefacts of the contemporary information sphere including research data and heritage visualisation [22]. Just adding a couple of additional data points to a visualisation does not do the job. We have to understand and preserve both formal standardised and informal information that are both critical elements of paradata that aspires to be complete enough to be usable for as many relevant stakeholders as feasible and as long time into the future as possible.

Acknowledgements. This work has received funding from the European Research Council (ERC) under the European Union's Horizon 2020 research and innovation programme grant agreement No 818210 as a part of the project CApturing Paradata for documenTing data creation and Use for the REsearch of the future (CAPTURE).

Disclosure of Interests. The author has no competing interests to declare that are relevant to the content of this article.

References

1. Amico, N., Ronzino, P., Felicetti, A., Niccolucci, F.: Quality management of 3D cultural heritage replicas with CIDOC-CRM. In: Alexiev, V., Ivanov, V., Grinberg, M. (eds.) Proceedings of the Workshop Practical Experiences with CIDOC CRM and Its Extensions (2013)
2. Bentkowska-Kafel, A., Denard, H.: Introduction. In: Bentkowska-Kafel, A., Denard, H., Baker, D. (eds.) Paradata and Transparency in Virtual Heritage, pp. 1–4. Ashgate, Farnham (2012)
3. Bentkowska-Kafel, A., MacDonald, L.W.: Digital Techniques for Documenting and Preserving Cultural Heritage. Arc Humanities Press, Kalamazoo (2017)
4. Blaise, J.Y., Dudek, I.: 3D as a Content, 3D as a Metaphor (2009)
5. Börjesson, L., Huvila, I., Sköld, O.: Information needs on research data creation. Inf. Res. **27**(Special Issue), isic2208 (2022). https://doi.org/10.47989/irisic2208
6. Börjesson, L., Sköld, O., Friberg, Z., Löwenborg, D., Pálsson, G., Huvila, I.: Re-purposing excavation database content as paradata: an explorative analysis of paradata identification challenges and opportunities. KULA Knowl. Creation Dissemination Preserv. Stud. **6**(3), 1–18 (2022). https://doi.org/10.18357/kula.221
7. Börjesson, L., Sköld, O., Huvila, I.: The politics of paradata in documentation standards and recommendations for digital archaeological visualisations. Digit. Cult. Soc. **6**(2), 191–220 (2020). https://doi.org/10.14361/dcs-2020-0210
8. Buchanan, S.: The assemblage of repository and museum work in archaeological curation. Inf. Res. **24**(2), 816 (2019)
9. Cameron, S., Franks, P., Hamidzadeh, B.: Positioning paradata: a conceptual frame for AI processual documentation in archives and recordkeeping contexts. J. Comput. Cult. Heritage **16**, 3594728 (2023). https://doi.org/10.1145/3594728
10. Carrillo Gea, J.M., Toval, A., Alemán, J.L.F., Nicolás, J., Flores, M.: The London charter and the seville principles as sources of requirements for e-archaeology systems development purposes. Virtual Archaeol. Rev. **4**(9), 205–211 (2013)
11. Crofts, N., Doerr, M., Gill, T., Stead, S., Stiff, M. (eds.): Definition of the CIDOC Conceptual Reference Model. ICOM/CIDOC Documentation Standards Group, Continued by the CIDOC CRM Special Interest Group (2007)
12. D'Andrea, A.: I Dati Archeologici Nella Società Dell'informazione. UniorPress, Napoli (2023)
13. Dell'Unto, N., Landeschi, G., Apel, J., Poggi, G.: 4D recording at the trowel's edge: using three-dimensional simulation platforms to support field interpretation. J. Archaeol. Sci. Rep. **12**, 632–645 (2017). https://doi.org/10.1016/j.jasrep.2017.03.011

14. Denard, H.: Implementing best practice in cultural heritage visualisation: the London charter. In: Good Practice in Archaeological Diagnostics: Non-invasive Survey of Complex Archaeological Sites, pp. 255–268. Springer, Cham (2013)
15. Fernie, K., Gavrilis, D., Angelis, S.: The CARARE Metadata Schema, v.2.0. CARARE Project (2013)
16. Hermon, S., Niccolucci, F., Bakirtzis, N., Gasanova, S.: A heritage digital twin ontology-based description of giovanni baronzio's "crucifixion of christ" analytical investigation. J. Cult. Herit. **66**, 48–58 (2024)
17. Huvila, I.: Ecology of archaeological information work. In: Huvila, I. (ed.) Archaeology and Archaeological Information in the Digital Society, pp. 121–141. Routledge, London (2018)
18. Huvila, I.: Information-making-related information needs and the credibility of information. Inf. Res. **25**(4), isic2002 (2020). https://doi.org/10.47989/irisic2002
19. Huvila, I.: Use-oriented information and knowledge management: information production and use practices as an element of the value and impact of information. J. Inf. Knowl. Manag. **18**(4), 1950046 (2020)
20. Huvila, I.: Documenting archaeological work processes for enabling future reuse of data: the CAPTURE project. Eur. Archaeologist **69**, 8–10 (2021)
21. Huvila, I.: Monstrous hybridity of social information technologies: through the lens of photorealism and non-photorealism in archaeological visualization. Inf. Soc. **37**(1), 46–59 (2021). https://doi.org/10.1080/01972243.2020.1830211
22. Huvila, I.: Improving the usefulness of research data with better paradata. Open Inf. Sci. **6**(1), 28–48 (2022). https://doi.org/10.1515/opis-2022-0129
23. Huvila, I.: Making and taking information. JASIST **73**(4), 528–541 (2022)
24. Huvila, I., Andersson, L., Sköld, O.: Citing methods literature: Citations to field manuals as paradata on archaeological fieldwork. Inf. Res. Int. Electron. J. **27**(3) (2022). https://doi.org/10.47989/irpaper941
25. Huvila, I., Andersson, L., Sköld, O.: Patterns in paradata preferences among the makers and reusers of archaeological data. Data Inf. Manage. 100077 (2024)
26. Huvila, I., Börjesson, L., Sköld, O.: Archaeological information-making activities according to field reports. Libr. Inf. Sci. Res. **44**(3), 101171 (2022)
27. Huvila, I., Sinnamon, L.: Sharing research design, methods and process information in and out of academia. Proc. Assoc. Inf. Sci. Technol. **59**(1), 132–144 (2022). https://doi.org/10.1002/pra2.611
28. Huvila, I., Sköld, O.: Choreographies of making archaeological data. Open Archaeol. **7**(1), 1602–1617 (2021). https://doi.org/10.1515/opar-2020-0212
29. Huvila, I., Sköld, O.: A fieldwork manual as a regulatory device: instructing, prescribing and describing documentation work. J. Inf. Sci. 01655515231203506 (2023). https://doi.org/10.1177/01655515231203506
30. Huvila, I., Sköld, O., Andersson, L.: Knowing-in-practice, its traces and ingredients. In: Cozza, M., Gherardi, S. (eds.) The Posthumanist Epistemology of Practice Theory: Reimagining Method in Organization Studies and Beyond, pp. 37–69. Palgrave MacMillan, Cham (2023)
31. Huvila, I., Sköld, O., Börjesson, L.: Documenting information making in archaeological field reports. J. Documentation **77**(5), 1107–1127 (2021). https://doi.org/10.1108/JD-11-2020-0188
32. Ioannides, M., Chatzigrigoriou, P., Bokolas, V., Nikolakopoulou, V., Athanasiou, V.: Educational use of 3D models and photogrammetry content: the Europeana space project for Cypriot UNESCO monuments. In: Fourth International Conference on Remote Sensing and Geoinformation of the Environment (RSCy2016), vol. 9688, pp. 284–292. SPIE (2016)

33. Ioannides, M., Patias, P.: The complexity and quality in 3D digitisation of the past: challenges and risks. In: Ioannides, M., Patias, P. (eds.) 3D Research Challenges in Cultural Heritage III: Complexity and Quality in Digitisation, pp. 1–33. Springer, Cham (2023)

34. Kreuter, F.: The Use of Paradata. In: Improving Survey Methods. Routledge, London (2014)

35. Kuroczyński, P., Hauck, O., Dworak, D.: 3D models on triple paths - new pathways for documenting and visualizing virtual reconstructions. In: Münster, S., Pfarr-Harfst, M., Kuroczyński, P., Ioannides, M. (eds.) 3D Research Challenges in Cultural Heritage II, pp. 149–172. Springer, Cham (2016)

36. Lombardi, M.: Sustainability of 3D heritage data: life cycle and impact. Archeologia e Calcolatori **34**(2), 339–356 (2023). https://doi.org/10.19282/ac.34.2.2023.18

37. Niccolucci, F., Markhoff, B., Theodoridou, M., Felicetti, A., Hermon, S.: The heritage digital twin: a bicycle made for two. Open Res. Eur. **3**, 64 (Apr 2023). https://doi.org/10.12688/ope nreseurope.15496.1

38. Olsson, M.: Beyond 'needy' individuals: conceptualizing information behavior. Proc. Am. Soc. Inf. Sci. Tech. **42**(1) (2005). https://doi.org/10.1002/meet.1450420161

39. Pletinckx, D.: Preservation of virtual reconstructions. In: Corsi, C., Slapšak, B., Vermeulen, F. (eds.) Good Practice in Archaeological Diagnostics, pp. 309–314. Springer, Cham (2013). https://doi.org/10.1007/978-3-319-01784-6_19

40. Reilly, P.: Three-dimensional modelling and primary archaeological data. In: Reilly, P., Rahtz, S. (eds.) Archaeology and the Information Age, pp. 92–106. Routledge, London (1992)

41. Sköld, O., Börjesson, L., Huvila, I.: Interrogating paradata. Information Research. In: Proceedings of the 11th International Conference on Conceptions of Library and Information Science, vol. 27, no. (Special Issue), p. colis2206 (2022). https://doi.org/10.47989/colis2206

42. Smith, J.: Practical approaches to managing messy data in archaeology. In: Watrall, E., Goldstein, L. (eds.) Digital Heritage and Archaeology in Practice: Data, Ethics, and Professionalism, pp. 98–108. University Press of Florida, Gainesville (2022)

43. The London Charter Organisation: The London charter for the computer-based visualisation of cultural heritage. Tech. Rep. 2.1, London (2009)

44. Thiery, F., Veller, J., Raddatz, L., Rokohl, L., Boochs, F., Mees, A.W.: A semi-automatic semantic-model-based comparison workflow for archaeological features on roman ceramics. ISPRS Int. J. Geo Inf. **12**(4), 167 (2023)

Paradata: The Digital Prometheus

Drew Baker[✉] [iD]

Cyprus University of Technology, Limassol, Cyprus
Drew.Baker@cut.ac.cy

Abstract. Paradata ['pær.ə 'deɪ.tə] Mass noun: From Ancient Greek παρά (pará) "beside" and the Classical Latin datum "that which is given". Paradata is a word that has become synonymous with good practice in the field of Digital Cultural Heritage over the past few years, but where did the concept of Paradata within cultural heritage come from, what is its significance, how has it evolved, and why is it relevant to our field today? This paper aims to answer some of those questions through the author's personal reflections on their relationship with developing Paradata as a concept and its use in current research practice.

Keywords: Paradata · Digital Cultural Heritage · 3D Visualisation

1 Introduction

Within Digital Cultural Heritage circles, Paradata has gained significant traction over the past few years; indeed, it is now considered by many to be an essential part of 3D digitisation along with a digital asset's metadata and the data describing the geometry of the analogue object digitised. The concept of 3D Paradata is not new and was formulated during the Arts and Humanities Research Council (UK)-funded project "Making Space" in 2005–2007 under the auspices of King's Visualisation Lab, King's College London. The Making Space project aimed to investigate a methodology for tracking and documenting the cognitive process in 3D visualisation-based research, and its results, including 3D Paradata, formed the basis of The London Charter for the computer-based visualisation of cultural heritage [6].

A key outcome of the project was the identification and acknowledgement that the creation of a digital 3D asset—that is, a data-enriched digital or virtual object typically representing an artefact, monument, or site—generated a significant amount of additional data during the process of research that informed the final form and content of the asset. Moreover, the project highlighted that a great deal of this data constituted information essential for the understanding, and evaluation of 3D assets, their method of creation, and the impact outcomes; further, this data was seldom documented or accessible from the finalised asset, making the creation process opaque. This lack of intellectual transparency, the project concluded, would hinder innovation in 3D visualisation-based research and result in an under-exploitation of created assets and a loss of intellectual capital if not addressed. The project proposed a solution to this: a new data-type called "paradata".

M. Ioannides et al. (Eds.): 3D Research Challenges in Cultural Heritage V, LNCS 15190, pp. 12–23, 2025.
https://doi.org/10.1007/978-3-031-78590-0_2

2   The Historical Context

To understand the need for this new data type, it is necessary to revisit the context and state of the art in 3D representation from which it arose circa 1994–2004. The use of computer-generated imagery (CGI) in the film industry had been well established by the 1990s, but with big budgets. It was not until the end of the decade that computer hardware and software became sufficiently powerful and affordable for more modestly funded institutions and individuals to create visually compelling images, graphics, and increasingly virtual worlds—the specific area of interest for the Making Space project.

In academia and especially in cultural heritage, this opened new and promising avenues of investigation; however, this presented several challenges to those working at the intersection between traditional research and this new digital frontier:

As a point of disambiguation, it is important to acknowledge that the term "paradata" pre-existed the Making Space project's definition and use of paradata. This can be attributed to Mick P. Couper 1998/2000 to describe the recording of "by-products" of automatic computer-assisted statistical survey systems. To quote Couper, "*I term these sources of information 'paradata' (auxiliary data describing the process) to distinguish them from metadata (describing the data).*" [2]. Paradata in the context of 3D documentation is *not* the same as that proposed by Couper, although there are similarities (Couper's own account of paradata within statistical surveys is an interesting read in its own right) [3]. Retrospectively, this inadvertent duplication of nomenclature may have put more emphasis on recording the quantitative aspects of digitisation rather than the qualitative than had been originally intended, although both are important.

2.1   Intent vs Illustration

Traditionally, representations of heritage had been purely illustrative, generally falling into one of three categories: diagrammatic or simplified technical drawings, artistic impressions, or photographic documentation. CGI was still widely viewed as an illustrative medium. With advances in computing, the ability to interactively explore 3D assets had become an area of increasing cultural heritage research. The use of the same or similar tools, methods, and terminologies, however, blurred the boundaries between illustrative and experimental or experiential research use of 3D assets and environments. To some extent, this was a misunderstanding or mis-implementation of the technological affordances of the new medium. As the primary interface with the data was visual, it was natural to present research visually, but the visual output of a project was not necessarily the intent or purpose of the study undertaken.

There was a perception that as the digital is infinitely mailable, changes can be made easily over their analogue counterparts (physical drawings, maquette models, etc.). This is partially true; the flexibility of the digital medium to change aspects of an asset is a clear advantage and allows the manipulation of the digital to explore assets through interaction and experimental experimentation. However, the digital asset, just like the analogue, still has to be defined and created, and depending on why and how the asset is developed, the ability to repurpose the visual output may or may not be 'easy'. Nothing spontaneously exists in the digital domain; the computer does not "create" the asset (even programmatically generated assets still need to be encoded); therefore, as much diligence is required in recording the process of creating digital assets as archaeologists take in recording the destructive process of excavation.

It was observed that the majority of these changes were made towards the end of the research, where the asset, having served its purpose, was being repurposed for dissemination. The nature of changes varied from changes in lighting to the addition of effects to make assets look more "realistic" and additional incidental props to "complete the scene." Unless the asset had been created in such a way that allowed or anticipated such changes—now commonly called reuse—it ran the risk of introducing unintentional errors or misrepresenting the purpose of the research objectives through 'gilding the lily,' detracting or distracting from the actual results.

Moreover, due to the time of introduction, such changes were frequently undocumented and insufficiently researched, and while only ever intended to be indicative, were presented (or worse, incorporated into the 3D data of the asset) as a *de facto* truth, bringing the underlying scholarship into question.

2.2 Research Innovation vs. Technological Fetishism

Closely aligned with the above was the pressure within academia, especially in the humanities, to demonstrate 'innovation' and 'cutting edge' research by exploiting new digital technologies to secure funding and show impact. While undoubtedly pushing the state of the art forward, the rapidity of technological change created an environment that promoted "wow moments" and proof-of-concept demonstrations rather than a more considered investigation into understanding the potential use of the new digital medium and its implications for scholarship and dissemination.

By definition, research into how the digital domain could enhance scholarship and research depended on a stable technological infrastructure available to be studied. At a time of high technological innovation, research constantly had to readjust and adapt to be seen as cutting-edge and, therefore, relevant. Arguably, the result was a culture of creating products showcasing technology using Cultural Heritage scholarship rather than showing how cultural heritage research could be enhanced through technology.

This does not imply that the scholarship produced at this time was somehow superficial, but that research was often judged on the technology *de jour* rather than its intellectual merits. Good results could be achieved but at the cost of understanding the medium and sustainability. Documentation of assets, if it happened at all, was seen as something done at the end of the development cycle, in much the same way as one might write a user manual for a computer programme, and tended to focus on specific implementations rather than developing best practices.

The rapidity of change in the technological infrastructure and the lack of documentation of both assets and practices meant that with almost every new project, a new piece of software or hardware would need to be implemented, compatibility with previously developed assets could not be guaranteed, skills and methods were not transferable, and research projects ran the risk of investing in technological dead ends.

2.3   The Transition from Paper to Screen

Again, it is important to stress the historical context here. In a pre-Web 2.0 world, in the middle of the first great digital transition, the uptake of new media presented new challenges to disseminating digital 3D results in an academic infrastructure that was primarily still geared towards paper publications.

CD-ROMs were frequent companions to publications, although seldom distributed with conference proceedings. Programmes were frequently bespoke applications or source code to be compiled to allow assets to be shown, but one could not guarantee the same hardware and software combinations needed to use assets at their point of delivery. The World Wide Web had been publicly available since 1993, but access to the Internet was neither ubiquitous nor fast, even within educational institutions. Producing a manifest of software-hardware specifications and setups, workarounds, and settings lists became an expectation.

Further, online dissemination of heritage assets via the internet highlighted issues surrounding sustainability, preservation, and concerns about the intellectual property rights of digitised objects. Asset manifests became outdated, software applications discontinued, links became broken, software discontinued, and key files (sometimes entire sites) were reorganised, moved, archived, or just deleted as space, and a more institutional approach to digital resource management became necessary.

A significant milestone occurred between 1994 and 1998 when a standard for the exchange and viewing of 3D assets, the Virtual Reality Modelling Language (VRML), was published (ISO/IEC 14772–1:1997). A plain text format that was both machine and human-readable, allowing in-line annotation and hyperlinking of data, providing control over the level of detail, and offering redundancy through the distribution of components addressed some of the challenges of documentation of 3D assets.

While VRML had potential and found favour in academic circles, it was ultimately surpassed but did provide a period of relative stability where serious research into 3D digitisation, virtual representation, and understanding of the medium could take place.

2.4   Citation, Referencing, and Acknowledgement

Perhaps the most pressing concern for researchers working in this emerging field of 3D Digital Cultural Heritage was how a 3D asset could be cited. It might take several months to research, develop, test, and review an asset for scholarly integrity, but ultimately, if the results were only ever perceived as being illustrative, supporting traditional publications, why invest time if the work could not be cited, referenced, and acknowledged as key performance indicators in a researcher's career?

Without the infrastructure to ensure that an asset could be found, reviewed, and evaluated by peers, bad scholarship would go unchallenged. This not only ran the risk of misrepresenting cultural heritage and propagating falsehood but also prejudiced good scholarship. If the power of the digital medium to be responsive and flexible in testing and incorporating new data was seen as being ephemeral (both in terms of documenting results and being able to find and build upon those results), then the implication was that 'digital was disposable' and needed to be recreated by each project, casting doubt on the justification of the cost of production and return on investment.

Without being able to show the logic and progression of an asset's development through documentation or publication records, researchers were vulnerable to criticism, especially as outputs often challenged established mental models held by colleagues in the academy. Months of work could be undone in an instant by an expert pointing out a visual error unrelated to the subject matter, while scholarly output was frequently dismissed as being of 'poor quality' when compared to large-budget commercial offerings like film animation and video games.

If the transdisciplinary skills, research, and development needed to leverage the potential of 3D visualisation of cultural heritage were to be realised, if 3D assets were to be more than just a form of 3D photocopying, and if the communication of the scholarship and research was to be more than a Barnumesque "dog and pony show" and make a meaningful contribution to understanding the past, things would have to change.

3   The Paradata Model of Data Metamorphosis

As a concept, paradata can be seen as tracking the progression of understanding through the stages of data metamorphosis. This model followed the 'classic' Data-Information-Knowledge-Wisdom (DIKW) model proposed by Ackoff [1], with paradata being recorded at key transitional points during the research process.

- Data that is structured becomes information through contextualisation.
- Information that is interpreted becomes knowledge through hypothesis.
- Knowledge that provides insight becomes Wisdom (or Foresight) through understanding.

While the DIKW model is traditionally depicted as a pyramid with a large baseline of data refined to a pinnacle of wisdom through a linear progression, the paradata concept considers data metamorphosis as part of the development cycle with a non-linear progression. This cycle is intentionally collaborative, with lines of investigation being suspended, queried, or bifurcated due to deviation. Data metamorphosis within the paradata concept can therefore be conceptualised as an onion diagram with the core (data) at the innermost circle positioned at the base of the concentric rings (see Fig. 1).

The development of an asset will start somewhere within the innermost circle of the Data section and progress through the processes of data structuring (including metadata) and contextualisation until it metamorphoses into information. This transition—and other transitions—is not a predetermined barrier but is characterised by the point at which data items can be combined, analysed, and compared, i.e., interpreted, the process that paradata aims to capture. It also marks the point at which the data/information may be rejected or included during the interpretation stage; another process paradata aims to capture along with the details of how the conclusion was reached (including methods used). As the asset is developed, each boundary provides similar opportunities to record the research methods, process, and rationale for progressing, increasing the 'data load' of the asset and providing points where deviation can occur.

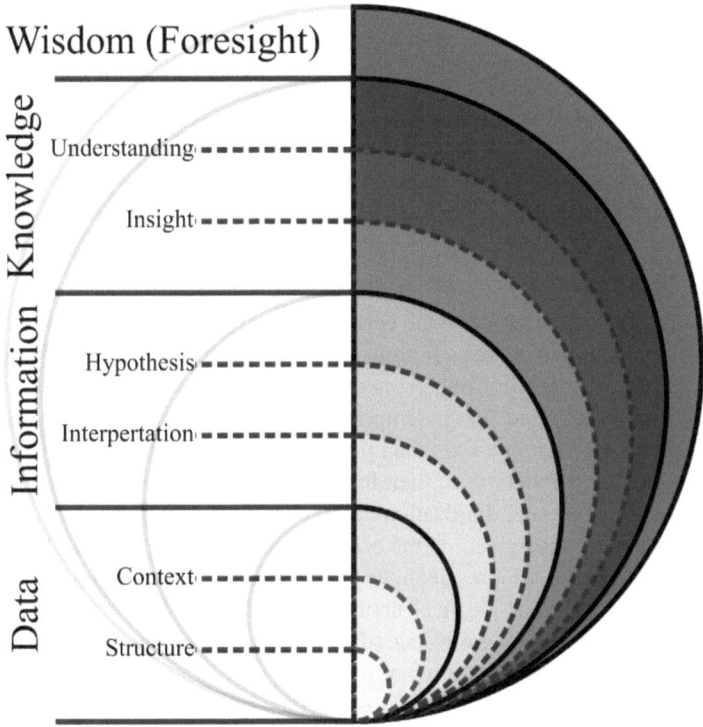

Fig. 1. The Paradata Conceptual Model of Data Metamorphosis

4   The Paradata Concept

As noted in the introduction, the objective of the Making Space project had a specific focus on 3D representations of cultural heritage within virtual worlds; however, as those worlds consisted of multiple individual 3D assets, the observations made during the project were still considered valid whether the digital representation was a single discrete object or part of a portmanteau scene.

The project concluded that a new type of data arose out of the digitisation of cultural heritage. This was not strictly metadata, as it was not information about the asset per se, but rather it was information about the development of the raw data from data capture, refinements, and enrichment, including vital information regarding the interpretation and selection of sources and deductive/inductive reasoning arising from the process of 3D modelling itself. This data fuelled the research and development of an asset while informing and, in turn, being assessed, validated, or rejected through experimentation. As such, the term "paradata" was used to describe this dynamic dialogue between source data sets and their digital manifestation.

Before we progress further, it is important to note one further point of language. The Paradata concept rejects the idea of digital or virtual "reconstruction" of cultural heritage but uses the term visualisation to distinguish the processes and outputs of digitisation. This is a subtle distinction, but fundamental to the paradata concept.

- Reconstruction is a process of rebuilding, repairing, or restoring something, the implication being that it is a faithful facsimile of the original, i.e., representing *the* truth.
- Visualisation, however, is the representation of the available data set to create a hypothetical version of the subject based on an identified and traceable decision-making process used to create the asset, in other words, *a possible* truth constructed on evidence. Visualisation communicates message and meaning not just imagery.

This shift in perspective is essential in representing cultural heritage where evidence may be missing, conflicting, unclear, its provenance is in question, or any form of interpretation as it changes the nature of the data. Even data acquired through high-precision data techniques cannot guarantee a faithful digital facsimile of an object. A multitude of factors may influence the recording process, and once raw data is compiled, errors can be included and proliferated. In contemporary parlance, visualisation is more aligned with the concept of a Memory Twin than that of a Digital Twin.

The principle of paradata was, therefore, not to simply record, define, and quantify cultural heritage through digitisation but to understand the context and significance of the object, including insights into the original creation process through digital affordances. One can measure, weigh, chemically analyse, and even grind down the Parthenon Marbles to understand their physical nature but will never find a single atom of the artistry, impact, meaning, or significance of their creation and how those innately human characteristics are still meaningful today.

This does not dismiss the quantifiable as that data is an intrinsic part of the Parthenon Marbles; but Cultural Heritage is not empirically based antiquarianism; it is the study of intellectual achievements and ideas, customs, and social behaviour of a particular people or society that exist from the past and their continued importance, impact and relevance to modern society.

In its simplest form, recording paradata echoes the schoolmaster's cry to "*Show your working out.*", perhaps a better analogy would be Karl Popper's statement, "*Those among us who are unwilling to expose their ideas to the hazard of refutation do not take part in the game* [of science]." [3]. While it is arguably impossible to apply the objective empirical-based scientific method to the subjective humanities, paradata offered a way to show the intellectual and creative narrative, which supported the development of a visual hypothesis presenting the results not as 'fact' but as 'possibility'.

Paradata would therefore introduce the possibility of falsification of the visual hypothesis presented, demanding a rigorous approach to the research employed in its creation and crucially providing information to allow meaningful scholarly debate surrounding conclusions by providing clear evidence of which elements of the visualisation were relevant and which were ancillary (but necessary) within the scene. The intent was to address five particular concerns:

4.1 Recording the Research Process

It was noted that little information was recorded about the processes undertaken in creating a visualisation. By this, we are not referring to data sources that form part of the research rationale but rather the variables that constitute the research process. Recording variables and constraints such as equipment and software used, personnel engaged in the development, methods employed, and purpose of the visualisation paradata would provide a clear *mise en scène* of the research process. This record would allow the visualisation context to be understood; for example, providing details of hardware and software would identify constraints (and potential issues) that may impact the results of digitisation, while stating the intent of a visualisation is to understand connectivity within an archaeological site allows the work to be judged on spatial representation rather than visual presentation.

4.2 Documenting Research Rationale and Logic

As a visualisation is an intentional creation, nothing exists within it without purpose. By recording the reason for a data object's inclusion within a visualisation, the rationale and logic of the research and creation processes become transparent. This documentation provides multiple services within the paradata concept:

- If an asset cannot be justified, it is superfluous to the needs of the visualisation and can be removed, increasing the communicative value and focus of the visualisation.[1]
- If everything can be justified, then the purpose of the visualisation is more understandable, defendable, with a higher potential for reuse as its confidence is increased.
- If the rationale and logic behind a visualisation are exposed and understandable—including alternative sources considered but rejected—the scholarly value of the visualisation (and its assets) is increased due to the inherent intellectual transparency.

Consider the case of digitising an example of standing archaeology; scanning provides state documentation; nothing more, nothing less. If digitisation intends to provide such a record, this can be stated within the paradata with details of the processes undertaken to produce that record. Future scholars can understand the intent and process through the paradata record assessing the digital record against their research criteria.

However, if the purpose is to provide a basis for interpretation, the digital scan is just one of multiple data sources required to construct a visual hypothesis. Indeed, such a scan may not be indicative of the structure in the past and may itself have been interpreted through physical reconstruction or interventions. Other sources—excavation reports, photographs, and testimonies—must be considered to prepare the visualisation. In the case of a room, the visualisation may need to consider the interpretation of walls and ceilings (possibly floors) that no longer remain; there may be doors, windows, or other features for which there is evidence but no longer exists or at least exists in situ.

4.3 Providing Mechanisms for Review of 3D Digital Assets

The reliance on traditional review methods of research was not considered robust enough to allow peer review of 3D visualisations, especially where the presented hypotheses

---

[1] It should be noted that this justification may be as simple as "required to complete the scene"—the point here was to encourage structured, thoughtful practice into asset creation and visualisation of cultural heritage.

involved multiple dimensions (spatial, temporal, and probabilistic). Paradata would provide the basis for a framework where visualisation-based research could be audited and assessed for scholarly integrity based on the documentation of the research rationale and process. Through such a mechanism, a reviewer would be able to follow the development of the research argument, the hypothesis made, and the resulting conclusions drawn without being distracted by any ancillary (but justified) elements needed to create a cohesive representation.

For example, a visualisation of a room for which there is strong evidence of a door but for which physical evidence does not exist will inform aspects of the visualisation of the room, such as minimum ceiling height, direction of ingress, illumination, etc. Acknowledging the existence of the door and its possible impact and effect on the hypothesis is a factor of review, not necessarily the appearance, materials, or construction of the door itself.

4.4   Support for Citation of 3D Digital Assets

Paradata was intended to show that the visible output of a visualisation was only a fraction of the research that contributed to the process. Without such recognition, it was considered (and arguably still is) that the serious scholarship required to create visualisations is ignored or less relevant than the (primarily) visual output.

As a new medium for scholarly investigation of cultural heritage (and other disciplines), a method that allows the citation of visualisations is critical to developing a sustainable career path for researchers using visualisation as part of digital scholarship. Paradata was seen as part of that solution, along with the review provision.

Without being able to cite visualisations and constituent assets, researchers would not receive the academic recognition vital for a sustainable career within the academy. Without such recognition, this new medium for scholarly investigation of cultural heritage would bifurcate: on the one hand, academics who would only consume or commission visualisations—repeating the illustration fallacy—and on the other, technically adept developers who would lack the necessary background for robust intellectual enquiry in the cultural heritage domain. Worse, those able to maintain a career in Cultural Heritage visualisation would be perceived as dilettantes, being neither one nor the other.

4.5   Accelerate the Research and Development Process

The final point paradata sought to address was the long development times for visualisations. The paradata concept, significantly influenced by The Berlin Declaration [4], took a two-fold strategy in tackling this issue: first the disciplined creation of visualisations and second the reusability of assets through open access.

The paradata concept's requirement for documentation and justification of assets and visualisation placed a quantifiable cost/benefit on development through the triple constraint 'iron triangle' principle of *"good, quick, cheap—pick two."* The intent was to focus development on implementing clear research agendas but not restricting intellectual curiosity. Understanding that deviation from the core research statement, would need to be documented would have implications for resource allocation, acting as a deterrent to 'additional extras'. However, by requiring the recording the development process (both intellectual and creative), high-quality assets based on sound reasoning would be created. The return on investment would be twofold:

First the paradata record would provide an audit trail to understand the point of deviation between the requirements of researchers.

- Researcher B could either accept Researcher A's work by assessing and agreeing with their conclusions manifested in the asset and include it within their visualisations (with appropriate citation). Increasing the confidence or value of the asset.
- Or B could create a version of A's asset and produce an alternative view based on the paradata record. Researcher B would only need to work from the point of deviation saving time and effort. This would stimulate scholarly debate.
- If B rejected A's research *in toto*, a new asset would need to be produced by B. This would be available for review and, therefore, the scrutiny of other scholars, reducing digital plagiarism. This would help prevent ersatz assets and research.

Critically, the paradata for an asset would not change but be expanded by revisions, only the manifestation of the asset; geometry, textures, behavioural scripts, etc. This would permit researchers to draw on a common research pool and present alternatives of the asset (including lower graphical or polygon count versions).

Secondly, the lacunae in the research corpus or those paths not investigated would be exposed and exploited by future research. Again, this provision offered the potential for accelerating and expanding research, not only through the addition of new material but also through establishing a record of the process that documents the approaches taken and methods employed that could be reassessed as technology advanced and new research paradigms emerged.

This second benefit was considered instrumental in opening up intellectual transparency in digital cultural heritage research to a wider audience. The multi-disciplinary nature of the field implicitly requires cooperation and collaboration from the inception of a project until its conclusion (and preparation for its future accessibility and use beyond). The implication is that the research data, processes, and methods documented in paradata offer other uses cross-domain. Understanding which structures survived (and why) on a site may be of interest to civil engineers in assessing the durability of materials, but only if they are confident that the structures are contemporary with the timespan they are investigating, not earlier or later (or modern interventions).

5   Conclusion and Reflection

While paradata was adopted into the London Charter as part of its principles, the ideals of the concept were never fully realised. Astute readers will have noted that some of the proposals within the paradata concept bear similarities to existing methods; DOI 2000, Dublin Core ISO standard in 2003, Linked Data 2006, GitHub branching 2008, FAIR Data Principles 2016 etc. Many of these innovations were in their infancy when the paradata concept was being formulated contributing to the technological zeitgeist.

Despite initial interest, failure to capitalise on these nascent technologies severely retarded the progression of the concept as a whole. That is not to say that paradata research and development has not been undertaken in the two decades elapsed as witnessed by the contributors to this volume; however, the full potential of paradata has yet to be realised as it was originally conceived. One criticism of the paradata concept was that it was 'too forward thinking'—a solution looking for a problem—but time moves on and the demand for the digitalisation of cultural heritage has only increased.

As we move into the second quarter of the twenty-first century, cultural heritage is increasingly under threat, not only from the climate crisis, natural disasters, and destruction through conflict and ideology but also through authenticity and misappropriation. In his book, 1984, George Orwell wrote, *"Who controls the past controls the future. Who controls the present controls the past."* If the democratisation of access, understanding, and memory of our shared past is the aim of cultural heritage's drive for 'digital transformation', then we have a moral obligation to undertake digitalisation with diligence, intellectual integrity, and transparency to facilitate democratisation.

Ultimately, however it is described, realised, implemented, branded, or renamed, the concept behind paradata, intellectual integrity, transparency and responsibility in digitising Cultural Heritage remains. It is part of the process and part of the solution—a Promethean spark with the potential to ignite novel scholarship in the digital data space.

Acknowledgments. The Making Space Project 2005–2007 was funded through the ICT Strategy Projects scheme of the UK's Arts and Humanities Research Council.

Disclosure of Interests. The author has no competing interests to declare that are relevant to the content of this article.

References

1. Ackoff, R.L.: From data to wisdom. J. Appl. Syst. Anal. **16**, 3–9 (1989)
2. Couper, M.P.: Usability evaluation of computer-assisted survey instruments. Soc. Sci. Comput. Rev. **18**(4), 384–396 (2000)
3. Couper, M.P.: Birth and diffusion of the concept of paradata. Adv. Soc. Res. **18**, 14–26 (2000). https://jasr.or.jp/english/JASR_Birth%20and%20Diffusion%20of%20the%20Concept%20of%20Paradata.pdf. Accessed 06 Jun 2024
4. Popper, K.R.: The Logic of Scientific Discovery. Routledge, London (2002)
5. The Berlin declaration on open access to knowledge in the sciences and humanities (2003). https://openaccess.mpg.de/67605/berlin_declaration_engl.pdf. Accessed 06 Jun 2024
6. The London charter (2006). https://www.london-charter.org. Accessed 06 Jun 2024

Integrating Paradata, Metadata, and Data for an Effective Memory Twin in the Field of Digital Cultural Heritage

Marinos Ioannides(✉) ⓘ, Elena Karittevli ⓘ, Panayiotis Panayiotou ⓘ, and Drew Baker ⓘ

Department of Electrical Engineering, Computer Engineering and Informatics, UNESCO Chair on Digital Cultural Heritage, Cyprus University of Technology, Arch. Kyprianou 31, 3036 Limassol, CY, Cyprus
{marinos.ioannides,elena.karittevli,p.panayiotou, drew.baker}@cut.ac.cy

Abstract. The extension of the concept of Digital Twin to Memory Twin offers an innovative approach to preserving and interacting in the field of Digital Cultural Heritage. This paper explores the integration of paradata, metadata and data to construct an effective Memory twin, providing a representation of cultural heritage. Paradata, together with metadata and data, greatly enriches the digital representation of cultural assets. By integrating these layers of information, we aim to develop a framework that enhances the preservation, accessibility and interpretability of digital cultural heritage. This approach enables advanced archival practices, personalised user experiences and improved data authenticity. Through case studies, we demonstrate the potential of this methodology to transform the management and dissemination of cultural heritage in the digital future.

Keywords: Memory Twin · Digital Cultural Heritage · Paradata · Cultural Heritage Preservation

1 Introduction

A Digital twin is a concept that has been applied widely in various sectors inclusive of digital cultural heritage. This means that digital twins are virtual replicas of cultural objects, which allow for tracking, analysis and simulation of such things within digital environments. They provide dynamic and interactive representations, thus advancing the preservation and dissemination of cultural heritage. For instance, through the creation of detailed 3D models for historical sites and artefacts, they have made virtual tours possible thus improving learning. The Memory twin on the other hand is not just an artefact performing this function but one which also considers factors such as contextuality, temporality and experience of archaeological sites and cultures. The main intention behind this technique is not only to replicate the material characteristics of cultural artefacts but also consider their use and historical settings. However, the Memory twin approach maintains attributes pertaining to their physical nature as well as historical backgrounds associated with them (Ioannides et al., 2021).

M. Ioannides et al. (Eds.): 3D Research Challenges in Cultural Heritage V, LNCS 15190, pp. 24–35, 2025.
https://doi.org/10.1007/978-3-031-78590-0_3

The Memory twin approach preserves the physical characteristics of cultural objects and incorporates their historical significance and the stories associated with them. This layered integration ensures more holistic preservation, facilitating advanced archival practices, personalized user experiences, and improved data authenticity. Through Memory twins, cultural institutions can change the way cultural heritage is managed and shared in the digital environment. This paper aims to discuss this concept and the corresponding theoretical background and practical examples of their use and possibilities. By incorporating paradata, metadata, and data in the creation of Memory Twins, the future of archival practices and engaging cultural history experiences are opened, thus enhancing the learning and appreciation of history.

2 Theoretical Background

The concept of a digital twin has been a transformative development in various industries, creating virtual replicas of physical objects or systems that allow for real-time monitoring, simulation, and optimization. Originally pioneered in the fields of manufacturing and engineering, digital twins have found applications in smart cities, healthcare, and beyond, providing dynamic, data-driven representations that enhance efficiency and decision-making (Grieves, 2014; Tao et al., 2018).

In the realm of digital cultural heritage, the digital twin paradigm has enabled the creation of virtual models of artefacts, sites, and monuments. These models facilitate preservation by allowing detailed study and interaction without the need to physically handle or be present at the actual sites. For instance, detailed 3D models of historical buildings and artefacts have been created, allowing for virtual tours and educational experiences that bring cultural heritage to a global audience (Bruno et al., 2016; Bekele et al., 2018).

3 Memory Twin Concept

Human history, art and achievements become a rich tapestry of cultural heritage. It is necessary to preserve and document these invaluable assets for our collective memory. Memory Twin is not just an idea but the digital copy of our culture enabling us to keep our past alive and make it accessible worldwide. This innovative approach goes beyond the possibilities of digital twins by introducing paradata, metadata, and data thereby giving a more comprehensive and enhanced view of what constitutes cultural heritage. Paradata involves contextual information that surrounds data creation as well as its application thus provides insights into the reasons why cultural items were made in such way. Metadata indicates the content, quality, condition, among other characteristics of data thus allowing better organization and retrieval. Data involves actual digital representations of cultural objects like 3D scans, photographs and textual records.

By integrating these three layers of information, the Memory Twin approach not only replicates the physical attributes of cultural artefacts but also preserves their historical significance and usage contexts. This multi-dimensional representation enriches the digital artefacts with narratives that are crucial for understanding their full value.

The combination of paradata and metadata ensures that users can access comprehensive information about how and why the artefacts were created, their journey through history, and their current digital state. This holistic integration transforms static digital copies into dynamic, informative, and interactive resources, making cultural heritage more engaging and accessible to a global audience. This methodology not only supports advanced archival practices but also fosters personalized user experiences and enhances the authenticity and interpretability of digital cultural heritage.

While digital twins have significantly advanced the preservation and accessibility of cultural heritage, they primarily focus on replicating the physical attributes and operational behaviours of artefacts. This approach, while valuable, often overlooks the deeper, more nuanced aspects of cultural heritage—its historical significance, usage contexts, and the experiential dimensions that are integral to understanding its full value.

The Memory Twin concept emerges as an evolution of the digital twin, addressing these gaps by creating a more comprehensive and enriched digital representation of cultural heritage. A Memory Twin goes beyond the mere replication of physical characteristics to incorporate the historical, contextual, and experiential information associated with cultural artefacts. This evolution reflects a shift from a focus on physical accuracy to a broader, more holistic understanding of cultural heritage.

The workflow chart (Fig. 1) included in this paper illustrates the comprehensive process of converting primary stakeholder requirements into publishable knowledge on platforms like Europeana and national aggregators. This process is systematically structured to address both the complexity of data gathering and the quality assurance necessary for preserving and disseminating digital cultural heritage.

The process begins by understanding and documenting the requirements of primary stakeholders. These requirements form the basis for developing digital tangible objects that accurately represent cultural heritage. The stakeholder requirements are transformed into digital tangible objects, which act as the foundational elements for further data processing and digitization.

The data gathering process involves converting physical cultural objects into digital formats using techniques like 3D scanning, photogrammetry, and other digitization methods. Contributions from experts and practitioners are integrated, encompassing comprehensive research utilizing both published and unpublished sources to enrich the digital representation. Practical insights and historical context are provided by individuals with relevant expertise.

The gathered information is classified into three primary components: paradata, metadata, and data. Paradata includes data about the processes and methodologies used to create the digital objects, offering insights into the digitization and decision-making processes. Metadata is structured information that describes the content, context, and attributes of the data, facilitating easier retrieval and management. Data refers to the actual digital content, such as 3D models, photographs, and textual records.

Paradata, metadata, and data are combined to create comprehensive information that serves multiple purposes, enhancing the overall understanding and utility of the digital objects. This information is evaluated and refined through several quality parameters to ensure its accuracy, relevance, and completeness. This includes developing and testing hypotheses based on the information, formulating research questions to guide further investigation, conducting experiments and analyses to validate the information, creating narratives to provide context and storytelling elements, ensuring the information is suitable for educational purposes, assessing the condition of the materials involved, and monitoring the structural integrity of the physical objects represented digitally.

The final product is validated knowledge, ready for dissemination and publication. The validated knowledge is published on online platforms like Europeana and national aggregators to ensure broad accessibility and engagement.

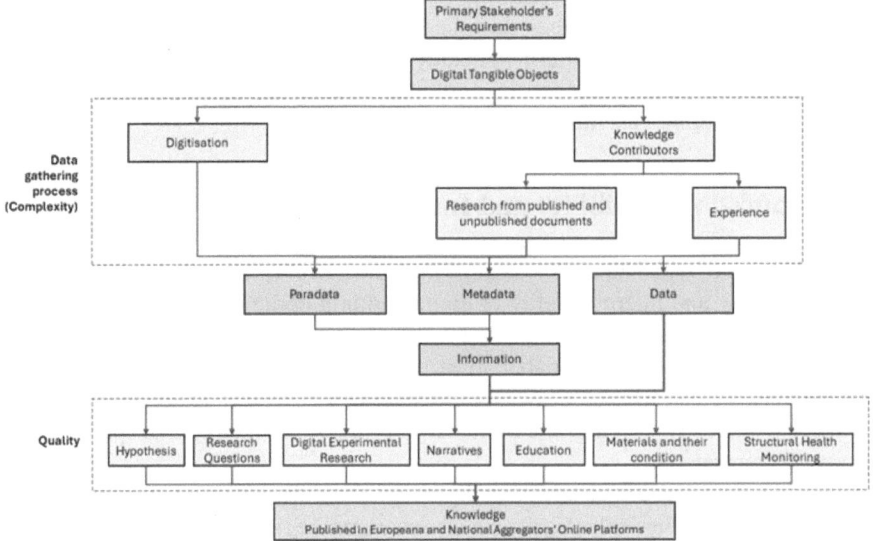

Fig. 1. The Memory Twin approach

4 Holistic Preservation

The Memory Twin approach integrates paradata, metadata, and data to ensure a holistic preservation of cultural heritage. Paradata provides more information than merely preserving data as it documents the way information was developed; hence, digital representations can capture methods employed, tools utilized and even circumstances under which the research was conducted. It is this kind of contextual information that helps us understand how decision making or other conditions shaped digitization processes, with such insights being very valuable for future investigation and conservation purposes.

Metadata on the other hand offers the necessary structural and descriptive details required to efficiently organize, retrieve and manage data. Metadata provides a way of describing different attributes of digital objects like their content, format, and where they came from thus ensuring that they are well organized and accessible. That is what makes browsing better by allowing advanced searching capabilities while ensuring effective retrieval to access interactive artefacts online.

This approach also adds to the experience of users by opening multiple avenues for engagement. The paradata can be used by researchers with a view to understand digitization methods, complexity and quality, metadata can be exploited by educators to come up with structured learning modules while at the same time the public can play around with high fidelity data for enhanced participation. Memory Twins is meant to serve different user requirements by offering a much more inclusive and engaging heritage experience. Memory Twins holistic preservation is not only about protecting the past but rather about aiding future research and conservation initiatives as well. Detailed paradata and metadata provide robust frameworks that will enable future scholars conducting digitization processes to understand how they have been done and may potentially reproduce or continue building on them. In terms of studying and conserving cultural heritage, this continuum is important because it allows digital representations to remain apposite and informative for future generations.

5   Enhanced Accessibility and Interpretability

The integration of paradata and metadata within the Memory Twin framework enhances the accessibility and interpretability of digital cultural heritage. Comprehensive metadata allows for sophisticated search and retrieval functionalities, making it easier for researchers, educators, and the public to access and engage with digital artefacts. Paradata enriches the narrative by providing the necessary context to understand the conditions and methods involved in the digitization process, facilitating a deeper and more informed interpretation.

This layered approach ensures that digital artefacts are not only preserved in a way that maintains their physical integrity but also captures the rich, contextual narratives that give them meaning. By providing a detailed account of the historical and cultural contexts in which these artefacts were created and used, the Memory Twin approach enables a more nuanced understanding and appreciation of cultural heritage. The evolution from digital twins to Memory Twins represents a significant advancement in digital cultural heritage. Memory Twins provide a richer, more nuanced representation of cultural artefacts, ensuring that both their physical properties and their historical and contextual significance are preserved. This comprehensive approach enhances the preservation, accessibility, and interpretability of digital cultural heritage, paving the way for more advanced archival practices and engaging cultural experiences.

The transformative potential of Memory Twins lies in their ability to create digital representations that are not only accurate and detailed but also rich in context and meaning. This allows for a deeper engagement with cultural heritage, fostering a greater understanding and appreciation of the past. Through theoretical exploration and practical application, Memory Twins offer new opportunities for cultural institutions to preserve and share their heritage in innovative and impactful ways, ensuring that the rich tapestry of human history is accessible to future generations.

6 Case Studies: Memory Twin of Lambousa Fishing Trawler and Fikardou Village

The Lambousa fishing trawler (Fig. 2), a significant piece of Cyprus's maritime history, serves as a prime example of how a Memory Twin can encapsulate both physical and historical dimensions of cultural heritage. Originally built in 1955 by Dimitrios Zacharias in Perama, Piraeus, Greece, and later named Lambousa upon its arrival in Famagusta in 1965, this 25-m vessel has been an integral part of the Mediterranean fishing narrative. The Lambousa was a marvel of naval architecture, measuring 25 m in length with a gross tonnage of 48 tons, and capable of reaching speeds of up to 10 knots.

The Lambousa was renowned for its use of bottom trawling, a fishing method involving a robust net designed to sink to the ocean floor. This method required a high degree of skill and knowledge from the captain and crew, who meticulously navigated the complex apparatus to avoid underwater hazards. The net could hoist up to four tons of catch, demonstrating the vessel's efficiency and the crew's expertise.

Throughout its operational life, the Lambousa witnessed numerous historical events and adventures. One such incident occurred in the summer before 1963 when the crew ventured into Turkish waters and encountered Turkish port authorities. The quick thinking and bravery of Captain Kyriakos Kastenis, who orchestrated a dramatic escape under gunfire, underscored the vessel's significance as a symbol of resilience and resourcefulness. The Turkish invasion of Cyprus in 1974 marked a turning point for the Lambousa. Prior to the invasion, the vessel operated across the entirety of Cyprus, but the conflict forced it to seek refuge in the Ormidia fishing harbour. Post-war, the Lambousa continued its fishing operations primarily from Limassol and Larnaca, contributing to the revival of the fishing industry in the free areas of the island. However, overfishing and environmental changes posed significant challenges to the sustainability of the marine ecosystem.

Recognizing the cultural and historical value of the Lambousa, the Municipality of Limassol undertook efforts to preserve the vessel as a floating museum. This initiative, funded by the European operational program 'Sea' for the period 2014–2020, included extensive restoration work to maintain the vessel in its original condition. The restoration not only preserved the physical structure of the Lambousa but also ensured its legacy would be accessible to future generations.

The preservation efforts for Lambousa are also driven by significant regulatory frameworks. According to Regulation (EU) No 508/2014 of the European Maritime and Fisheries Fund, certain fishing boats, including traditional vessels like the Lambousa, were required to be decommissioned to reduce fishing capacities and protect marine life. This regulation posed a threat to the existence of many historic vessels. However, recognizing the Lambousa's unique cultural and historical value, an exception was made to preserve it as part of Cyprus's maritime heritage. This legal framework highlights the importance of balancing conservation efforts with regulatory compliance, ensuring that significant cultural assets are not lost to stringent regulations.

The UNESCO Chair on Digital Cultural Heritage, with the support of the EU-funded project EUreka3D and MNEMOSYNE, has spearheaded the digitization and preservation of the Lambousa fishing boat. This initiative employs advanced 3D digitization techniques to create a detailed digital model of the vessel, ensuring its historical integrity and accessibility for future generations. Specifically, a Photogrammetric survey was made in January 2023 when the Trawler was in a decayed condition. Moreover, in October 2023, while the boat was under restoration, a Terrestrial Laser Scanning survey was made to capture the geometry of its timber structure. The point cloud data from both surveys was further processed, for the creation of a CAD 3D model, which includes all the elements of the boat which are 440 in total. By integrating these digital assets into the Europeana platform, the project enhances the visibility and educational potential of the Lambousa, promoting a broader appreciation of Cyprus's maritime heritage and contributing to the preservation of European cultural history. Further details on the holistic documentation approach of the Lambousa can be found on elambousa.eu (Fig. 3). This platform allows the user to learn about the history of the vessel, through a 360 virtual interaction, educational games, eBook, and a portfolio with photos, videos, interviews and drawings.

Fig. 2. The Lambousa Fishing Trawler

Fikardou Village (Fig. 4), a UNESCO Tentative List World Heritage Site, exemplifies the Memory Twin approach in a different but equally compelling context. This traditional Cypriot mountain settlement, with its origins tracing back to the Byzantine era, offers a rich tapestry of cultural narratives. Fikardou Village stands as a prime example of a traditional rural settlement, meticulously conserving its 18th- and 19th-century architecture amidst its pristine natural environment. Named after its noble lineage during the Frankish rule in Cyprus, Fikardou embodies a rich cultural heritage that has endured through the ages.

Fig. 3. Holistic documentation – eLambousa.eu platform

The trend of urbanization and abandonment had left many houses deserted, threatening the village's unique architectural features and cultural practices. The Department of Antiquities took charge of the village in 1978, declaring it an "Ancient Monument" and establishing strict regulations through a "Controlled Area" designation. In 1984, a comprehensive revitalization effort was launched, focusing on the restoration of dilapidated structures and the enhancement of the village's infrastructure. These endeavours have garnered recognition, with Fikardou now proudly listed on the tentative UNESCO World Heritage Sites roster, underscoring its cultural significance and potential for global acclaim. Notably, the meticulous restoration of key residences, such as the "Residence of Katsinioros" and the "Residence of Achilleas Dimitri," earned international acclaim, affirming the village's status as a beacon of architectural heritage.

The Memory Twin of Fikardou involves extensive 3D scanning to capture the village's architectural intricacies and spatial layout. Paradata collected includes the methodologies employed in scanning the narrow, cobbled streets and traditional houses, the historical research on the village's founding and development, and the community's input on cultural practices and traditions. Metadata for Fikardou details the architectural styles, the historical significance of various buildings, and the socio-economic history of its inhabitants. This integration of paradata and metadata with high-fidelity digital models ensures that the Memory Twin provides a holistic and immersive experience, preserving both the physical and cultural essence of the village.

The digital documentation process employed by the UNESCO Chair on Digital Cultural Heritage team commenced with data acquisition, utilizing advanced technologies such as laser scanners, 360° photography, and drones to capture the intricate details of Fikardou's built environment. This initial phase was critical in creating a comprehensive digital representation of the village, facilitating subsequent data processing stages. Data preparation involved the meticulous cleaning and organization of acquired data, ensuring its suitability for analysis and interpretation.

The subsequent processing stages included registration, interpretation, and storage, culminating in the creation of structured digital assets that accurately represent Fikardou's architectural and cultural heritage. Data modelling played a pivotal role in structuring the digitized information, providing a robust framework for database management and application development. By establishing clear relationships between data entities and attributes, data models ensured the coherence and accessibility of the village's digital archives.

Central to the preservation efforts was the implementation of digital preservation strategies aimed at ensuring the longevity and accessibility of Fikardou's digital materials. Adhering to best practices, including metadata documentation, controlled storage environments, and proactive management, safeguarded the integrity and authenticity of the village's cultural heritage in the digital realm.

Additionally, the team engaged deeply with the community, conducting interviews with villagers spanning generations. These interviews were invaluable in capturing the intangible heritage of Fikardou, including stories, traditions, and cultural practices passed down through oral tradition. Each voice added depth to the digital archive, weaving together a rich tapestry of intangible heritage that defines the village's unique identity.

Furthermore, the development of the online platform efikardou.eu (Fig. 5) emerged as a strategic avenue for disseminating Fikardou's cultural legacy to a global audience. Through immersive virtual tours, interactive exhibits, and educational resources, the platform serves as a dynamic portal for engaging with the village's rich history and architectural splendour. By harnessing digital technologies, the team fosters cultural awareness, promotes sustainable tourism, and ensures the enduring legacy of the village for future generations.

Fig. 4. Drone Image, overview of the Fikardou village

Fig. 5. Holistic documentation - efikardou.eu platform

7   Conclusion

The integration of paradata, metadata, and data into the creation of Memory Twins presents a pioneering approach to preserving and interacting with digital cultural heritage. This paper introduces the concept of the Memory Twin as an evolution of the Digital Twin, offering an innovative methodology that enhances the representation of cultural assets by capturing both their physical and contextual aspects. This comprehensive approach ensures a more holistic preservation of cultural heritage.

Memory Twins not only replicate the physical attributes of cultural artefacts but also encompass their historical significance, usage contexts, and experiential dimensions. This richer and more nuanced representation enables cultural institutions to transform the management and dissemination of cultural heritage. By providing detailed accounts of the historical and cultural contexts, Memory Twin facilitates a deeper understanding and appreciation of cultural artefacts.

Through detailed case studies, such as the Lambousa fishing trawler and Fikardou village, the transformative potential of Memory Twins is demonstrated. These case studies highlight how Memory Twins provide enriched and accessible digital representations that support advanced archival practices, personalized user experiences, and improved data authenticity. The Lambousa fishing trawler Memory Twin preserves not only the vessel's physical structure but also its maritime history, while the Memory Twin of Fikardou village captures its architectural intricacies and cultural narratives.

The development of Memory Twins paves the way for innovative and impactful ways to preserve and share cultural heritage. This approach enhances the visibility and educational potential of cultural assets, promoting a broader appreciation of cultural history and contributing to the preservation of European cultural heritage. The advancements in digital documentation and preservation techniques embodied in Memory Twins ensure that the rich tapestry of human history is accessible to future generations. This evolution from Digital Twins to Memory Twins represents a paradigm shift towards a more holistic understanding of cultural heritage, providing new opportunities for cultural institutions to engage with and preserve their heritage in the digital age.

Acknowledgments. **EUreka3D** project is co-financed by the Digital Europe Programme of the European Union, GA n. 101100685. **ExhiBIT** project is co-financed by the ERASMUS+ programme of the European Union. Project number: 2023–1-CY01-KA220-ADU-000152821. **IMPACTOUR** project has received funding from the European Union's Horizon 2020 research and innovation programme under grant agreement No. 870747. **MNEMOSYNE** project has received funding from the European Union's H2020 Framework Programme for Research and Innovation under Grant agreement no. 810857. **TExTOUR** project has received funding from the European Union's Horizon 2020 research and innovation programme under grant agreement No.101004687. **VIGIE 2020/654** Study on quality in 3D digitisation of tangible cultural heritage: mapping parameters, formats, standards, benchmarks, methodologies, and guidelines, Cyprus University of Technology, European Union, 2022.

Disclosure of Interests. The authors have no competing interests to declare that are relevant to the content of this article.

References

Bekele, M.K., Pierdicca, R., Frontoni, E., Malinverni, E.S., Gain, J.: A survey of augmented, virtual, and mixed reality for cultural heritage. J. Comput. Cult. Heritage (JOCCH) **11**(2), 1–36 (2018). https://doi.org/10.1145/3145534

Bruno, F., Bruno, S., De Sensi, G., Luchi, M.L., Mancuso, S., Muzzupappa, M.: From 3D reconstruction to virtual reality: a complete methodology for digital archaeological exhibition. J. Cult. Herit. **11**(1), 42–49 (2016). https://doi.org/10.1016/j.culher.2015.02.006

Charlotte, J.: Threats to Our Ocean Heritage: Bottom Trawling. Springer Briefs in Archaeology. Springer, Cham (2024). https://doi.org/10.1007/978-3-031-57953-0

Common fisheries policy (CFP) (2023). https://oceans-and-fisheries.ec.europa.eu/policy/common-fisheries-policy-cfp_en

Department of Antiquities – Museums. (n.d.) (2022). http://www.mcw.gov.cy/mcw/da/da.nsf/All/8865F898FAA8A275C22571990020EEAA?OpenDocument

European Maritime and Fisheries Fund (2014–2020). https://eur-lex.europa.eu/legal-content/EN/TXT/?uri=LEGISSUM%3A0202_1

Fishing boats destruction (2021). https://woodenboats.gr/en/fishing-boats-destruction/

Grieves, M.: Digital twin: manufacturing excellence through virtual factory replication. White Paper **1**, 1–7 (2014). https://www.researchgate.net/publication/275211047_Digital_Twin_Manufacturing_Excellence_through_Virtual_Factory_Replication

Ioannides, M., Fink, E., Cantoni, L., Champion, E.: Digital heritage: progress in cultural heritage documentation, preservation, and protection. In: Proceedings of the 8th International Conference, EuroMed 2020, vol. 12719. Springer Nature (2021). https://doi.org/10.1007/978-3-030-73043-7

Ioannides, M.: Study on quality in 3D digitisation of tangible cultural heritage: mapping parameters, formats, standards, benchmarks, methodologies, and guidelines [VIGIE 2020/654], Final Study Report. Cyprus University of Technology, European Union (2022). https://doi.org/10.2759/471776

Tao, F., Zhang, H., Liu, A., Nee, A.Y.C.: Digital twin in industry: state-of-the-art. IEEE Trans. Industr. Inf. **15**(4), 2405–2415 (2018). https://doi.org/10.1109/TII.2018.2873186

UNESCO: The rural settlement of Fikardou – UNESCO World Heritage Centre. (n.d.) (2022). https://whc.unesco.org/en/tentativelists/1673/

Traditional Boats Destroyed According to European Directive, https://greekreporter.com/2011/08/10/traditional-boats-destroyed-according-to-european-directive/

Pavlou, L.: Traditional Earth Sheltered Buildings on Five Finger Mountain (Cyprus) Evaluation of the Energy Efficiency by Computer Simulating the Rectangular Plan Typology

Πλοιάριο, "Λάμπουσα." (n.d.) (2022). https://www.limassol.org.cy/en/ploiario-Lambousa

Dive into Heritage: Paradata and Metadata in an Immersive Digital Heritage Experience

Luisa Ammirati[1]([✉]), Bethany Watrous[1], Amira Ftaita[1], Thomas Rigauts[2], and Michelle de Gruchy[1]

[1] United Nations Satellite Centre (UNOSAT), United Nations Institute for Training and Research (UNITAR), 7 bis, Avenue de la Paix, CH-1202 Geneva, Switzerland
`luisa.ammirati@unitar.org`
[2] UNESCO World Heritage Centre, 7, Place de Fontenoy, 75352 Paris, SP, France

Abstract. The importance of paradata and metadata in fully complying with FAIR data principles is clear, particularly within the context of 3D models that are shared online through platforms such as Sketchfab [1], where it is expected that other users will want to use/reuse the models.

Paradata and metadata serve crucial roles in elucidating the decision-making process behind the design and reconstruction of 3D models depicting historical sites or objects. The process of optimizing 3D models significantly impacts the documentary value and authenticity of the final model. Understanding the dynamics is essential for transparency and reliability in representing cultural heritage. At the same time, integrating metadata into an immersive web-based platform presents challenges as it risks disrupting the narrative flow.

This paper uses the case study of the UNESCO Dive into Heritage (DIH) project, which combines reused existing 3D models, newly acquired 3D data captured by UNESCO, and original 3D models by UNOSAT to create an immersive experience. This paper aims to start a discussion about best practices on the representation of paradata on websites like the DIH platform that will enrich the user experience while ensuring scholarly rigor and authenticity are maintained throughout the exploration of cultural heritage and their narratives.

Keywords: Digital Twin · Interactive Immersive experience · Scrollytelling

1 Introduction

Immersive digital technologies are increasingly used as communication tools for educating general audiences about cultural heritage [4]. Researchers affirm that when visual data, like 3D models of artefacts, are augmented with standardized descriptions and connected to trustworthy sources, it enables users to have a deeper comprehension of the related project [20]. This enhanced comprehension provides deeper insights into the original object and its 3D twin than merely visualizing the 3D model [20]. While images and visualizations play a crucial role in shaping (pre-)historical understanding [5], numerous cultural heritage visualizations, including 3D models and other visual elements, often

M. Ioannides et al. (Eds.): 3D Research Challenges in Cultural Heritage V, LNCS 15190, pp. 36–51, 2025.
https://doi.org/10.1007/978-3-031-78590-0_4

lack sufficient descriptive information about their creation process [9]. Scrollytelling is a narrative technique that combines scrolling interactions with dynamic multimedia elements such as text, images, videos, and animations, further enriches these educational experiences.

Paradata and metadata are vital for clarifying the decision-making process in designing and reconstructing 3D models of historical sites or objects. Hence, in the graphical reconstruction of heritage, stages include gathering material for replication, determining shape and dimensions, crafting the mesh and textures, and adjusting lighting as needed [21]. Paradata provides insights into the steps, choices, and interpretations made during the modeling, while metadata offers essential contextual information about the model's origin, purpose, and technical details. Interpretation is pivotal throughout, especially in crafting original models, where subjective decisions shape the outcome based on available information and expertise. These decisions significantly influence the documentary value and authenticity of the final model.

Thus, both metadata and paradata serve as a critical tool for validating the accuracy and authenticity of 3D models by shedding light on the documentation process involved in their creation. This transparency allows researchers to cross-reference the model with primary sources and compare it to the original heritage sites and objects, ensuring fidelity to historical facts and enhancing trustworthiness in digital reconstructions [21]. For these reasons, research emphasizes the parallel importance of documenting methodologies [5]. Additionally, digital cultural heritage endeavours often involve collaborations across different disciplines, requiring interoperability and the adoption of shared languages and systems [20].

The London Charter was established in 2006 to ensure that the principles of transparency, academic rigor, and sustainability were followed in the use and sharing of 'computer-based visualization methods and outcomes' when researching and communicating cultural heritage [17]. Meanwhile, across data science, FAIR data principles (Findable, Accessible, Interoperable, and Reuseable) have become established best practice [28]. While CARE data principles for indigenous data governance (Collective benefit, Authority to control, Responsibility, and Ethics), build upon the United Nations Declaration on the Rights of Indigenous Peoples (UNDRIP), [6, 7]. Full adherence to these data principles involves many considerations and steps, including the recording and sharing of detailed paradata and metadata. This can lead to challenges in presentation, particularly in immersive digital experiences, due to the volume of information required.

For projects that cater to diverse audiences ranging from heritage enthusiasts to novices, integrating metadata into an immersive web-based platform requires users to shift their focus from the narrative to detailed informational content. This shift can disrupt the narrative flow, fragmenting the experience so it is less immersive.

This paper explores this challenge through the UNESCO DIH project case study, aiming to create immersive experiences of UNESCO World Heritage sites using a mix of reused, third-party, and original 3D data, along with 3D models produced from reference materials.

2   UNESCO Dive into Heritage

The project, DIH is a UNESCO-led project generously funded by the Kingdom of Saudi Arabia that aims to educate general audiences about our world's cultural and natural heritage globally by using technology to create an immersive web experience. It invites users from all over the world to discover World Heritage and its Outstanding Universal Value through the latest technologies such as 3D models, high-resolution videos, and interactive maps. UNESCO has partnered with UNOSAT to develop a functional prototype of the platform.

In its first phase (2022–2024), the project focuses on a selection of 10 pilot World Heritage sites in the Arab States region with the aim to eventually digitize all World Heritage sites inscribed on the World Heritage List, which includes 1199 sites around the world at the time of writing. The first version of the DIH web platform is currently scheduled for release online in early 2025.

The DIH web platform aims to deliver an accessible experience, inviting a wide audience to explore World Heritage sites in new ways with multiple entry points. One key feature is a space with responsive 3D viewers for each site, allowing users to freely navigate, zoom, pan, and rotate 3D models of architecture and artifacts. This interactive exploration fosters a deeper connection with the heritage represented.

Another feature, located on the website landing page, is an interactive 3D globe developed using Cesium, an open-source Javascript library, that allows users to locate and explore all the World Heritage sites within their geographic context. The 3D globe is covered with 3D terrain tiles to simulate the earth's differentiating elevation, overlaid with photographic representations of the built and natural environments. The 3D models of architecture from each of the World Heritage sites have added geospatial information embedded to integrate them accurately and to scale within the 3D globe, producing a kind of digital twin of each World Heritage site.

Later phases of DIH may add additional components for Augmented Reality (AR) or Virtual Reality (VR), which should be considered when devising a solution for sharing paradata and metadata on the DIH web platform. AR overlays digital information onto the physical world, seamlessly integrating computer-generated elements with real-world surroundings in real-time. Conversely, VR immerses users in synthetic content that closely simulates real-world environments, enhancing visual perception, auditory sensations, and tactile experiences to replicate the feeling of being present in a physical environment [29]. Like the 3D globe, this will require accurately placing multiple 3D models, potentially with additional embedded media (e.g. images, videos), within their geographic context.

Finally, the project also requires combining multiple types of data to enrich the 3D models and create narrative, scrollytelling experiences for each World Heritage site, including 3D data, satellite imagery, photographs, videos, animations, and interactive maps. Scrollytelling is a web-based storytelling technique which has users scroll to navigate through text and mixed media content (e.g. 3D models, images, videos, animations, etc.). This mixed media approach creates the potential for constructing memory twins of each World Heritage site for users to engage with both the tangible and intangible heritages connected to the sites.

3 Data Acquisition and Processing

The many 3D models for each site included in the DIH experience were procured from multiple sources with variations in file sizes, levels of detail, and geometric complexities. Additionally, to be complete, metadata for a 3D object must include information about the cultural heritage asset (European Commission, 2019). UNESCO World Heritage sites are globally recognized for their Outstanding Universal Value, transcending national importance and representing the collective heritage of humanity. As such, these sites are accompanied by specific metadata that provides detailed contextual information essential for their documentation and preservation (see Fig. 1).

Metadata for UNESCO World Heritage sites	
• ID number	• Category (cultural, natural, mixed)
• World Heritage property name (EN/FR)	• World Heritage Criteria (i-x)
• Date inscribed	• State(s) Party(ies)
• Danger List (incl. dates)	• Region
• Coordinates centre point (long, lat)	• Transboundary site (Y/N)
• Area (ha) of property and buffer zone (if applicable)	

Fig. 1. Metadata specific to UNESCO World Heritage sites

These metadata are crucial for accurately representing each World Heritage site and are indispensable for the ongoing monitoring of the state of conservation as mandated by the 1972 UNESCO World Heritage Convention. To populate the DIH web platform, the 3D models fall into three categories that each require different workflows and have, therefore, different implications for metadata and paradata:

1. reused 3D digitization
2. newly acquired 3D digitization
3. original 3D models and 3D reconstructions

In some cases, the 3D models acquired, generated, or produced by DIH during this first phase can be considered digital twins or, at least, partial digital twins. As Grieves [14] describes, a digital twin is a dynamic model that mirrors the real-world counterpart in real-time, allowing for monitoring, analysis, and simulation. In practice, work on digital twins in cultural heritage currently fall into one of three categories: (1) a 3D record of a cultural heritage site or component, (2) a digital replica of a cultural heritage site that can facilitate virtual visits, and (3) a full digital twin that can facilitate site conservation and management [15, 18, 19, 27]. The 3D models on the DIH platform do not necessarily record all historic elements of a structure, nor are they dynamic with real-time information. Nonetheless, all of the models digitise in 3D data, monuments and structures on the World Heritage sites in entirety or in part at a specific point in time.

In some instances, the 3D models on the DIH platform may also be considered a form of memory twin, particularly when combined with additional media within the scrollytelling narrative experiences on the DIH platform. Unlike a digital twin that documents the physical, tangible heritage, a memory twin involves more holistic recording to document the intangible heritage, history and heritage values associated with the physical site.

The scope and volume of paradata and metadata produced by these complexities (in addition to the large quantity of 3D models) are outlined by 3D model source.

3.1 Reused 3D Digitization

In the framework of the project, UNESCO contacted State Parties to the World Heritage Convention who were identified as having existing 3D digitisations of World Heritage sites within their territories. Several States Parties generously contributed many 3D digitisations (models) of these sites to DIH. These digitisations and other 3D models freely available from Sketchfab were created from laser scan data and photogrammetry (the process of creating a 3D model using photography and specialized software). A common issue encountered was the presence of gaps or missing components within the 3D datasets that required filling in to adhere to the standards of the DIH web platform and its aim as an immersive experience. In instances where the initial data was shared in its raw form, such as with point clouds, the UNOSAT team engaged in a process of refining the initial dataset, then generating a mesh and texture (occasionally texture painting adjustments). For models integrated directly in the DIH web platform, rather than embedded from Sketchfab, it was necessary to optimize the 3D data without sacrificing quality and ensure compatibility with various digital environments and browsers. This could involve:

- the use of polygon reduction tools across the whole 3D model
- selective polygon reduction
- manual retouching and editing to rectify and refine meshes
- re-topologization
- file format conversion

For mobile versions of the 3D models, optimization included reducing the mesh and polygon count and focusing the area of interest closer to the highlighted object. For larger models, key areas were extracted to fit the scrollytelling experience, slightly altering the narrative. Texture sizes and weights were compressed, often omitting the "Normal map" and keeping only the "Diffuse map".

For the 3D models of structures included in the 3D globe, additional steps were required to embed geographic information (spatial coordinates) and bring the models to a consistent scale.In the cases of both models received by State Parties and those acquired from Sketchfab, the DIH project team relies on received paradata and metadata as a baseline, but also generates new paradata and metadata as the models are adapted for use on the web platform. The volume of paradata and metadata that can be recorded and shared is lengthy (see Fig. 2).

Metadata for reused 3D digitisations	Paradata for reused 3D digitisations

Photogrammetry models
  • Site location/GPS data*
  • Time and date*
  • Number of vertices/triangles
  • File size
  • Scale
  • Vertex colour
  • Material
  • Light source information
 	
Laser scan models
  • Site location/GPS data*
  • Time and date*
  • Number of points
  • File size
  • Scale
  • Light source information
	Data Acquisition
	Photogrammetry models
	  • Image capture/scan methodology*
	  • Image capture/scan parameters* (such as camera settings, resolution, and sampling frequency)
	  • Image capture/scan conditions (e.g. weather, environmental)*
	  • Number of photos/scans*
	  • Average camera/scanner distance to subject*
	  • Camera/scanner positions*
	  • Targets used* (Y/N)
	
	Data Pre- and Post-Processing*
	  • How missing information is handled (e.g. whether gaps in data were filled)
	  • The data used/not used to construct the model (e.g. which, if not all, photos were used, if the model/point cloud was cropped)
	  • Steps taken to clean up or optimize the data (i.e., removing artefacts, aligning features, enhancing visual quality)
	  • Computer specifications (processor, RAM, video card, VRAM, storage)

*May be missing, if not recorded and provided by the original data provider	

Fig. 2. Metadata and paradata for reused 3D digitisations

3.2 Newly Acquired 3D Digitisations

In addition to collecting and reusing existing data, UNESCO and its teams are deployed on the ground to capture new data. This approach ensures comprehensive and up-to-date digital documentation of World Heritage sites, following the Guidelines, Standards, and Criteria developed by the project [26] with input from leading experts in the field of Digital Cultural Heritage such as the UNESCO Chair on Digital Cultural Heritage at the Cyprus University of Technology.

In the first phase of the project, UNESCO collaborated with the UNESCO Chair for World Heritage Management and Sustainable Tourism at the German University of Technology in Muscat (GUTech), the Arab Regional Centre for World Heritage (ARC-WH), and the Ministry of Heritage and Tourism in Oman to digitally record the World Heritage site Bahla Fort. Data acquisition over three days included 3D laser scanning, capturing coordinate points with a Total Station, and aerial and terrestrial photogrammetry. The team conducted 64 Faro laser scans of the fort, surrounding area, and some interiors, resulting in a unified 3D point cloud. Targets linked 3D scanning data with photogrammetry data. Over fifteen thousand photos were taken: 2,768 of interiors and door details with a mirrorless camera, and 13,361 drone images from 30 and 80 m above ground, plus detailed shots of the inner fort façades.

Like other models integrated into the DIH web platform, a process of optimization was required to ensure compatibility with various digital environments and browsers, which produced additional paradata and metadata (Fig. 3). Several opimization techniques were employed depending on the target version (desktop or mobile) of the platform, its requirements and the desired output quality:

- Polygon reduction, including selective polygon reduction
- Re-topologization
- Manual retouching and editing

Additional paradata and metadata were produced during this optimization phase (Fig. 3).

Metadata for reused 3D digitisations	Paradata for reused 3D digitisations
Photogrammetry models	*Data Acquisition*
• Site location/GPS data	• Image capture/scan methodology
• Time and date	• Image capture/scan parameters (such as camera settings, resolution, and sampling frequency)
• Number of vertices/triangles	
• File size	
• Scale	• Image capture/scan conditions (e.g. weather, environmental)
• Vertex colour	
• Material	• Number of photos/scans
• Light source information	• Average camera/scanner distance to subject
	• Camera/scanner positions
Laser scan models	• Targets used (Y/N)
• Site location/GPS data	
• Time and date	*Data Pre- and Post-Processing*
• Number of points	• How missing information is handled (e.g. whether gaps in data were filled)
• File size	
• Scale	• The data used/not used to construct the model (e.g. which, if not all, photos were used, if the model/point cloud was cropped)
• Light source information	
	• Steps taken to clean up or optimize the data (i.e., removing artefacts, aligning features, enhancing visual quality)
	• Computer specifications (processor, RAM, video card, VRAM, storage)

Fig. 3. Metadata and paradata for newly acquired 3D digitisations.

3.3   Original 3D Models and 3D Reconstructions

Occasionally during the first phase of the project, the scrollytelling narrative experiences asked for 3D models to illustrate specific objects or architectural features that were not offered to the project through partnership and were not freely available online on platforms like Sketchfab. In these instances, the 3D modelling team within UNOSAT's heritage unit produced original 3D models and 3D reconstructions. Both the models and reconstructions were produced using a variety of reference materials, including drawings, photographs, and, in one instance, an incomplete point cloud.

An example of metadata and paradata collection for a DIH web platform 3D model is the *Khufu Solar Ship*, produced for the Memphis and its Necropolis narrative experience and 3D viewer. A 3D model was sought as the best method of introducing this historical object to audiences, but the project lacked such a model. The creation of this model provided the team with the opportunity to develop best practices and a unique information collection system to carry forward throughout the project based on FAIR data standards, as well as those laid out by the London Charter (Fig. 4).

A dense point cloud was found on Sketchfab available to download under CC Attribution [3]. Like other 3D digitisations reused for DIH, the paradata and metadata found and stored on the Sketchfab page for the point cloud was partial, consisting of: the creator's username, the name and location of the ship, the number of triangles and vertices, a brief description of the quality of the point cloud and the history of the ship, the available download formats, a few tags for identification through Sketchfab, and the time of publication.

The Sketchfab dense point cloud was used as a reference in the creation of an original 3D model of the ship, thus creating the following additional paradata: the methodology of using the Sketchfab pointcloud as a reference for size and element placement, and the use of images of the actual artefact found in Google searches; the choices made when sections of the ship were not visible from any reference available; the selection and placement of textures; the length of time it took to model; the difference in size between the point cloud and the 3D model (see Fig. 5).

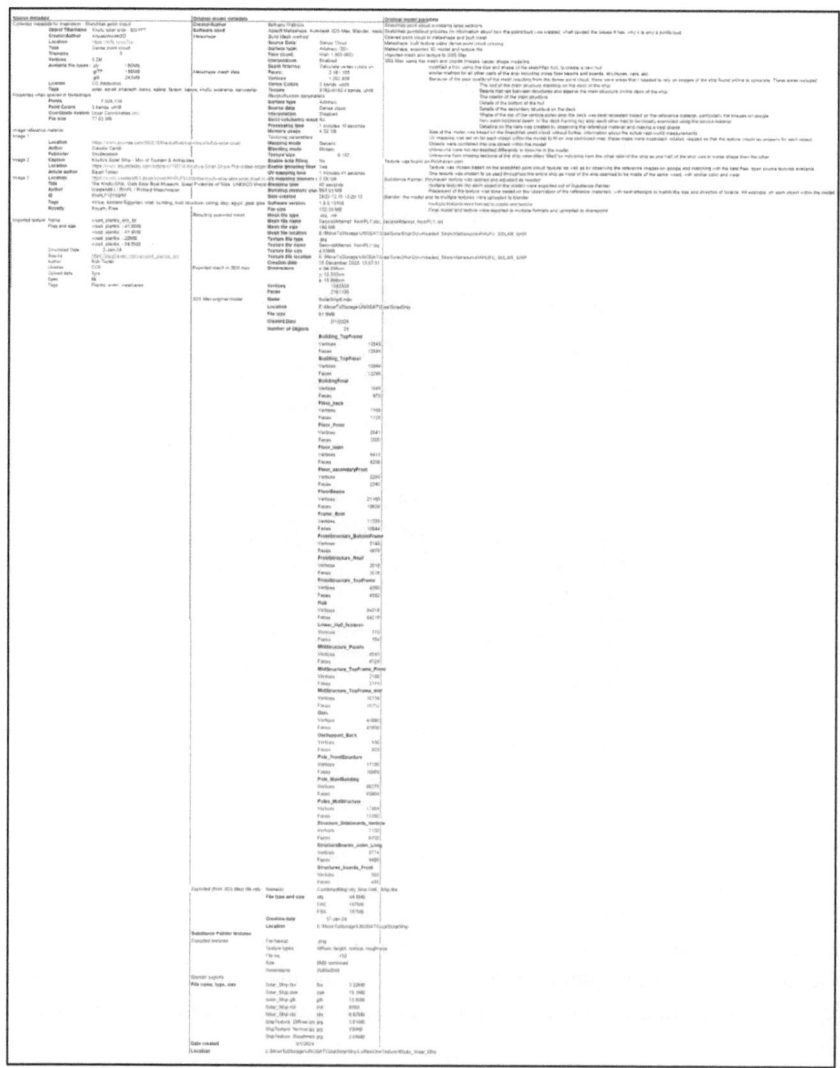

Fig. 4. Khufu Solar Ship 3D model and its metadata/paradata

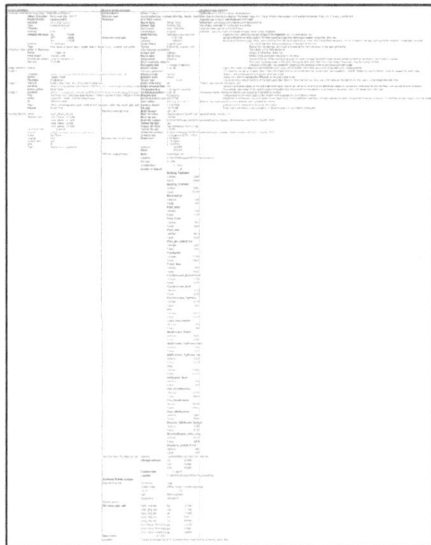

Fig. 4. (*continued*)

• Reference materials and data used to create the 3D models or reconstruction	• Any inferences made inherent to the reconstruction of the model based on available metadata
• Information about the 3D modeller(s) who created the model	• Whether weight was given to one source over another where contradictory information occurs
• Date of modelling	
• The software used	• How unknowns are represented in the final model
• Number of vertices/triangles	
• File size	• Computer specifications (processor, RAM, video card, VRAM, storage)
• Scale and level of detail	
• Whether or not missing information was reconstructed and, if so, on what basis	
• Textures used	
• Lighting source and accuracy	
• Licensing information	

Fig. 5. Metadata and paradata for original 3D models and 3D reconstructions

4 Including Metadata and Paradata in an Immersive Experience

The volume of paradata and metadata produced and recorded for each individual model can amount to pages of information. Even a concise summary of the paradata and metadata comprises multiple lines of text that would be difficult to place within an immersive digital environment without distracting from the experience. DIH is unique in creating an immersive experience that could eventually contain thousands of 3D models recorded using different methods, each requiring a unique set of additional steps to further adapt them for use and cohesion within composite scenes.

Metadata serves little purpose unless it is made available to the user, either by being embedded in the digital file or through an easy lookup method [21]. Thus, incorporating metadata and paradata into the DIH platform while maintaining immersion requires careful design and integration. As we seek a solution, we focus on three primary considerations:

1. Contextual integration – the paradata and metadata must be seamlessly integrated into the user interface without disrupting the immersive experience.
2. Interactive exploration – implemented interactive features that allow users to access additional information on demand.
3. Provide users with an ability to choose the amount or type of data provided based on their "perceptions of the usefulness of specific types of paradata" [16].

Without any precedent to reference, here we explore a number of potentially effective methods for incorporating the paradata and metadata.

4.1 Information Panels

Curated summaries of paradata and metadata could be placed on information panels alongside the 3D models. Taking advantage of the platform's spatial design, the panels could be distributed strategically in different places for users to discover organically as they navigate the virtual environment. Pre-determined settings can allow for the kinds of data presented to the user through this option. It is unclear how to apply this approach in a composite scene with more than one 3D model. Furthermore, this solution on a smaller mobile screen would not be ideal when screen space is already limited.

4.2 An Annex

The creation of a dedicated section of the web platform for gathering all pertinent information in an annex would separate the many lines of paradata and metadata from the spaces of the web platform where visitors engage with the 3D models (and other data/media). It requires assigning an identifier to each 3D model that visitors could use to look up paradata and metadata information in the annex. As the DIH project is not the owner of the majority of 3D data on the web platform, it is not appropriate for the project team to publish the models or assign them DOIs. Rather, the created identifier and annex would necessarily be an internal organisation system. Data presented in an annex could also be organized or filtered based on particular types of information.

4.3 Integration of a Button

A third possibility would be the use of a button displayed by each 3D model that leads to either a pop-up window or a separate page with the full paradata and metadata for the models. A similar approach is already employed on the website where an "i" symbol is utilized to embed additional media or information overtop 3D models within the immersive DIH experience allowing users the option to delve deeper. A second button would provide users the choice to view this additional information. Choices could also be provided as to the level or type of information presented. A concern with this approach is the cluttering of 3D scenes with buttons which could disrupt the immersive flow and divert the user's attention from the narrative. Within the 3D globe, this clutter could be reduced by limiting the appearance of buttons to a particular zoom level. Nonetheless, the potential for distraction remains.

4.4 References Section or Credits Screen

Instead of aiming to present the paradata and metadata either alongside the 3D models or in a centralised annex in a separate space on the DIH platform, information could be stored at the end of each experience. This lengthy documentation would cover only the 3D models on that page or experience.

5 Discussion

A key discussion point is how and when knowledge is created and gathered. Metadata-based descriptions usually appear in digital heritage projects when data are ready for dissemination. Proactively incorporating this need during image capture and model creation can enhance data manageability, integration, and traceability accuracy [23]. A multimodal approach, involving cooperation between several modalities [23], can address the complexity of engaging with digital cultural heritage assets through various phases, though it requires careful initial planning.

For ideal collection and recording each person in the process of the data collection or creation would need to conform to rigorous standards and a unified system to accurately and accessibly collect and store metadata and paradata for each project, each site, and each model. This becomes challenging when using external sources without similar rigor. Unconscious inferences in 3D model creation can lead to incomplete paradata records [5], making it difficult to track all paradata accurately.

A possible solution is a system that automatically tracks and records paradata and metadata, though achieving this in a 3D modeling environment is currently unclear. Best practices emphasize transparency and accuracy, typically seen in academic work. The best systems are those that are well established and agreed upon organization-wide prior to the gathering of any data. Predetermined key terms, collected data points, terminology, and organizational structures are fundamental to achieving FAIR principles. This terminology should be sufficiently inclusive to record all manual, semi-automated, and automated methods used in the digitisation or creation of the 3D model [8]. Additionally, the system must be able to account for variations in the metadata being collected [4]. Within 3D modelling, the metadata for photogrammetry differs significantly from the metadata of a 3D model that is designed from scratch by a modeller. The latter relies on visual references such as photographs, illustrations, or sometimes other 3D models, rather than on direct physical measurements or scans.

The datasets recording paradata and metadata should be scalable and kept in standardized formats for preservation and accessibility [15]. Beyond 3D modelling, FAIR data principles and the push for open science encourage all data scientists, whether working with 3D data or 2D data, to share equivalents of paradata and metadata (although the terms vary by field). In geospatial data sciences for archaeology and cultural heritage, this has led to adopting R and Python, which record all steps to final results without manual documentation. Platforms like GitHub or GitLab automatically document all steps, including failures. While this hasn't yet shifted to 3D modeling, current efforts focus on standardized methods for paradata and metadata [16], and ongoing projects need careful planning to manage these data.

In the specific case of DIH creation of the project, involved collaboration among various entities, along with different specialists' participation. Interoperability is thus an intrinsic feature of DIH. Given this characteristic, while the method for disseminating metadata and paradata to the project's audience has yet to be decided, this informational material has been collected and documented, making it useful for sharing with the main participants in the project.

For the DIH project, a spreadsheet template was set up to collect metadata and paradata as the UNOSAT team created 3D models. This template keeps data points and terminology organized. Since automated methods are not yet available, manual recording remains necessary, which is time-consuming and care needs to be taken to avoid missing details. There is also no automated way to integrate this data into the DIH experience, so the templates, designed for internal use, require additional effort to be user-friendly and accessible – in line with The London Charter Principle 4. Thus, efforts must focus on transforming internal templates into easily accessible formats that are understandable for the public, supporting transparency and evaluation of the visualizations.

This leads to the second point of discussion which is the sharing of metadata and paradata with the audience in a way that is accessible and non-disruptive. It can be hard to find similar online experiences like DIH which incorporates 3D models into an online storytelling experience. Many organizations are turning to existing 3D model repositories with built-in metadata presentation for their 3D model storage and interaction. One example is the British Museum's Sketchfab page which holds over 250 models of objects from their collection [24]. Beyond the standard information captured by Sketchfab, information provided by the museum includes links to websites with further information about the objects. In this way, these organizations are sharing some of the metadata about their models but not enough to allow for deeper scrutiny as to how they were created and how accurate they are as digital twins to the real-world objects. In line with The London Charter Principles 3 and 4.5, it is essential to systematically identify and evaluate research sources, include a comprehensive list of these sources, and disseminate their provenance to ensure the intellectual integrity of original 3D models and reconstructions. A second example is OpenHeritage3D, which functions primarily as a repository, providing free access to high-resolution 3D data of cultural heritage sites worldwide [22]. The repository approach allows for extensive metadata and paradata to be included for each dataset without overloading the user, as the platform is designed for detailed data exploration rather than narrative-driven experiences. Users can download these detailed datasets for deeper scrutiny. Global Digital Heritage (GDH) offers a third practical approach by allowing users to download a detailed report containing metadata and paradata [12]. This practise ensures that the essential context and creation details are available to those who seek it without overwhelming the casual viewer. Within Google Arts and Culture, another scrollytelling platform, research references are provided but very little metadata or paradata is linked for public use [13]. Nor have we, on DIH, arrived at a definitive solution that satisfactorily combines searchability, immesive storytelling, and clarity. Instead, in hindsight, we argue that paradata and metadata must be considered from the earliest phases of a web project.

Though integrating metadata and paradata appears to be rare for online experiences such as DIH, it is clear is that presentation needs to suit the experience. Before User Experience (UX)/User Interface (UI) design takes place for a new web platform, the project should identify the paradata and metadata that will be shared on the platform, so that the team can work with the UX/UI designer to find solutions for including the information into the website. With careful and well-thought-out design, users could access this information, if they choose, in an organic way.

6   Conclusion

In conclusion, the integration of paradata and metadata into immersive 3D experiences is crucial for advancing the field and enhancing user engagement. However, it is clear that more automated methods for collecting this data from the 3D modeling process are needed. Additionally, UX design should play a central role in discussions about how to integrate metadata and paradata into the user experience effectively.

Maintaining a connection with the project is essential, as the collection of metadata and paradata can generate valuable insights and applications for other purposes. Although challenges and gaps remain, addressing these issues will help advance the subject in the coming years.

If the strategy of sharing metadata and paradata is adopted to provide a high-value experience and material for the user, with associated benefits of transparency and interoperability, careful planning is required. This data should be managed and compiled with the same level of importance as storytelling and multimedia quality. Moreover, a standardized framework for producing and presenting this data must be devised to ensure its proper visibility and usability. Investing time in collecting metadata and paradata is worthwhile only if done correctly; otherwise, it becomes a wasted effort.

Currently, there are no existing experiences like DIH that serve as strong examples of how to integrate this information. Developing a system that best suits the online web-browser experience is necessary. If similar projects exist, they are likely limited to research rather than designed for broader audiences. Indeed, most other online experiences with 3D models do not emphasize the provision of metadata. Large dissemination projects aimed at the general public, often initiated by private entities for commercial purposes, typically do not prioritize the scientific dissemination of paradata and metadata as research-focused projects like DIH do.

In summary, while the challenges are significant, the integration of paradata and metadata into immersive 3D experiences holds great potential for enhancing transparency, interoperability, and user engagement. With thoughtful planning and innovative approaches, projects like DIH can set new standards in the digital representation of cultural heritage.

Acknowledgments. DIH is a UNESCO-led project generously funded by the Kingdom of Saudi Arabia. Phase I (2022–2024) of the project is conducted in collaboration with the United Nations Satellite Centre (UNOSAT).

Disclosure of Interests. The authors have no competing interests to declare that are relevant to the content of this article.

References

1. Sketchfab: Sketchfab platform. https://sketchfab.com. Accessed 15 Jul 2024
2. Antonietti, M.: Interactive storytelling for cultural heritage. In: Proceedings of the International Conference on Digital Heritage, pp. 281–288 (2017)
3. Arqueomodel3D: Khufu solar ship – Egypt. 3D Model (2022). https://sketchfab.com/3d-models/khufu-solar-ship-egypt-5c56a4feeb8e4c67b5a4d903b4a96e5a
4. Bertrand, S. et al.: From readership to usership: communicating heritage digitally through presence, embodiment and aesthetic experience. Front. Commun. **6**, 676446 (2021). https://doi.org/10.3389/fcomm.2021.676446
5. Borjesson, L., Sköld, O., Huvila, I.: Paradata in documentation standards and recommendations for digital archaeological visualisations. Digit. Cult. Soc. **6**, 191–220 (2020). https://doi.org/10.14361/dcs-2020-0210
6. Carroll, S.R., et al.: The CARE principles for indigenous data governance. Data Sci. J. **19**, 43 (2020). https://doi.org/10.5334/dsj-2020-043
7. Carroll, S.R. et al.: Operationalizing the CARE and FAIR principles for indigenous data futures. Sci. Data **8**(1), 108 (2021). https://doi.org/10.1038/s41597-021-00892-0
8. CBHC_RCAHMW: Sketchfab. https://sketchfab.com/CBHC_RCAHMW. Accessed 21 May 2024
9. Champion, E.: The role of 3D models in virtual heritage infrastructures. In: Benardou, A., Champion, E., Dallas, C., Hughes, L. (eds.) Cultural Heritage Infrastructures in Digital Humanities. Routledge, London (2018)
10. Pritchard, D., et al.: Study on quality in 3D digitisation of tangible cultural heritage, which contains all the relevant mentioned guidelines', with « European Commission, Directorate-General for Communications Networks, Content and Technology, Study on quality in 3D digitisation of tangible cultural heritage – Mapping parameters, formats, standards, benchmarks, methodologies, and guidelines –Publications Office of the European Union (2022) https://doi.org/10.2759/581678
11. Gabellone, F.: Digital twin: a new perspective for cultural heritage management and fruition. Acta Imeko **11**(1), 1–7 (2022). https://doi.org/10.21014/acta_imeko.v11i1.1085
12. GDH Homepage. http://globaldigitalheritage.org/. Accessed 22 May 2024
13. Google.: 3D models - google arts & culture. Google Arts & Culture. https://artsandculture.google.com/project/3d-models
14. Grieves, M.: Digital twin: manufacturing excellence through virtual factory replication. White Paper **1**, 1–7 (2014)
15. Hardesty, J.L., et al.: 3D data repository features, best practices, and implications for preservation models: findings from a national forum. College Res. Libr. **81**(5) (2020). https://crl.acrl.org/index.php/crl/article/view/24512/32346. Accessed 4 Apr 2024
16. Kuroczyński, P., Apollinio, F.I., Bajena, I.P., Cazzaro, I.: Scientific reference model - defining standards, methodology and implementation of serious 3D models in archaeology, art, and architectural history. In: The International Archives of the Photogrammetry, Remote

Sensing and Spatial Information Sciences, XLVIII-M-2–2023, 29th CIPA Symposium "Documenting, Understanding, Preserving Cultural Heritage: Humanities and Digital Technologies for Shaping the Future", Florence, Italy. https://cris.unibo.it/bitstream/11585/934635/1/SCIENTIFIC_REFERENCE_MODEL_-_DEFINING_STANDARDS_ME.pdf. Accessed 22 May 2024

17. London Charter: Objectives. London Charter. http://www.londoncharter.org/objectives.html. Accessed 24 Apr 2024

18. Luther, W., Baloian, N., Bielle, D., Sacher, D.: Digital twins and enabling technologies in museums and cultural heritage: an overview. Sensors **23**(3), 1583 (2023). https://doi.org/10.3390/s23031583

19. Massafra, A., Predari, G., Riccardo, G.: Towards digital twin driven cultural heritage management: a HBIM-based workflow for energy improvement of modern buildings. Int. Arch. Photogrammetry Remote Sens. Spat. Inf. Sci. **XLVI-5/W1-2022**, 149–157 (2022). https://doi.org/10.5194/isprs-archives-XLVI-5-W1-2022-149-2022

20. Mi, X., Pollock, B.M.: Metadata schema to facilitate linked data for 3D digital models of cultural heritage collections: a university of South Florida libraries case study. Cataloging Classif. Q. **56**(2–3), 273–286 (2018). https://doi.org/10.1080/01639374.2017.1388894

21. Ogleby, C.: The "truthlikeness" of virtual reality reconstructions of architectural heritage: concepts and metadata. In: Proceedings of the 3DARCH, p. 3D (2007)

22. OpenHeritage3D Homepage. http://openheritage3d.org/. Accessed 22 May 2024

23. Pamart, A., De Luca, L., Véron, P.: Metadata enriched system for the documentation of multi-modal digital imaging surveys. Stud. Digit. Heritage **6**, 1 (2022)

24. The British Museum: Sketchfab. https://sketchfab.com/britishmuseum. Accessed 21 May 2024

25. UNESCO: Convention concerning the protection of the world cultural and natural heritage. https://whc.unesco.org/en/conventiontext/. Accessed 22 May 2024

26. Vileikis, O., Rigauts, T., Rouhani, B., Ziane Bouziane, M., Santana Quintero, M.: Dive into heritage: a digital documentation platform of world heritage properties in the Arab States region. Int. Arch. Photogrammetry Remote Sens. Spat. Inf. Sci. **XLVIII-M-2-2023**, 1613–1620 (2023)

27. Vuoto, A., Funari, M.F., Lourenço, P.B.: Shaping digital twin concept for built cultural heritage conservation: a systematic literature review. Int. J. Architectural Heritage **18**, 1–34 (2023). https://doi.org/10.1080/15583058.2023.2258084

28. Wilkinson, M.D., et al.: The FAIR guiding principles for scientific data management and stewardship. Sci. Data **3**, 160018 (2016). https://doi.org/10.1038/sdata.2016.18

29. Zhao, Q.: A survey on virtual reality. Sci. China Ser. F Inf. Sci. **52**(3), 348–400 (2009)

Digital Representations of Cultural Heritage: Enabling the Quality to Speak for Itself

Mark Mudge[(✉)] [iD] and Carla Schroer [iD]

Cultural Heritage Imaging, 2325 3rd Street, Suite 337, San Francisco, CA 94107, USA
info@c-h-i.org

Abstract. Humanities and scientific collections institutions and cultural memory organizations around the world are incorporating advanced digital representations of their materials into their conservation practice, service to the public, and materials preservation strategy. Understanding the reliability of digital assets is key to the success of these activities. Imaging tools and methods are now available that produce 2D and 3D digital representations which carry a metadata record describing the process of their creation. The open-source Digital Lab Notebook software simplifies the creation of such a metadata record and assists in its long-term archiving and preservation. This transparent record allows users, both within and outside of collection organizations, to evaluate the quality of the representation, understand its precision, and determine its utility for their own purposes.

Keywords: Digital Lab Notebook · photogrammetry · digital preservation

1 Reliable Documentation of Cultural Heritage

1.1 Introduction

Reliable digital representations give scholars, cultural communities, and the interested public access to knowledge assets that pay dividends each time they are reused. Curators and collections managers employ 3D representations and their associated orthographic 2D representations in many exhibit-related ways. Museum visitors can enjoy the participatory experience of manipulating 3D models, bringing collection materials to life. Advanced digital representations allow the public new ways to experience the imaging subject if they are unable to visit it and, if previously viewed remotely, enjoy a richer, more nuanced experience when encountered in person. Conservators now use 3D measurements to monitor changes to collection materials, aid in the planning of conservation treatments, and record their interventions. Distributed scholarship and study are enabled when reliable 3D assets are made available. Both the research of students and senior scholars benefit from the wealth of information carried by reliably produced digital representations. The use of 3D representations means that subjects can be examined in detail over and over again; delicate, valuable, sensitive, and cumbersome subjects can be examined while the physical objects remain safely un-handled. This is a key to successful collections care and preventive conservation, and it helps to bridge the difficult gap between preservation and access.

M. Ioannides et al. (Eds.): 3D Research Challenges in Cultural Heritage V, LNCS 15190, pp. 52–62, 2025.
https://doi.org/10.1007/978-3-031-78590-0_5

Advanced digital representations are part of a cultural memory institution's long-term preservation strategy. For example, photogrammetry uses well-captured sets of digital photographs as its source data. The technology can scientifically exploit the information present in the photographs using the laws of physics and optics. A well-captured photogrammetric data set can be processed in any competent photogrammetry software package and can produce 3D digital representations with the same level of surface shape precision each time they are built. Archivists understand the long-term preservation of digital photographs. When photogrammetric photo sets and the metadata describing their acquisition are placed in an archival preservation environment, they become a robust record of the imaging subject's surface shape and color. This means that collecting a well-acquired photographic data set and the associated metadata is enough: An organization with limited resources can collect the image data of at-risk materials or sites, defer the processing, and bank the photographs, along with their associated metadata, for future use.

The great value of cultural materials is that they carry the memory of past human experience. Reliable digital documentation can retain some of this memory in the event of the unthinkable. This data becomes invaluable in case of catastrophic loss; the subject is stolen, damaged, or destroyed. Notre Dame burned. Archived 3D digital representations of its internal and external structure, along with newly captured post-fire photogrammetric data, along with information from a variety of other data collection modalities, now guide its reconstruction [1].

1.2 The Reliability Problem

Widespread adoption of robust digital representations by the humanities and science in all fields, including the multi-disciplinary study of our cultural heritage, requires confidence that the data being used is reliable. For a scholar to use a digital representation built by someone else, in their own work, they need to know that what's shown in the representation is what's observed on the physical original. If archaeologists are relying on virtual 3D models to study Paleolithic stone tools, they must be able to judge the likelihood that a feature on the model will also be on the original and vice versa. If they can't trust that it's an authentic representation, they won't use it in their work. This means reusable digital representations must be acquired in a transparent way to enable its qualitative and quantitative evaluation.

Transparency is a necessary element for the use of digital representations in scholarly and scientific discourse. Humanities collections management, digital-based scholarship, distributed research collaboration, and future reuse of today's investment in digitization require the means to evaluate a digital representation's quality and reliability. Reuse and repurposing are a fundamental test for digital information. If contemporary and future scholars can evaluate a digital representation's trustworthiness, it has passed this test. If not, its value, other than as a source of entertainment, is doubtful.

Understanding that digital representations require transparency has little value unless it is possible to build transparent digital representations using the tools and practices available to both cultural heritage practitioners and cultural and indigenous communities. If there is to be widespread adoption of digital practices, these practitioners must be able to generate transparent, trustworthy digital representations as a normal part of their practice without significant disruption to their working cultures. Whether this happens or not will determine the digital future, or lack of it, in the cultural heritage domain.

The need for transparent methods of evaluating reliability is illustrated clearly in the case of 3D models. Photogrammetry is a leading technology for digitalizing 3D subjects. Photogrammetry is fundamentally about the measurement of surface color, shape, and position to produce 3D assets and 3D-derived, 2D representations of subjects and sites. The key to successful photogrammetric practice is knowing where and how to take the photographs. The person capturing photos for a photogrammetry data set must configure, position, and orient the camera towards the subject in a rule-based way that provides low-error information to the photogrammetry processing software [2].

When collected using good practices, these photographic image sets can be processed to produce millions or billions of high precision measured points in 3D space that represent the imaging subject's 3D shape and color. The level of confidence that these measured points are in the "right place" can be reliably determined using scientific statistical methods and expressed in terms of root mean square errors and standard deviations. Similarly, distance measurement precisions can be demonstrated by using carefully calibrated "real world" scales, photographed along with the imaging subject. These scale values can be used to scale 3D assets in virtual 3D space. The scale's known distance values can also be compared against the photogrammetry software's internal estimate of their distance to add another, independent demonstration of the asset's measurement precision. However, these statistical determinations of surface shape precisions and measurement uncertainty can be rendered unreliable if the image data is collected using poor practices.

Photogrammetry software's increasing ease of use has encouraged many photogrammetry practitioners to claim, "All you need to do is take a bunch of photos." This advice often results in data sets comprised of haphazardly collected photos. This poorly collected data can produce 3D models that look fine, but have, in fact, large measurement errors with undiscoverable origins. Computer scientists have long known that "The extraordinary extent to which weak geometry and lack of redundancy can mask gross errors is too seldom appreciated [3]." High levels of error introduced into the photogrammetry processing pipeline lead to high error in the statistical characterization of the results. This means that the photogrammetry software's reported scientific statistics can only be trusted when combined with a record of the means and circumstances employed in the photographic data's collection and, when needed, a practical way to find and review the archived photographic data.

Poor data collection practices similarly impact the reliability of most forms of advanced digital documentary methods. This problem is also present in models built with lasers, structured light, and other means. In 2024, most 3D and other advanced digital representations of cultural materials lack metadata describing how the representation's data was acquired and how the representation was constructed using the captured information. Access to this knowledge is critically important because, as in the case of photogrammetry, poor data capture and processing practices make it easy to introduce major, often unfixable, and hard-to-recognize errors. In all these forms of empirically-based 3D digitization, the resulting model could have been produced from low error data using good processing practices; but, without a metadata record describing the data capture context and methods along with the associated processing history, there is no way to know the model's reliability.

There is an ancient conversation about how people can learn from their experience and what this experience lets us know about ourselves and our world. In this very old and still vigorously pursued discussion about the nature of human knowledge, a fundamental question remains; how to determine if the observations of the senses (or the extension of our senses through tools, such as cameras and microphones) are reliable.

Science has grappled with the reliability problem since its inception. The reliability of data and the robustness of inferences drawn from that data are core scientific issues. When the scientific method is reduced to its essentials, two requirements remain: empirical observations, the experience of the senses, must be inter-subjectively observable by two or more people and lab notebook accounts must be present to describe the observations' acquisition, and subsequent processing. The process of scientific inquiry indicates that what is needed to demonstrate the reliability of a documentary digital representation is the digital equivalent of a scientific lab notebook account describing the representation's creation.

The metadata record contained in such a digital lab notebook is sometimes called "paradata". The utility, or lack thereof, associated with use of the term paradata is discussed at length in the book, *Paradata and Transparency in Virtual Heritage,* published in 2012 [4]. In the book, London Charter co-author Drew Baker, who coined the term "paradata", describes the case for its use [5]. In the book's next chapter [6], the present chapter's authors argue that the analysis of linguistic usage [7, 8] demonstrates that the difference between the terms metadata and paradata is essentially a distinction without a difference and that the confusion caused by the introduction of a new word to characterize a concept that can be simply described without it outweighs any clarity gained. Consequently, the present chapter's authors choose to use the term "metadata" instead of the term "paradata".

The need for reliable, reusable digital representations of material culture and the encoding of well-structured digital lab notebook metadata is understood worldwide. With the widespread emergence of digital 3D models, initial efforts began to inject rigor into their academic use [9, 10]. In 2004, the authors began their advocacy to associate digital lab notebook metadata with documentary digital representations on a panel titled *Cultural Heritage and Computer Graphics* at the SIGGRAPH Conference [11]. At the European Union sponsored EPOCH project [12] member meeting, held during the 2005 VAST Conference, the authors continued this advocacy. The discussions at the EPOCH meeting directly led [13] to the first iteration in 2006 of the London Charter [14]. The London Charter called for explicit disclosure of the means and circumstances involved with the use of digital visualizations in archaeology. The authors participated in the subsequent iteration of the London Charter [15], and the associated book [4], and the following Seville Principles (2012) [16], which extended the analysis of the London Charter to the general scientific use of digital representations in archaeology.

This decade of widespread international collaboration led to what became *FAIR Guiding Principles for cultural heritage digital documentary management and stewardship* [17]. FAIR stands for Findable, Accessible, Interoperable, and Reusable. The goal of the FAIR principles is the widespread creation and reuse of transparent data and digital representations of cultural heritage.

In North America, the authors participated in the US Institute of Museum and Library Services (IMLS) funded Community Standards for 3D Data Preservation (CS3DP) project [18], which culminated in the 2022 book: *3D Data Creation to Curation: Community Standards for 3D Data Preservation* [19]. The book, offered as a free PDF download, repeatedly stresses the importance the project placed on good documentation for 3D work, along with the importance of data sustainability and implementing an archival preservation strategy. In the chapter dedicated to *Metadata,* and in the *Sustainability* section of the *Management and Storage* chapter, CHI's Digital Lab Notebook software is referenced and recommended.

Between 2012 and 2022, the author's employer, the California non-profit organization (NGO) Cultural Heritage Imaging [20], engaged in an international software development collaboration with the Center for Cultural Informatics (CCI) [21] of the Institute of Computer Science (ICS) at the Foundation for Research and Technology Hellas (FORTH) based in Heraklion, Crete. In July 2022, the collaborators released a powerful software tool to collect and record digital data acquisition context and processing metadata called the Digital Lab Notebook (DLN) [22]. The free DLN open-source software and its *User Guide* is available for download here [23].

2   The Digital Lab Notebook

2.1   Simplifying Documentary Imaging

The DLN dramatically simplifies the scientific imaging workflows used to build advanced, image-based digital representations of material culture. It provides automatic semantic knowledge management (more explanation below) for the photographic data, generated digital representations, and context metadata used in photogrammetry, multispectral imaging (MSI), Reflectance Transformation Imaging (RTI), and various types of documentary photography, including single photos, photo sets, panoramas, object movies, HDR, DStretch, focus stacking, and high-resolution stitching. If used throughout the scientific imaging workflow, the DLN can automatically build Open Archive Information System (OAIS), ISO 14721, standards-based Submission Information Packages (SIPs) [24] to prepare this information for archival deposit in a user-selected preservation environment.

Many advanced digital representations of cultural heritage materials now come from a family of technologies called computational photography. This family of technologies gathers information about the imaging subject using sequences of digital photographs. Generally requiring only off-the-shelf digital camera equipment for data capture, these dynamically developing computational photography technologies are now undergoing rapid, worldwide adoption. Information found in the photographic sequences is extracted by computer algorithms and used to generate new, information-rich representations. This new information can come in many forms: measurable 3D models of Hawaiian petroglyphs; the interactive panorama of an ancient landscape, increased readability of a charred papyrus text; the revelation of a previously indecipherable date on a coin; the infrared-based picture of an oil painting's under drawing; or an up-close 3D view of Diego Rivera's brushstrokes in a fresco's once-wet plaster.

The DLN software makes the collection of metadata during documentary imaging faster and more efficient. The DLN, at the user's discretion, can record information about the imaging subjects, the photographic equipment used to document them, the capture methodology, the imaging operators, project purposes, project stakeholders, locations, date ranges, individual processing steps, entire processing workflows, work products, and related documents.

The DLN simplifies the scientific imaging process through a plain language easy-to-use working experience. It is designed so that much of an imaging team's relevant metadata can be entered during a preparation phase before the image acquisition work begins. For example, the team can enter the information about their photographic equipment into an installed private database [25], using easy-to-understand data entry fields. Using the DLN, data entry is done only once because the information is stored internally by the software. The metadata is then accessible through the DLN software for reuse during subsequent documentary work. Equipment data, for example, can be grouped into typical equipment configurations. When capturing a new documentary subject, the user can select the previously entered metadata that describes the equipment they will use with just a few mouse clicks. Processing workflows are handled in a similar way. Processing steps are entered into the database, described individually. And then grouped into temporally-ordered workflows. When a process is modified, the modification is entered into the database and placed into its position in the temporal order. The metadata, describing as many workflows as needed, can be saved and selected as the situation demands.

The DLN makes the collected metadata available to users in human-readable and machine-readable formats. These metadata formats are saved together with the associated image data and digital work products during the DLN's preparation of the archival Submission Information Package (SIP).

The software automatically builds human-readable reports in the HTML format of the collected metadata describing the processed 3D representations and their associated sets of photographic image data. The reports enable the user to interactively expand high-level metadata topics to gain access to underlying information. In reuse scenarios, the potential users of the 3D asset can use these reports as an initial reliability check.

The DLN also automatically transforms the metadata into machine-readable metadata formats. It does this "under the hood," away from the user, and requires no user knowledge of metadata structures or advanced knowledge management techniques. The DLN's automatic metadata generation begins with mapping the plain language metadata, collected in its private database, to the DLN's internal, XML-based [26] data structure. The architecture of the DLN then uses the X3ML framework [27], developed at FORTH's Center for Cultural Informatics, to transform this XML format information into several different formats. As there are a variety of metadata formats employed by long-term preservation environments around the world, the DLN currently provides metadata in three different forms: XML-based Light Information Descriptive Objects (LIDO) [28]; Linked Data [29] mapped to the Dublin Core format [30] and stored in the Resource Description Framework (RDF) [31]; along with the most descriptively powerful form, recommended by both the International Council of Museums (ICOM) and the International Federation of Library Associations (IFLA)—Linked Data mapped to the Conceptual Reference Model (CRM), ISO 21127, [32] and stored as RDF (more explanation below). It is possible to add new metadata formats to the DLN by supplying a new X3ML mapping definition language file [27] containing the necessary transformation instructions. While the preparation of this file requires expert knowledge, the DLN can produce machine-readable information to meet nearly any metadata format requirement.

2.2 Knowledge Management

The DLN builds metadata records designed to use the international knowledge management infrastructure. The DLN tools produce structured Linked Data, which has the ability to integrate knowledge within, and potentially across, repositories. Computers can parse this Linked Data, make connections with other related information, and enable humans to understand and exploit it. Researchers can follow this thread of connections between information elements to find new and serendipitous knowledge.

Linked Data relationships gain their greatest power to represent highly organized knowledge, such as the process history describing the generation of a 3D representation, by "mapping" or referring the information they represent to an underlying knowledge structure. The DLN's metadata format with the most descriptive power uses the Conceptual Reference Model (CRM). This model is an abstracted and generic way to describe what exists and happens in our world. When two related pieces of information are mapped to their corresponding concepts in the model, the documented relationships between the concepts in the model will preserve the "real world" relationships between the two individual pieces of information in the metadata record. If humans had to link and map all this data by hand, it would only rarely get done. Thankfully, this is all handled automatically by the DLN software without needing user involvement. Reliably built, complex digital representations, described with semantically managed Linked Data, can become a valued resource for use now and in the future.

2.3 Efficient Archival Submission and Preservation

The DLN workflow also supports streamlined archival submission practices by automatically building standards-compliant Submission Information Packages (SIPs).

The SIPs contain the original photographic data, the user-selected photogrammetric 3D and 2D work products, the standards-compliant, machine-readable metadata, and the human-readable reports. Both the linked data and the SIPs OAIS compliant structure help to maintain the relationships between documentary digital representations, their metadata, and their photographic data. The maintenance of these relationships simplifies the process of finding a digital representation's metadata, querying it to evaluate reliability, and examining the original data. If these relationships are broken or cannot be found efficiently, the reliability question cannot be answered.

The DLN's archival support helps to get humanities documentation off of isolated hard drives and into long-term preservation environments. It also simplifies repository work by packaging complex media into well-organized and familiar forms that can be ingested into the repository using standardized, automated OAIS tools.

2.4 Future Directions

The Digital Lab Notebook (DLN) 1.0 software was designed to run as standalone desktop software. This both serves to keep the adoption of the software simple and removes the need for internet access to use the tools. However, larger organizations have indicated that a networked version, which can maintain a shared and synchronized database, would encourage adoption. Because the system is designed to be flexible, many organizations have requested a facility to support the creation of internal requirements, along with tools to check that all the required information is present before creating a final archival package.

Making the DLN available in additional languages is also a priority. The DLN software is internationalized. This structure to reduces the barriers and costs associated with translation.

Other requested features for a future version include more database management tools, and more human readable reports of user data. DLN users can ask questions and request features in the free CHIForums.

3 The Democratization of Cultural Heritage Documentation

3.1 The Reliability of Information Must Become Self-evident

CHI supports the widespread decentralization of the documentation and preservation of humanity's cultural legacy. There is not one human story, there are many. The goal of the DLN and the information management system it employs is not to build one narrative of human culture but to provide a means for creating, exploring, evaluating, and integrating many human narratives.

What makes the DLN special is its ability to enable digital representations to prove their own reliability. The DLN, and potentially future tools serving the same purpose, can have a profound impact on the breadth and depth of humanity's cultural narrative that is preserved for future generations. The participation of cultural and indigenous communities as documentation providers enriches humanity's cultural knowledge.

In today's world, there is a general absence of metadata records of the means and circumstances used during the creation of advanced digital representations. The result is that those wishing to evaluate a representation's reliability for reuse often fall back on dubious considerations of the "authority" or "reputation" of the representation's author or associated institution. In addition to this approach's obvious and numerous uncertainties, the determination of reliability based on reputation or authority has insidious downstream impacts. As a basis for reliable knowledge, institutional authority can reinforce the structures and attitudes that support a dominant cultural and political power. This fundamental need for information reliability has given extraordinary influence to those working for, or carrying the credentials of, authoritative institutions. In current practice, as the arbiters of reliability, the viewpoints of these authorities influence the general narrative of human culture and often shape the primary cultural narrative of indigenous and formerly colonized communities. Linking reliability to institutional authority reduces the potential sources of human cultural documentary knowledge and the diversity of values present in it.

The DLN's transparent documentary workflow makes it possible for people to represent humanity's cultural legacy and demonstrate to others the quality of their work. The workflow creates digital data that is designed to separate the evaluation of the representation's *empirical reliability* from the representation maker's *institutional authority*. This permits the documentary work from someone working at a small collection or from an uncredentialed local cultural caretaker, who learns a good practice-based imaging workflow and does it properly, to stand toe to toe with the work from the most respected and authoritative sources. The DLN's rich, structured metadata allows a digital representation's quality (or lack thereof) to speak for itself. Over time, this will improve access to reliable digital representations from sources representing a range of collections organizations, cultural and indigenous communities, and citizen scholars.

3.2   Expanding the Sources of Cultural Heritage Documentation

For widespread decentralization of the documentation and preservation of humanity's cultural legacy to occur, the cultural heritage practitioners and indigenous and cultural communities who want to use advanced digital representations must be able to employ these new tools themselves.

The means by which robust digital information is captured and synthesized into reliable digital representations must scale quickly by being straightforward, inexpensive, and compatible with the existing local values. In light of the increasing impacts of climate change, Cultural Heritage Imaging (CHI) believes that spreading documentary technology skills to the widest possible user-base is necessary to preserve even a significant minority of our increasingly at-risk cultural legacy.

The way we document our past is important. The transfer of digital documentary imaging and repository technology to local users around the world is the key to preserving and understanding the richness of humanity's diverse cultural narratives.

Acknowledgments. Many thanks to the DLN's developers and concept designers, Erich Leisch, Stelios Sfakianakis, Ron Bourret, Martin Doerr, and Steve Stead. Thank you to our case study and Beta testing participants especially Adam Rabinowitz and Jon Blundell. Thanks also to the US National Endowment for the Humanities, grant # PR-258746-18, and Cultural Heritage Imaging donors for funding this project.

Disclosure of Interests.   The authors have no competing interests.

References

1. Roussel, R., De Luca, L.: An approach to build a complete digital report of the notre dame after the fire using the aioli platform. Int. Arch. Photogrammetry Remote Sens. Spat. Sci. **48**, 1359–1365 (2023)
2. Photogrammetric data acquisition. https://culturalheritageimaging.org/Technologies/Photog rammetry/. Accessed 15 Jun 2024

3. Triggs, B., Mclauchlan,P., Hartley, R., Fitzgibbon, A.: Bundle Ajustment – A Modern Synthesis, p.300. In: Triggs, B., Zisserman, A., Szeliski, R. Vision Algorithms: Theory and Practice, Springer-Verlag, pp.298–372 (2000)
4. Bentkowska-Kafel, A., Denard, H., Baker, D.: Paradata and Transparency in Virtual Heritage, Routledge, London and New York (2012)
5. Baker, D.: Chapter 14: Defining Paradata in Heritage Visualization. In: Paradata and Transparency in Virtual Heritage, Routledge, London and New York (2012)
6. Mudge, M.: Chapter 15: transparency for empirical data. In: Paradata and Transparency in Virtual Heritage, Routledge, London and New York (2012)
7. Wittgenstein, L.: The Blue and Brown Books. Harper, New York (1965)
8. Quine, W.V.O.: Word & Object. MIT Press, Cambridge, MA (1964)
9. Ryan, N.: Documenting and validating virtual archaeology. Archeologia e Calcolatori **12**, 245–273 (2001). ISSN 1120–6861
10. Eiteljorg, H., II., Fernie, K., Huggett, J., Robinson, D.: CAD: A Guide to Good Practice. Oxbow Books, Oxford (2003)
11. Mudge, M.: Cultural heritage and computer graphics panel. In: SIGGRAPH 2004 Conference Presentations, Web Graphics/Special Sessions/Panels (2004)
12. EPOCH. http://epoch-net.org/. Accessed 15 Jun 2024
13. Beacham, R., Denard, H., Niccolucci, F.: An introduction to the London charter. In: Ioannides, M., et al. (eds.), The E-volution of Information Communication Technology in Cultural Heritage: Where Hi-Tech Touches the Past: Risks and Challenges for the 21st Century, Short Papers from the Joint Event CIPA/VAST/EG/EuroMed, Budapest: Archaeolingua (2006)
14. London Charter. https://www.london-charter.org/downloads.html. Accessed 15 Jun 2024
15. London charter. https://www.london-charter.org/media/files/london_charter_2_1_en.pdf. Accessed 15 Jun 2024
16. Principles of seville. https://icomos.es/wp-content/uploads/2020/06/Seville-Principles-IN-ES-FR.pdf. Accessed 15 Jun 2024
17. FAIR Principles. https://www.go-fair.org/wp-content/uploads/2022/01/FAIRPrinciples_overview.pdf. Accessed 15 Jun 2024
18. Community standards for 3D data preservation. https://cs3dp.org/. Accessed 15 Jun 2024
19. 3D data creation to curation: community standards for 3D data preservation. https://cs3dp.org/2022/06/29/cs3dp-book-now-available/. Accessed 15 Jun 2024
20. Cultural heritage imaging. https://culturalheritageimaging.org/. Accessed 15 Jun 2024
21. Center for cultural informatics. https://www.ics.forth.gr/isl/centre-cultural-informatics. Accessed 15 Jun 2024
22. Digital lab notebook. https://culturalheritageimaging.org/Technologies/Digtal_Lab_Notebook/. Accessed 15 Jun 2024
23. Digital Lab Notebook free download. https://culturalheritageimaging.org/What_We_Offer/Downloads/DLN/index.html. Accessed 15 Jun 2024
24. Open Archive Information System (OAIS) Standard. https://www2.archivists.org/groups/standards-committee/open-archival-information-system-oais. Accessed 15 Jun 2024
25. Postgres Database. https://www.postgresql.org/. Accessed 15 Jun 2024
26. XML format. https://www.w3.org/XML/. Accessed 15 Jun 2024
27. Minadakis, N., et al.: X3ML framework: an effective suite for supporting data mappings. In: 19th International Conference on Theory and Practice of Digital Libraries (2015)
28. LIDO. http://lido-schema.org/schema/v1.0/lido-v1.0-specification.pdf. Accessed 15 Jun 2024
29. Linked Data. https://www.w3.org/wiki/LinkedData. Accessed 15 Jun 2024
30. Dublin Core. https://www.dublincore.org/specifications/dublin-core/. Accessed 15 Jun 2024

31. Resource Description Framework. https://www.w3.org/RDF/. Accessed 15 Jun 2024
32. Conceptual Reference Model (CRM). https://cidoc-crm.org. Accessed 1 Jun 2024

Making the Europeana Data Model a Better Fit for Documentation of 3D Objects

Antoine Isaac[1]([⊠]) [iD], Kate Fernie[2] [iD], Valentina Bachi[3], Eleftheria Tsoupra[1],
Marco Medici[4] [iD], Henk Alkemade[2][iD], Sander Münster[5], Valentine Charles[1],
and Lianne Heslinga[2]

[1] Europeana Foundation, 2595 BE The Hague, The Netherlands
antoine.isaac@europeana.eu
[2] CARARE, Dublin, Ireland
[3] Photoconsortium, via della Bonifica 69, 56037 Peccioli, Italy
[4] INCEPTION s.r.l., Via Ghiara 36, 44121 Ferrara, Italy
[5] Friedrich-Schiller-Universität Jena, Am Fürstengraben 1, 07743 Jena, Germany

Abstract. The current effort in 3D digitisation of heritage items poses new challenges in accommodating more and higher quality information to be associated with the 3D models that are of interest to users and stakeholders. The Europeana Data Model (EDM) is a metadata schema that distinguishes between the information related to the cultural heritage object as such (represented by the class edm:ProvidedCHO) and the information related to its digital representation (edm:WebResource), brought together in the class ore:Aggregation. Work done in the context of the new common European data space for cultural heritage collected inputs from various experts and initiatives working on 3D data, metadata and paradata, in the light of studying requirements for the extension and adaptation of EDM classes to the more complex scenario of representing and sharing 3D digitised cultural heritage collections.

Keywords: 3D digitisation · 3D models · metadata schema · paradata · cultural heritage collections

1 Introduction

This paper presents an analysis of the Europeana Data Model (EDM) from the perspective of enhancing representation of 3D in Europeana, both in terms of accommodating a larger quantity of items and representations, and higher quality of information, considering the growing recognition of the importance of paradata in 3D documentation in the light of supporting reuse. it is the product of a working group gathering representatives from the Europeana Initiative, most of whom are also involved in data space projects[1] currently ongoing on 3D (5D Culture [2] and EUreka3D [3]).

---

[1] The common European data space for cultural heritage [1] is an initiative of the European Union.

© The Author(s) 2025
M. Ioannides et al. (Eds.): 3D Research Challenges in Cultural Heritage V, LNCS 15190, pp. 63–74, 2025.
https://doi.org/10.1007/978-3-031-78590-0_6

In the process, we have looked at relevant related work - some of which involving the members of the group producing this report: EC 3D studies [4], deliverables of the 4CH initiative [5], other past Europeana outcomes and work, like the report of the EuropeanaTech task force on 3D content in Europeana [6], and concrete examples of metadata coming from projects like Share3D [7] and WEAVE [8].

2   Basic Modelling Principles for 3D in EDM

2.1   Modelling Distinctions that Matter: Cultural Objects, Digital Representations and the One-to-One Principle

As shown in Fig. 1, the basis of EDM's modelling approach is the distinction between a Cultural Heritage Object (represented by the class edm:ProvidedCHO[2]), digital representations of that object (edm:WebResource) and the "package" that brings them together (ore:aggregation). The one-to-one principle [10] is then applied with the aim that each resource "carries" information that belongs to it and not to another resource. This means, for example, that the date of when a "real-world" object was digitised, which resulted in the creation of some media (an image, an audio file...), is attached to the WebResource that stands for the resulting media file, while the date of creation of the original object is attached to the ProvidedCHO, even though both are expressed using a same metadata element (dcterms:created).

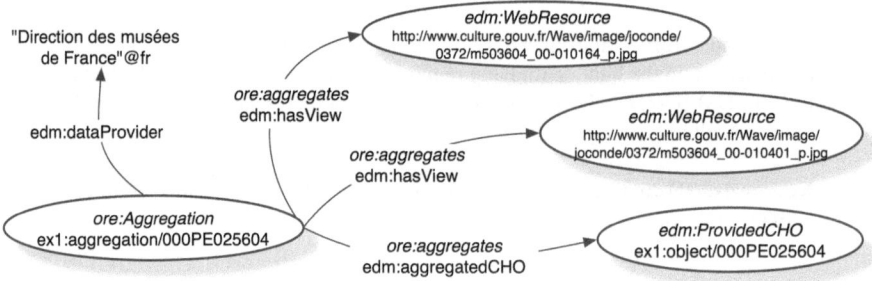

Fig. 1. Basic EDM pattern representing an aggregation of a cultural object together with digital representations.

There are some known issues with the application of the one-to-one principle in EDM. Especially, there is a long-standing issue in that the ProvidedCHO carries the edm:type attribute that belongs on the WebResource (cf. Sect. 3).

We argue that better applying the one-to-one principle can be the basis for handling the case of 3D representations of cultural objects in EDM. Our approach has taken into account relevant work such as (1) 4CH's analysis of 3D data generation and creation for Cultural Heritage (cf. [11], Sec. 2) and (2) previous experiments in preparing for

---

[2] EDM is based on the RDF(S) model [9], where resources are represented as instances of *classes* and attributes and relationships of resources are represented using *properties*.

Europeana objects that have been represented by 3D models, notably in the Share3D project. Let us exemplify it with the example of a Japanese Arita Ware porcelain figure from the Hunt Museum, whose 3D model has been published on Sketchfab [12]. This case corresponds to a "reality-captured" 3D model in the 4CH report, as "the source data are directly coming from the original asset". We propose to represent the "real world" porcelain figure as an instance of edm:ProvidedCHO, whose metadata can include a title like "Japanese Arita Ware porcelain figure of a puppy" and "17th century" as date of creation. The 3D model itself can be represented as an instance of edm:WebResource carrying metadata statements like "Models processed using Meshlab and Blender" under description with "2022" as date of creation. The different metadata statements for the date of creation, especially, exemplify the application of the one-to-one principle, as they use the same property dcterms:created but with different values when they are used for different resources (Fig. 2).

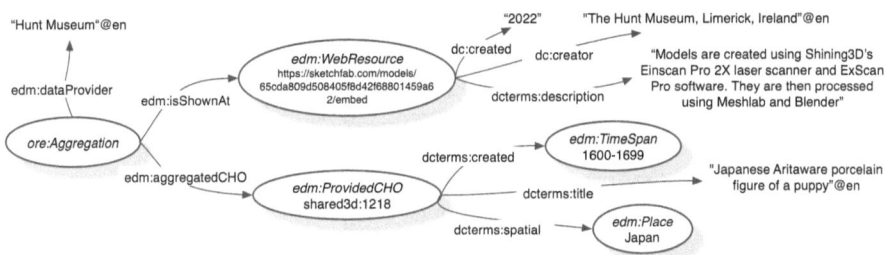

Fig. 2. Distribution of some metadata values onto the main EDM classes.

A main motivation for following the one-to-one approach strictly is its consistency and wide applicability: the same pattern can be employed for various types of 3D model, and is compatible with the approach undertaken in EDM for non-3D representations. As a matter of fact it also allows for "mixed" situations where an object is provided with 3D representations and non-3D ones[3]. It seamlessly enables the representation of objects that are provided with different 3D models, or versions of a 3D model (for example with different numbers of polygons or points, and different rights).

Note that the distribution of (meta)data onto the various resources brought together in the EDM Aggregation, and with descriptions of digital representations separate from the description of the heritage asset, is very much in line with ontological approaches to *digital twins*[4] in Cultural Heritage. See for example [14], which defines a digital twin as "the digital representation of the complex of knowledge about [an] heritage asset" and proposes to model it as a resource that points both to the asset and includes various documents, e.g., 3D models and other visual imagery.

---

[3] For example when a building is provided both with a 3D model and "traditional" 2D photographs.

[4] A Digital Twin can be generally defined as "a virtual replica of a physical product, process or system" [13].

2.2   From Reality-Captured 3D Models to Born-Digital Objects

The pattern can extend to the process of creating a 3D reconstruction of a heritage asset at a moment in time in the past. In the case of 3D, as the 4CH report elaborates, some 3D models include elements that are not directly extracted from reality but instead come from interpretations of cultural objects, for example based on historical documentation (see Appendix "Sample metadata for 3D reconstruction" in our technical report [15]). In this case we speak of 3D reconstructions or "born-digital-reconstructions".

These models have a more complex workflow in comparison to reality-captured models. For example, the workflow may include data capture on the surviving fragments of a CHO, followed by data processing and modelling to reconstruct aspects of a building based on information from plans or drawings which show how it may have looked like in the past. A reconstruction is a representation of the object at a moment in time in the past.

Take for example a digital reconstruction of Wojsławice town in the 1930s [16]. A first EDM interpretation of this case would be to claim that the historical town itself is the CHO, and the 3D model is a digital web resource that is directly associated with it (i.e., linking an instance of an `ore:Aggregation` to the 3D model via one of the properties `edm:isShownBy`, `edm:isShownAt` or `edm:hasView`). However, the nature of the reconstruction (i.e. not purely based on captured reality) would argue for not only focusing on the "original" real-world object as the CHO. The reconstruction of the original object – as an "information object" created following research and interpretation – could also be treated as CHO. There would be CHOs for both the town and the reconstruction related via the `edm:isRepresentationOf` property, or the more general property `dc:subject`. The `edm:ProvidedCHO` resource would carry metadata that applies to the representation (information object), i.e. the creator would be the creator of the model, not the founder of the town. Note that this still does not mean that the `ProvidedCHO` resource should have metadata that belongs to the level of a specific `WebResource`. In fact the reconstruction may not be entirely born digital: there might be analog or digital archives that were employed during the process of creating the (3D) representation, which are also contributed as web resources. In this case, the "reconstruction CHO" should not have metadata statements that hint that it is only a 3D representation. For that to happen, a provider would have to distinguish between distinct CHOs for the 3D representation and the analog sketches (Fig. 3).

The same approach applies similarly to other important cases where the object itself is born digital, as for an abstraction of a design or the work of an artist's imagination that does not represent any pre-existing real world object (this may also include AI-generated objects). This can happen, among others, for architectural (and other) design drawings. For example, in the case of a competition to design a major public building[5], only one of the designs is built. The other designs are proposals which do not represent a real-world object but which may be preserved as part of an architect's archive - ideas that may be reused and re-interpreted in future buildings. In the past the designs would have been done on paper, as with the analogue room design at [18]. Today more and more are born-digital.

---

[5] E.g., the Re-imagining Cappadocia as an Eco-District Architecture competition mentions 3D visualisations among the media that can be submitted [17].

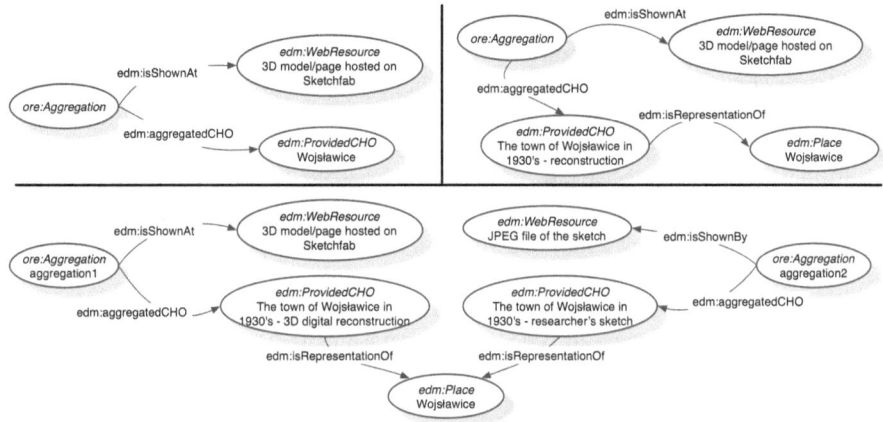

Fig. 3. Variants for reconstructions of an object: (top left) with a cultural object representing the town, (top right) treating the 3D reconstruction as a cultural object; (bottom) With both 3D reconstruction and 2D sketches as cultural objects.

In this case of a born-digital object the CHO is also described at a conceptual level and the digital representation is the "materialisation" of it, e.g., as a file. One object/concept/intention may have different representations and different media files - for example providing different views, offering different types of 3D modelling, different quality, different rights.

3   Identifying and Addressing Basic Limitations for 3D in EDM

When we started discussing the approach above, we knew that there are discrepancies between the current EDM - and especially, the way it is often applied - and the theoretical approach. To further identify limitations, we have applied the above principles to an example from the Share3D project (see appendix in our technical report [15]). The metadata shown there tries to respect the one-to-one principle and the distinction between the original object and the 3D representation. It also represents some data that we believe is important, either present in the original example or mentioned in the literature.

First, we observed that some important information like description or file format are already supported in EDM.

Other requirements would be met by relatively straightforward additions to the current EDM `WebResource` class:

- allowing the representation of types of model by high-level categorisation between "reality captured" models and "3D reconstruction"
- allowing the representation of types of model by technical aspect of the representation (cf. slide 13 of [19]): point cloud, mesh with higher or lower polygon count, with or without textures, BIM and parametric models, etc. (from a controlled list of types, preferably)
- (maybe) enabling `dc:title` and `dcterms:provenance`

For the first two requirements, the example in the appendix at [15] uses dc:type. However, we have made this choice merely to illustrate the matter at hand. Both could be addressed by using a different property, either reused from an existing namespace or newly created in the EDM vocabulary (similarly to edm:type). This will have to be discussed in the next steps of our work. In any case, both requirements probably require establishing a controlled vocabulary of possible values. Such endeavour relates to a more general effort to inspect whether existing EDM properties need to be provided with recommendations on using controlled vocabularies that are specific to the 3D context - for example on foreseen file formats.

We then identified a fundamental issue with the usage of the existing property edm:type, which is meant to reflect the general media category of an object, like TEXT or IMAGE, for Europeana purposes. This type should not be attached to ProvidedCHO as it is currently. For example, in the case of a statue that has some digital images, edm:type is set to IMAGE. But if the same statue in a different context would have been provided with a 3D model, edm:type should be set to 3D. It would be more appropriate to attach the type of media to the resource that stands for the media representation of the cultural object, i.e., the edm:WebResource.

As an alternative (or in addition), the property could be attached to the ore:Aggregation[6]. But we should then probably allow for multiple edm:type statements on the ore:Aggregation class, to cater for the cases where an object has representations of different types (say, a 3D model and some more classical photographs that dictate using IMAGE as value for edm:type). However, even though this option meets simple user information needs like "retrieve objects that have at least one 3D representation", it would complicate rather than improve the model. If edm:type is moved to the level of edm:WebResource, the type of each representation for an object is clear. If it is moved to the ore:Aggregation and we allow multiple types, the type of each representation is not clear.

4 Advanced 3D Requirements for EDM

The previous section seeks to address common, basic needs of characterization of 3D objects. We identified more advanced requirements that can play a crucial role, too.

The first category regards the intended usage of representations available on the web for 3D objects. When sharing 3D models in a context like that of the data space, it makes a big difference whether a representation is meant for a specific (technical) purpose, (such as preservation) or for viewing. This distinction could be made explicit in EDM. A specific case is that of content accessed via a viewer, for example Sketchfab's, which can be embedded in another page, for example on europeana.eu. Another example is when a provider would like to give a link to the raw/full version of a 3D model instead of relying on re-users asking for it via another process. From a user perspective it would be useful to have access to information about how such - often very large - resources may

---

[6] This case would be similar to what happens for the edm:rights property, which is used to express controlled rights statements. An edm:rights statement must be attached to the Aggregation in order to apply as a "default" to the WebResources attached to it, in case these do not have their own edm:rights statement.

be consumed (e.g., the software, media bundles, contexts etc.). We do not know yet from the perspective of the data space, how best to support this access. These requirements are not specific to 3D but they can play a significant role in the 3D context.

The second category of desirable extension of EDM regards context and especially the paradata; "auxiliary information [..] that describe the data acquisition process" [4]. For us, paradata is a kind of metadata that can be crucial to some types of data space users, especially those who rely on rich and trusted provenance information on the 3D content for professional research or re-use. While the collection and management of paradata is highly valued by the scientific community, in cultural heritage it often represents an innovation in the institutions' workflows, which brings added value in terms of enabling the digital transformation of the sector.

We do not foresee that EDM will be extended to cope with all the possible paradata collected at source, which can be very rich and specific. Yet, we recognise that a subset of this information can be very useful in the data space for access and re-use scenarios, especially to inform about the authenticity of the model, relevant technical aspects of the model's creation process and re-use conditions. For example information on motivation (e.g., "research") and limitations of digitisation projects give hints about the quality and trustworthiness of the 3D model. Examples of such provenance aspects could include the indication that a model results from a general "research" (project) motivation, that it is generated from AI training datasets and has not been curated, or that it was created photogrammetrically from user-generated images.

A survey of existing metadata schemas for 3D objects has led us to identify the general categories of paradata that are most relevant for the data space: identification of creation process, methodology followed, people involved, temporal and spatial information, and identification of the various digital resources produced as well as their lineage. Based on this survey, a "core" set of elements from these paradata categories will be considered for inclusion in an EDM extension for 3D for easier consumption. EDM already provides a generic mechanism that allows the creators of 3D content to provide a relation to the full paradata (e.g. in a document expressing the information in the relevant standards or more specific formats) where it can be accessed by data re-users.

Note that some "simple" provenance requirements such as capturing the roles of the people or organisations involved in the life cycle of 3D models[7] may need significant extensions of EDM. The issue of representing roles of agents, for instance, has been identified for a long time as a general limitation of EDM, and it requires non-lightweight solutions such as introducing events [20].

5 Supporting Work Needed

This section gathers issues that are not about data modelling proper, but, which should be addressed so that providers are encouraged to follow best practices.

---

[7] This is especially important to give indication on the authenticity and trustworthiness of the model, e.g., whether it is created by a research team based on data with high geometric accuracy, or by a project with other motivations and more limited resources.

Review of Documentation and Guidelines. Our experience tells that more guidance on specific (mapping) points will be useful. Many issues relate to the one-to-one principle. EDM provides the ability to distinguish the cultural asset (ProvidedCHO) from its specific digital representations. Statements that apply to the asset or the digital representations should be attributed to the specific EDM resources that stand for it. It is crucial to decide whether the ProvidedCHO is the original object or a digital representation[8]. Metadata statements such as the creation date should follow that choice. Note that we do not claim that statements of one kind are more important than others. Of course, users will often benefit much from knowing the date of creation of the original CH asset. But some users will also need to know when the 3D model of that asset was created.

Consider an item that represents a real-world object/monument, as hinted by the use of "church" in the ProvidedCHO's dc:title (without any mention of a "3D model" in it) and a date like "13th century" as the date of creation. Here are some examples of possible other statements for the ProvidedCHO that would raise a discrepancy issue:

- a dc:subject with "3D model": in this example the church is the subject of the ProvidedCHO, the format of the digital representation is best entered into the WebResource.
- a dcterms:extent describing the number of polygons in the 3D model: technical data about the model is best entered into the WebResource. A church's extent would rather consist of its physical dimensions.
- a dc:rights that mention the creator of the 3D model in some project, not the creators of the church. Here it is best to include rights information about the 3D model in the WebResource.

These metadata statements should be present on an instance of the WebResource class, not the ProvidedCHO, when that ProvidedCHO is meant to stand for an (analog) heritage asset[9]. These are not specific to the case of 3D, but for 3D their impact can be significant - especially as they could happen very often.

It is worth noting that the existing EDM guidelines can be confusing. Echoing the issue of edm:type mentioned in the previous section, the EDM mapping guidelines for dc:format on the edm:ProvidedCHO include the instruction "Use the value 3D-PDF if appropriate". This is actually not compatible with following the one-to-one principle and should be removed.

Separating these elements of information would require creating a new instance of the EDM WebResource class when it is not present in the provided metadata. This is an extra effort, but it is very much in line with the needs to represent valuable, 3D-specific information (type of model, digital provenance) introduced in the earlier parts of this report. Guidelines should emphasise this.

---

[8] This concern also holds in the case of objects with non-3D representations, where attributes of the digital representation should not be mixed with those of the original cultural object.

[9] The situation of a ProvidedCHO standing for a born-digital object would be different. There, for example, the dc:creator of the ProvidedCHO is likely to be also the creator of the model itself (which should still be also represented on the WebResource).

Recommendations for the Delivery of 3D. Specific care is needed to articulate recommendations on the web resources themselves, which are provided for an object. For example, it is sometimes not possible to give access to a "raw" 3D model, due to the size of these files. In any case, it is important to provide alternatives to the raw model, such as with an `edm:isShownBy` linking to an embeddable viewer which is supported by Europeana, and/or an `edm:isShownAt` pointing to a view of the objects at the data provider's website. In case the provider wants to point to the raw model (e.g., for specific types of professional users, such as architects or conservators), this is possible by including a relation in the metadata, for example to an archive published on Zenodo or to the provider's own website.

Exploitation of Enhanced Metadata on 3D Representations. Several of the issues that we have observed for representing 3D objects can be traced back to concerns of display in the Europeana website. For example a record can have the `dc:format` and `dc:type` duplicated across a `WebResource` and the `ProvidedCHO`. This is certainly not because these attributes cannot be used with `WebResources`. It is rather because they are not displayed on the europeana.eu portal when they are used only on the `WebResource`. Even the `dc:creator` field is not displayed when it is attached to the `WebResource`. This is a barrier for data providers that seek to convey to users information that they feel is important. Adapting display and search (indexing) to better surface information about (3D) web resources should be implemented at the same time as the data model is deployed and documentation is updated.

6   Roadmap for Future Work

As next steps, we will work on confirming the proposals and progress on their implementation. The main elements of work are:

Identify Requirements for Paradata and Technical Metadata on 3D Models in the Data Space. These requirements will include the representation of:

- types of model by high-level categorisation ("reality captured" vs. "3D reconstruction")
- types of model by technical aspect of the representation (cf. Slide 13 of [19]): point cloud, mesh with higher or lower polygon count, with or without textures, etc. (from a controlled list of types, preferably)
- types of model by project/motivation/limitations (esp., provenance info that could give hints about the quality and trustworthiness of the 3D model)
- intended usage of 3D models, especially, for links to embeddable viewers
- any other context information (digital provenance) is relevant to capture for basic access and re-use scenarios in Europeana (including and beyond dcterms:provenance). This could focus on elements which are in existing established schema for paradata (e.g., CIDOC-CRM dig, CARARE 2.0 etc.) or which can be detected automatically.

We will seek to identify these requirements from studying (re-)user applications[10], earlier reports[11], more record examples[12], existing and coming metadata schema inventories and mappings. We will check whether additional requirements would arise from other efforts in the data space that are not specific to 3D but may have a relation, such as work on enrichment, provenance and annotations.

Identify which new elements should be included in the EDM model, trying to re-use as much as possible existing metadata standards used in the domain. E.g., for context/provenance, re-using Dublin Core's `dcterms:provenance`[13] (for more EDM classes), the proposed extension for events in EDM and/or specific modelling support for software processes, like `dcterms:Software`. Emphasis should be given on use of Linked Open Data data models and vocabularies.

Identify first 3D-centred quality criteria for metadata on 3D objects, especially identifying mandatory or recommended metadata elements. These could be included in the Europeana Publishing Framework[14]. For instance we can include information about 3D objects such as file format, number of vertices, etc., in the calculation of EPF Metadata tiers. The type/motivation for 3D models as discussed in Sec. 4 could also be relevant with regards to setting up quality requirements on the provenance metadata. For this effort it will be useful to re-use works that seek to define completeness of 3D information, such as the 4CH report mentioned above and the VIGIE 2020/654 Study on quality in 3D digitisation of tangible cultural heritage [1].

Supporting Work. In line with the directions raised in the previous section, we will discuss with the designers of the europeana.eu website, how the new metadata and content could be accessed and displayed. This includes how to download and display different versions of a 3D model, embeddable viewers ([6] includes a list of viewers in Sec. 5.2 and Appendix 1) as well as provenance information represented via the corresponding `WebResources`. We shall also review documentation and guidelines to properly reflect adherence to the one-to-one principle and avoid problematic mappings mentioned in Sec. 4. We will also seek feedback from other experts. This would allow more interested stakeholders to be involved, for example from the EuropeanaTech community.

---

[10] We could use IDOVIR [21] as case study. The portal presents some structured data on 3D digitization projects and the software they use, but it seems that it also has a free-form description of paradata and a link to a fuller representation.

[11] We could draw an inventory of types of 3D content relevant for Europeana and a first analysis of digital provenance information from the report of the EuropeanaTech task force on 3D content [4] (e.g., Sec. 2.2.1, 5.1, 5.2 and Appendix 1).

[12] It will be interesting to present cases where different versions of a 3D model are available and hierarchical objects where an object is embedded in another object.

[13] Note that the current dcterms:provenance is focused on "ownership and custody" while we need to represent paradata.

[14] Europeana Publishing Framework. https://pro.europeana.eu/post/publishing-framework. Accessed 31 July 2024.

7   Conclusion

In this paper we report on an analysis of EDM and its support for 3D in Europeana and the common data space for cultural heritage. Such analysis follows the need of maximising the impact of heritage digitisation as highlighted in the EC Recommendation 2021/1970 which, among others, poses the focus on 3D to innovate workflows in digitization, reuse and digital preservation of heritage across the EU. Europeana, as the coordinator of the data space, leads the digital transformation process that the sector is undergoing by adapting the existing tools to the new requirements and needs connected to sharing 3D models and fostering their use and reuse. In this light, we have identified several areas in which EDM may be adapted or extended in future to offer better support for 3D models, Digital Twins and paradata. This analysis is a first step that will support further actions: reflecting on existing metadata and paradata practices, identifying strategies to provide the datasets published in Europeana with enriched information, and understanding current constraints and desired developments. Supporting work is needed to advance our recommendations both by Europeana Foundation and organisations which are creating and delivering 3D to the data space. Our roadmap for the future includes specific work on EDM, on Europeana's Publishing Framework and website, but also with the content creators and cultural heritage institutions building capacity to help ensure that high quality metadata and paradata are produced to support and enable re-use of high quality 3D content.

References

1. Common European data space for cultural heritage Homepage. https://www.dataspace-cultur alheritage.eu. Accessed 31 July 2024
2. 5D Culture Homepage. https://5dculture.eu. Accessed 31 July 2024
3. EUreka3D Homepage. https://eureka3d.eu. Accessed 31 July 2024
4. Ioannides, M., et al.: Study on quality in 3D digitisation of tangible cultural heritage. Technical report, VIGIE 2020/654 (2022). https://digital-strategy.ec.europa.eu/en/library/study-quality-3d-digitisation-tangible-cultural-heritage. Accessed 31 July 2024
5. 4CH Homepage. https://www.4ch-project.eu. Accessed 31 July 2024
6. Fernie, K.: 3D content in Europeana task force. Technical report, Europeana Network Association (2020). https://pro.europeana.eu/post/3d-content-in-europeana-task-force-review. Accessed 31 July 2024
7. Share3D Homepage. https://share3d.eu. Accessed 31 July 2024
8. WEAVE Homepage. https://weave-culture.eu. Accessed 31 July 2024
9. Brickley D., Guha R.V.: RDF Schema 1.1. W3C Recommendation (2022). http://www.w3.org/TR/rdf11-schema/
10. Dublin Core Metadata Initiative, One-to-One Principle. https://www.dublincore.org/resour ces/glossary/one-to-one_principle/. Accessed 31 July 2024
11. Medici M., et al.: D3.1 design of the CH cloud and 4CH platform. Technical report, 4CH (2022). https://doi.org/10.5281/zenodo.7701438
12. Japanese Aritaware porcelain figure of a puppy, The Hunt Museum, Ireland, Public Domain. https://sketchfab.com/models/65cda809d508405f8d42f68801459a62/embed. Accessed 31 July 2024

13. European Location Interoperability Solutions for e-Government (ELISE), Glossary. https://joinup.ec.europa.eu/collection/elise-european-location-interoperability-solutions-e-government/glossary/term/digital-twin. Accessed 31 July 2024

14. Niccolucci, F., Felicetti, A., Hermon, S.: Populating the data space for cultural heritage with heritage digital twins. Data **7**(8), 105 (2022). https://doi.org/10.3390/data7080105

15. Isaac, A. (ed.): Review of EDM to support 3D. Technical report, Common European data space for cultural heritage (2024). https://pro.europeana.eu/post/review-of-the-europeana-data-model-to-support-3d. Accessed 31 July 2024

16. The town of Wojsławice in 1930's - 3D digital reconstruction, Grodzka Gate – NN Theatre, Poland, CC BY. https://www.europeana.eu/en/item/814/https___biblioteka_teatrnn_pl_dlibra_publication_edition_139444_content. Accessed 31 July 2024

17. Re-imagining Cappadocia as an Eco-District Architecture Competition Project Submission Deadline Extended. https://www.archdaily.com/999941/open-call-re-imagining-cappadocia-as-an-eco-district-architecture-competition. Accessed 31 July 2024

18. Entwurf für eine Raumgestaltung, MAK – Museum of Applied Arts, Austria, In Copyright. https://www.europeana.eu/en/item/15514/KI_14388_38. Accessed 31 July 2024

19. Fernie, K.: Sharing with Europeana: depositing and publishing 3D datasets for preservation and future access. Twin it! Webinar 5: Storing, managing and visualising the 3D models (2024). https://europeana.atlassian.net/wiki/spaces/EF/pages/2407170152/Twin+it+3D+for+Europe+s+culture+webinar+series#Webinar-5:-Storing,-managing-and-visualising-the-3D-models. Accessed 31 July 2024

20. Tsoupra E., Charles V., Stein R. (eds.): Recommendations for the representation of EDM: Event in Europeana. Technical report, Europeana Network Association (2021). https://pro.europeana.eu/project/data-quality-committee#representing-events-in-edm. Accessed 31 July 2024

21. IDOVIR Homepage. https://idovir.com. Accessed 31 July 2024

Publishing and Long-Term Archiving 3D Data in Humanities

Matthieu Quantin[1]([⊠])[iD], Sarah Tournon[2][iD], Mehdi Chayani[2], Xavier Granier[3], and Florent Laroche[1]

[1] Laboratory of Digital Sciences (LS2N), École Centrale de Nantes, Nantes, France
`matthieu.quantin@ec-nantes.fr`
[2] Archeovision 3D SHS – Universities of Bordeaux Montaigne, Pessac, France
[3] LP2N – Universities of Bordeaux Montaigne, Pessac, France

Abstract. We present here the French solution for long-term archiving combined with online publication of 3D research data in the humanities. The focus is on the paradata that document the technical process involved in obtaining the 3D result. Our schema, initially limited to the fields of archaeology and cultural heritage, is now open to other areas of the human sciences. The choice of data organization, metadata, paradata, standards and infrastructure is in line with the FAIR principles of the semantic web. It is aligned with standard vocabularies and mapped to the Europeana Data Model (EDM). The CINES (Centre Informatique National de l'Enseignement Supérieur.), the Open Archival Information System (OAIS) infrastructure for research data in France, is in charge of archiving. We take care of data documentation and propose to publish part of these documented data at the same time. On the user side, we developed aLTAG3D, a desktop UI software to help research teams to create their OAIS Submission Information Package (SIP). On the publication side, we provide a DOI and a 3D viewer on the online plateform to meet the needs of researchers and public communication. On the archiving side, long-term archiving has given direction to the way our description schema works: it is focused on reproducibility. The content of the SIP is centered on the 3D data, its build process and sources. Paradata describing the process to the 3D file is under development and several options are under study with CIDOC CRM-Dig or W3C *prov-O* ontologies.

Keywords: 3D · metadata · paradata · archiving · publishing

1 Introduction

1.1 Context

In 2014, on one hand, a set of laboratories in France have interest in long-term archiving their 3D data. All of them are working with cultural heritage or archaeology. On the other hand, the OAIS infrastructure for research in France

M. Ioannides et al. (Eds.): 3D Research Challenges in Cultural Heritage V, LNCS 15190, pp. 75–88, 2025.
https://doi.org/10.1007/978-3-031-78590-0_7

(CINES) has no specification for archiving 3D data. Our working group has emerged for creating a missing link between the production (3D data) of the laboratories and the capacities of the archiving infrastructure: a process and a metadata schema. Built upon the requirements of the CINES (for long-term archiving), the metadata schema quickly included publication matters. The idea is to create only once a package that can be published and archived.

Since 2017, our consortium *3D for Humanities* offers this service through the *French National 3D Data Repository for Humanities* (CND3D). Until 2021, our focus has been on the fields of archaeology and cultural heritage. In 2021, with more than one thousand (1000) projects registered, driven by laboratories from all over the country, open questions were posed to the community. In response, we have developed a new metadata schema that allows a more precise description of the research content, greater openness to other non-archaeological humanities fields, and better FAIR compliance.

1.2   Scope

Long-term archiving has given a direction to the way our description schema works. A technical point of view is adopted: we care about the data **until it becomes a 3D result**. We rely on other tools to document the content after this point, from a humanities point of view. The content of the OAIS Submission Information Packages (SIP) is focused on the **3D data**, its **sources** and **build process** (computing and human intervention). Figure 1 shows the simple chain of actions that leads to the creation of a 3D result. The description of the content of the 3D at a lower level: historical analysis of a 3D part, for example, is out of scope yet.

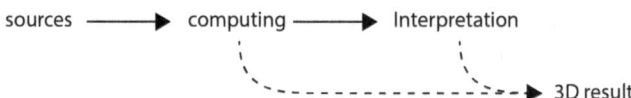

Fig. 1. Basic data life-cycle in the 3D producer (lab) view

The 3D content may be of 3D types as described in Table 1. "Reconstitution" and "Conception" are two types of digital born content. The last case, "3D Conception" is new, and few use-cases for this kind of 3D are yet recorded. So this article doesn't focus on them. Nevertheless, they create a singularity in the data model because the 3D result doesn't refer to any physical object. This case is taken into account in the Sect. 3.1.

1.3   Objectives

In this paper we present the whole process with a special focus on the paradata that document the technical process involved in obtaining the 3D result that should be archived and published.

Table 1. Content is of 3 types

Type	Example	Humanity field (example)	Particularity
Captured reality	3D scan of a cultural material heritage asset	archaeology	no Interpretation
Reconstitutions	3D of building according to plans and site scan	history	–
Conception	3D immersive environment for an experiment	theatre	no Sources

While publication is sharing at the present, it is based on instant capabilities (technologies); archiving means sharing with a distant future, it raises other issues like re-computing the results, understanding the context, the goals and the means of the production process, and many other issues that are not based on metadata and paradata topics. Reproducibility is a key concept in our archiving objectives for scienfic productions.

1.4   Workflow and Tools from User Point of View

From the user point of view, the workflow has several entry points as show in Fig. 2. Each of these entry points CND3D, aLTAG3D or Archeogrid is described below.

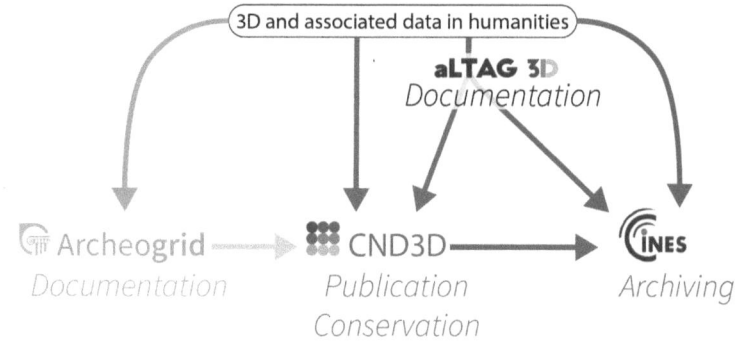

Fig. 2. User view: software and data within the proposed lifecycle

Archeogrid is an online software as a service (Saas)[1] for creating data documentation as the project progresses [15,17]. It is designed to be used during the project and to ensure data validation by multiple users.

---

[1] www.archeogrid.fr.

aLTAG3D is a GUI desktop app to create the SIP by documenting an entire project in one go [5]. It is designed to be use when the project is finished and the data are fully validated. The vantage of a desktop software is to work locally, avoiding latencies caused by delays in uploading large 3D files. The software is open-source and available for download[2]. Its interface is a node editor (see screenshot in Fig. 3) dedicated to the creation of XML files. An XSD file manages the content of the nodes, i.e. the boxes and fields to fulfil. After export, to ensure compliance of the produced 3D data package, a validation step is run against this XSD file. aLTAG3D adapts itself to a new schema when the XSD is updated.

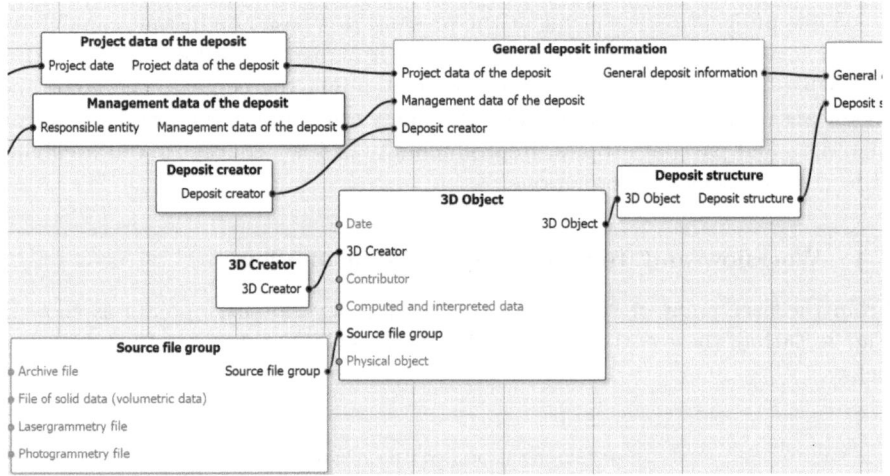

Fig. 3. aLTAG3D, a GUI node editor for creating SIP

CND3D Portal is the online publication portal[3]. It offers a form to directly create a new deposit online. The form is flat and doesn't allow nested and complex records. This alternative is designed to be used when projects are small and simple, and when the laboratory lacks the resources to invest time in the use of a software (aLTAG3D).

Only a subset of the metadata is published online. The publication portal embeds 3DHop [16], a 3D viewer for the web dedicated to cultural heritage assets, so published content can be viewed online side by side with basic metadata[4]. A distinct Digital Object Identifier (DOI) is assigned to each published project and associated 3D object.

---

[2] https://altag3d.huma-num.fr.
[3] https://3d.humanities.science/.
[4] for example: https://doi.org/10.34969/CND3D/417630.o.2023.

1.5   Related Works

About Archiving, the Community Owned digital Preservation Tool Registry (COPTR[5]) initiative of COST Action SEADDA (CA18128) combined with the Digital Research Infrastructure for the Arts and Humanities (DARIAH) SSH marketPlace[6] helped us to position our tools and digital preservation workflows among other European initiatives. These sources are updated regularly. Of the 594 archiving tools listed by the COPTR project and the 61 tools dedicated to archiving, only our 2 tools, *aLTAG3D* and *CND3D*, can create packages for archiving 3D data. Besides this core functionality, *aLTAG3D* appears to be the only XML visual programming node editor available.

Apart from tools, several institutions propose to archive 3D data in national OAIS repository, *DANS* in the Netherlands, *SND* in Sweden with their tool called *DORIS*, *DRI* in Ireland, *ADS* dedicated to archaeology in the UK, and *Zenodo* as an international option for archiving research data, quite poor for 3D content. They all offer online forms to create a new deposit for small projects, and most of the time a human process is triggered for large projects.

About describing, as we started our work in 2015, no 3D file from any research institution was archived in the French dedicated OAIS infrastructure (CINES). Now in France, many independent projects have built their own process and descriptors to archive 3D research data in other disciplinary fields. In 2017, the *Centre National de la Préhistoire* has published metadata recommendations for 3D scans [2]. Recently, the *eCol+* project for natural history museums is the closest work, because they care of similar objects. We reuse some of their results in metadata, for example tomography technical documentation (see Sect. 3.2).

Abroad, recent work [11] in Switzerland deplores lack of long-term standards for 3D data. Globally, few works are related to the challenge of documenting the 3D in humanities in an archiving perspective, and every work is very specific to a country or a use case.

The *Europeana Data Model* (EDM) is being updated soon to 3D data take into account [6]. This shows an interest for describing properly the 3D data with a specific data model, partially diverging from the one dedicated to still and moving 2D images. Europeana recently launched a campaign called *Twin It!* [10] (ending in June 2024) in order to collect 3D assets which nowadays only represent 0.01% of their published items [19].

Few tools are developed for description purpose, and the publishing matters are predominant. The *WEAVE* project[7] has developed WEAVEx "allowing the user to create holistic documentation of the cultural communities' heritage". It has listed best practices from international institution for handling 3D data within a community [20]. After the end of the *3D icons* project (2012–2015) many others started. Among them, recent European projects *4CH* [1], *WEAVE*,

---

[5] https://coptr.digipres.org.
[6] https://marketplace.sshopencloud.eu.
[7] https://weave-culture.eu/.

Eureka3D and *5Dculture* are concerned with describing the content of the 3D files with linked open vocabularies. They provide a great framework and challenging opportunities, but they don't focus neither on the archiving issues nor on the build process of the 3D. Publication and instant sharing remain the main goals for these projects.

About Publishing, many works offer an online platform for 3d content, including commercial services. Few of them attach importance to the quality of the data description. All the cited national archiving service offer a DOI and most of them propose a viewer for 3D content online. Europeana is the most advanced platform for publication of cultural heritage contents. They really cares about data description. In the case of 3D, recently Europeana decided to focus on metadata: they host the description, but the 3D data is hosted and managed by *Sketchfab* offering an embedded viewer (it may be also compatible with WEAVE 3D viewer). The basics of publication services are: indexing and displaying metadata, providing a DOI, offering to view the 3D content.

2   Global Process

2.1   The Process Architecture

The global process is described here in a complete version from aLTAG3D, which is the most common case. Figure 4 shows this process, each step is described below. The process is asynchronous, as the archiving branch (bottom in Fig. 4) is only triggered after the publication branch (top in Fig. 4) and validation loops have been completed.

1. It starts with the content of a research project with 3D results. This content has to be validated and is not supposed to be updated. This content is composed of many files gathered on the same computer. See Sect. 2.2 for more details about the file selection to archive.
2. Using aLTAG3D enables the user to create locally a SIP. The SIP is a package associating the selected content with its documentation: metadata and paradata. See Sect. 3.1 for more details about the content documentation. aLTAG3D helps in creating some of the metadata automatically, and lets the user focus on the human added-value part of the documentation.
3. The SIP is uploaded in a temporary file storage
4. The SIP is moved to an *ActiveCircle* secure file storage managed by Huma-Num. This buffer hierarchical storage manager (HSM) holds the SIP during the publication step, and until the archiving is triggered.
5. The SIP is unpacked, the files are converted to web formats and the XML documentation is parsed to create web compliant content. This content is stored in a postgreSQL database. Several jobs enrich the information:
   (a) Get a DOI for each of the 3D object and for the project itself.

(b) Request the authority lists and standard thesaurus: *Pactols* [14] and *Art and Architecture Thesaurus* for the descriptive concepts, *Virtual International Authority File* (VIAF) [8] for the persons, *periodo* [18] for the dates.

(c) Alignment and harvesting facilities: exposition with OAI-PMH in *Europeana Data Model* (EDM) expression.

6. The enriched documentation and 3d data is published online via the web portal (see Sect. 1.4). Only a small subset of the 3D object's or associated physical object's metadata is published. Among other items, the sources and their documentation are not published. This publication time is the opportunity to update and fix the enriched documentation.

7. The SIP is rebuilt with corrected and enriched documentation, and submitted to the OAIS store for long-term archiving. This may be triggered years after the first SIP creation.

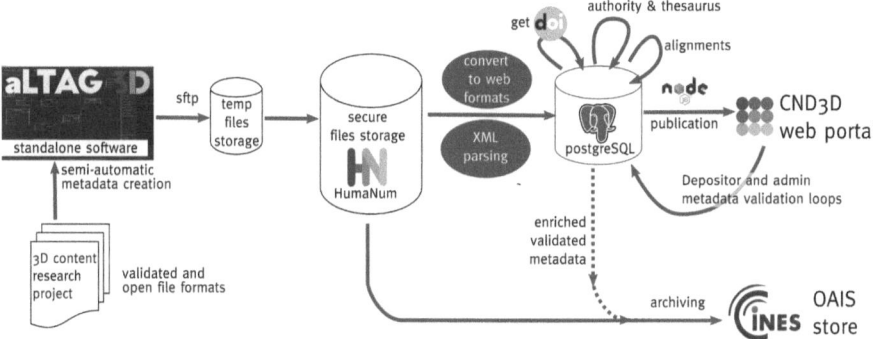

Fig. 4. Data process from aLTAG3D to publication and archiving

2.2 Data Selection for Archiving

Selection among the production is needed or economic and ecological reasons. The entire production chain is not intended to be archived. This selection is guided by the three (3) minimal principles of scientific "reproducibility":

– If they exist, the source files must be archived.
– The methodology leading to the 3D result should be recorded and archived (paradata).
– The scientific goals must be archived.

The following steps describe the selection along the production process and refer to Fig. 5.

[A0] If they exist, the source files must be archived. To avoid duplicates, they may be linked if they are already archived under equivalent conditions.

[V0] It only exists in case of scans. A first raw 3D content may be archived. This is the result of no human added-value. It is the fisrt "clean" 3D obtained.

[V1n] They are the intermediate results of the loop of hypothesis and restitution. They didn't receive validation but have been useful for the research project. They are **not** archived. But their production process may be documented.

[V2] This is the validated 3D model. Validation can be internal or, even better, external, in the form of a scientific publication. The derivatives of this 3D (deliverables) are not supposed to be archived because they can be recomputed and don't hold scientific information.

For example, in the (common) case of a photogrammetry with no added 3D content we should archive the sources (A0) which are the photographs, and the first computed and cleaned 3D (V0). Nothing else.

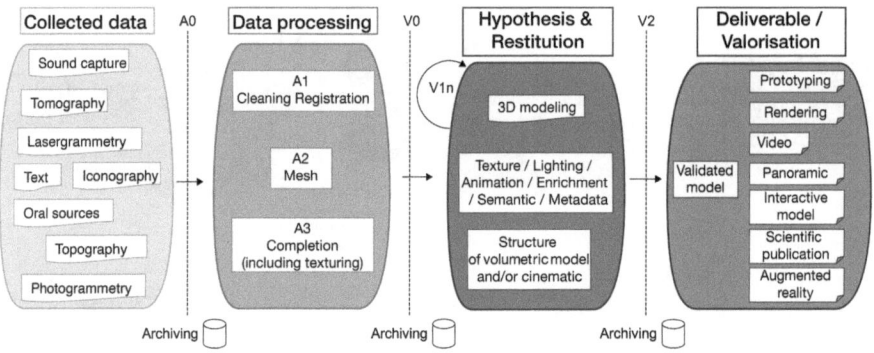

Fig. 5. Selection of files to be archived in each production step

Selection among file formats is mandatory for archiving purpose. In our case, the files must comply with the obligations set out by the CINES to allow migration and rewriting (and therefore ensure that they will still be readable in 30 years). Authorized file formats are standard, open source and with published specifications. The online software FACILE can be used to validate a file. For 3D, the PLY and DAE (collada) formats are the only ones available. The collada file validator is not yet available. On our platform, the vast majority of submissions contain 3D files in PLY. Of course, the online publication platform doesn't have such constraints, then GL Transmission Format Binary files (glb), streamed point clouds and other format may be used depending on the needs and evolution of the web technology.

3   The Data Model

3.1   Metadata and Paratada Schema

A data schema organizes the logical relationships in data, metadata and para-data. The Fig. 6 is a condensed representation of our global schema. Inspired by ADS UK guide of good practice [13] we can split the schema into 4 parts: (1) Project-level (● light gray on Fig. 6); (2) administrative (● dark gray parts); (3) File-level (● orange parts, not described by this figure); and (4) Resource-level (all the others). Resource-level information is the core of the schema. It can be split into 3 sub-parts: the physical object (● green); the sources (● purple); the computed and interpreted data (● blue).

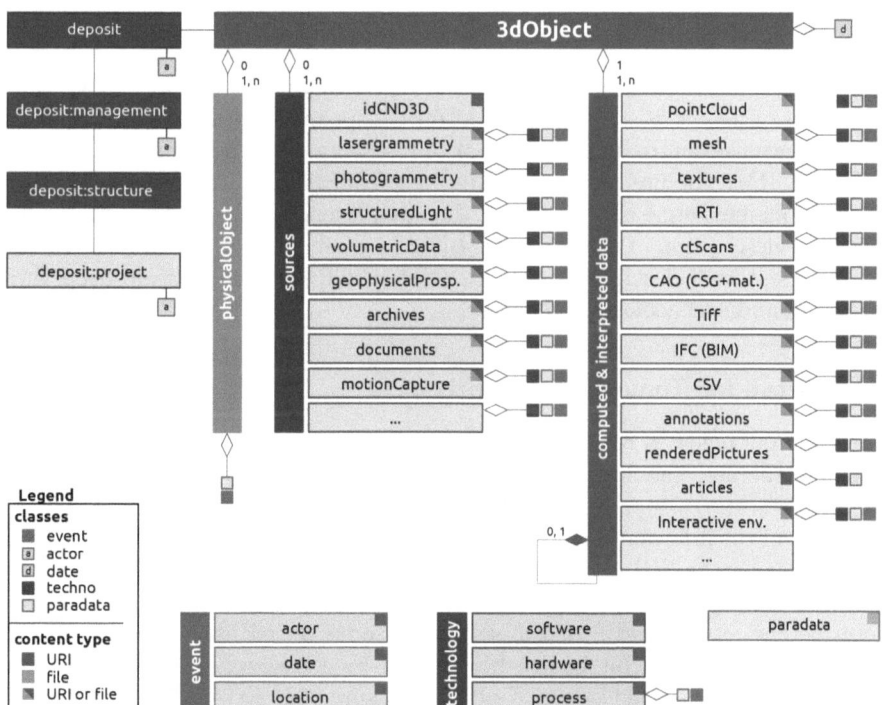

Fig. 6. Overview of our data model with main classes and their relations

At the bottom of the schema, 3 classes are mentioned: event (● brown), technology (● pink) and paradata (● orange). These classes are used in many situations in our schema. They standardize these generic descriptions and leave the more specific classes (e.g. tomography) to describe specifically their object (see below the tomography example Sect. 3.2.

Our schema is very flexible, in the case of a scan of material cultural heritage there should be one physical object, 3D sources and one computed data; in the case of immaterial heritage there may be no physical object but sources and interpreted data; in the case of the 3D restitution of a ruined site there may be a physical object, 3D and non-3D sources, computed and interpreted data.

In every case should be documented the paradata: technologies in use, process, actors involved etc.

The Paradata class (• orange) is a very versatile option to extend the description of the context. Our schema propose some generic paradata (actor, software, hardware, date, etc.) and specific ones to each technology (voxel depth used and unit for tomography acquisition). The paradata class offer to extend it with a file. Until now, the file content was only human-readable: text, drawings, etc. We are now thinking about using external descriptors to be more precise and standard (see Sect. 3.3).

Mappings are necessary to be compatible with main standards. Two mapping of our schema exists: one to EDM for europeana, another to CIDOC-CRM [3]. The event-oriented architecture of our schema ease the compatibility with CIDOC-CRM. The use of standards terms authority lists and thesaurus (VIAF, AAT, geonames, etc.) is in line with the open science and semantic web principles. The description of the physical object (• green part) is minimalist. We rely on other external descriptors such as CIDOC-CRM to describe in-deep these historical and archaeological aspects.

3.2 Detail for Tomography Source File

The example below is related to volumic data (tomography) 3D acquisition. In this case the user should describe a set of metadata and paradata as shown on the Fig. 7.

Much of the information is filled in and suggested automatically by aLTAG3D when creating the SIP. Some other information is based on Uniform Resource Identifier (URI). For example, we use the *Software Heritage project* [21] to describe the exact version of the software. Some closed list values are also in use, for example the unit has to be filled in by a case-sensitive term (column "C/s") from the Unified Code for Units of Measure code system [7]. For reasons of interoperability, as little data as possible is filled in manually using literals.

3.3 Perspective for Paradata Improvements

Two parts of the schema (Fig. 6) are related with complex paradata:

– *paradata* (• orange box). It is an option to extend the description of the context, process, or anything that the user considers important and that the schema has omitted. It is convenient but too permissive, and may lack of precision.

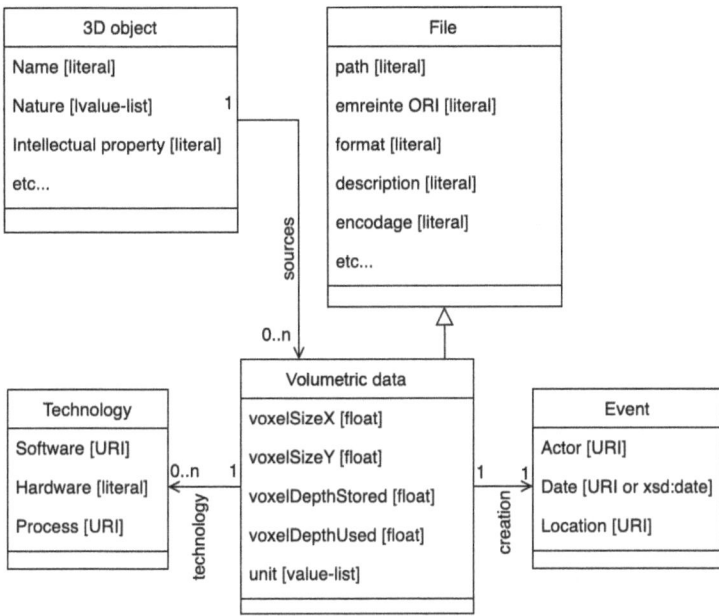

Fig. 7. Volumic data (tomography) source file, its descriptors and direct environment

– *process* in the *technology* (● pink box). It is the description of a process through a URI from *SSH Open Marketplace*. This is not a convenient tool.

In replacement of these 2 points, we plan to use external descriptors produced by an external software. The software *Memoria IS* [9] is an online tool with a user interface dedicated to the description of digital activities. Figure 8 shows the case of a specific photogrammetry protocol record (Notre-Dame de Paris fragment scanning). It is rich of details, user-friendly and fits exactly the requirements for paradata and process recording we need.

Memoria IS fits the requirement of a software to create rich paradata we could embed in our SIP. But the content created by the software cannot be archived, because nothing is standard. It doesn't fit the requirement of the OAIS store (see Sect. 2.2). There is a need to create exports in standards files. At this step, on our side, we are working on selecting the standard descriptors. Two (2) candidates have been selected: *CRM-dig* [4] an official extension of the CIDOC-CRM, dedicated to the provenance description in museums and cultural heritage contexts and *prov-O* [12] an official ontology for the World Wide Web provenance description.

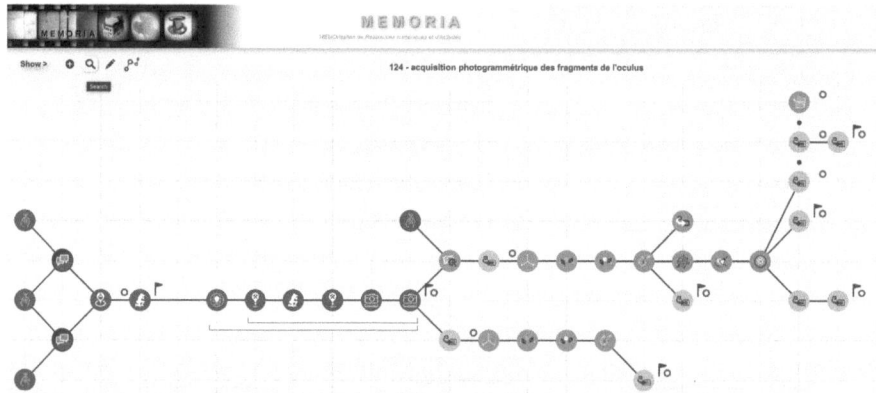

Fig. 8. User interface of the Memoria IS online software

4   Conclusion

We propose an integrated workflow with the experiences of hundreds of existing deposit. The metadata schema has evolved to fit the semantic-web compatibility and enhance the publication phase. Nevertheless, archiving is the core functionality of our pipeline, and therefore we plan to describe better the production process. Actually, recording the process is the key for scientific reproducibility. From a semantic-web perspective, the process record cannot be a simple schema, new tools and standard ontologies enable fine-grain descriptions and interoperability for these paradata.

Acknowledgments. This study was carried on by Consortium 3D for humanities funded by Huma-Num (CNRS UAR 3598).

References

1. Boeri, A., Orlandi, S., Roversi, R., Turillazzi, B.: The 4CH project and enabling technologies for safeguarding the Cultural Heritage. TECHNE - J. Technol. Archit. Environ. **25**, 162–172 (2023). https://doi.org/10.36253/techne-13711
2. CENTRE NATIONAL DE PREHISTOIRE: MAP (UMR 3495): Livret méthodologique: Description des métadonnées des acquisitions numériques. CNRS, Et quelques préconisations (2017)
3. Doerr, M., Ore, C.E., Stead, S.: The CIDOC conceptual reference model: a new standard for knowledge sharing. In: 26th International Conference on Conceptual Modeling, ER 2007, vol. 83, pp. 51–56. Australian Computer Society, Inc., Australia (2007)
4. Doerr, M., Stead, S., Theodoridou, M.: Definition of the CRMdig (2022). https://cidoc-crm.org/crmdig/sites/default/files/CRMdigv4.0.pdf
5. Dutailly, B., Tournon, S., Chayani, M., Grimaud, V., Granier, X.: aLTAG3D: a user-friendly metadata documentation software. In: Cultural Heritage Data as Humanities Research Data? (2023). https://hal.science/hal-04115897

6. Fernie, K., et al.: Review of EDM to support 3D (2024). https://pro.europeana. eu/post/review-of-the-europeana-data-model-to-support-3d. Version 1.1
7. Gunther, S., Clement, J.M.: UCUM/UCUM Specification (2017). https://ucum. org/ucum
8. Hickey, T.B., Toves, J.A.: Managing ambiguity in VIAF. D-Lib Mag. **20**(7/8) (Jul 2014). https://doi.org/10.1045/july2014-hickey
9. Iwona, D., Jean-Yves, B.: Research workflows, paradata, and information visualisation: feedback on an exploratory integration of issues and practices - MEMORIA IS. PCI Archaeol. (2023). https://doi.org/10.5281/zenodo.8311129, https:// zenodo.org/records/8311129
10. Kate Fernie: Sharing with Europeana 3D TwinIt (2023). https://docs.google.com/ presentation/d/1AeG8mFWl1gzIhEkFO_glOCud5SJW8_OI
11. Kruse, K., Schönenberger, E.: Archiving the third dimension: production, maintenance and use of 3D models in cultural heritage management. In: The 3 Dimensions of Digitalised Archaeology: State-of-the-Art, Data Management and Current Challenges in Archaeological 3D-Documentation, pp. 205–219. Springer, Cham (2024). https://library.oapen.org/bitstream/handle/20.500.12657/88397/1/978-3-031-53032-6.pdf#page=214
12. Lebo, T., et al.: Prov-o: The prov ontology. W3C (2013). https://core.ac.uk/ download/pdf/70283855.pdf
13. Niven, K., Pierce-McManamon, F.: Guides to good practice (2011)
14. Nouvel, B., Humbert, V., Sinigaglia, E.: PACTOLS the French terminological repository for archaeology. In: Back to the (Re)sources (2019). https://shs.hal. science/halshs-02421873
15. Néroulidis, A., et al.: A digital platform for the centralization and long-term preservation of multidisciplinary scientific data belonging to the Notre Dame de Paris scientific action. J. Cult. Heritage **65**, 210–220 (2024). https://doi.org/10.1016/j. culher.2023.09.016
16. Potenziani, M., Callieri, M., Dellepiane, M., Corsini, M., Ponchio, F., Scopigno, R.: 3DHOP: 3D heritage online presenter. Comput. Graph. **52**, 129–141 (2015). https://doi.org/10.1016/j.cag.2015.07.001
17. Robert Vergnieux: Archeogrid: towards a national conservatory of 3D data of cultural heritage. In: Robert Vergnieux (ed.) Virtual Retrospect 2005. Archeovision, vol. 2, pp. 163–167. Ausonius, Biarritz (2005). https://hal.science/hal-01764228
18. Shaw, R., Rabinowitz, A., Golden, P., Kansa, E.: A sharing-oriented design strategy for networked knowledge organization systems. Int. J. Digit. Libr. **17**(1), 49–61 (2016). https://doi.org/10.1007/s00799-015-0164-0
19. Thierry Breton: Twin it! 3D for Europe's culture (2023). https://pro.europeana. eu/page/twin-it-3d-for-europe-s-culture
20. Truyen, F., et al.: WEAVE best practices and guidelines for community management (2022)
21. Zacchiroli, S.: Software heritage: scholarly and educational synergies with preserving our software commons. In: Conference on Innovation and Technology in Computer Science Education - ITiCSE 2017, p. 3. ACM Press, New York (2017). https://doi.org/10.1145/3059009.3059066

Virtual Access to Fossil & Archival Material from the German Tendaguru Expedition (1909–1913): More Than 100 years of Data-Meta-paradata Management for Improved Standardisation

Marin Depraetere[1,3](✉) ⓘ, Sara Akhlaq[1,3] ⓘ, Verónica Díez Díaz[1,2] ⓘ,
Ina Heumann[1,2], and Daniela Schwarz[1,2] ⓘ

[1] Museum für Naturkunde, Leibniz Institute for Evolution and Biodiversity Science, Berlin,
Germany
Marion.Depraetere@mfn.berlin
[2] Department 1 - Dynamics of Nature, Berlin, Germany
[3] Department 2 - Collection Future, Berlin, Germany

Abstract. As the number of digital objects associated with scientific studies and collection objects of all kinds grows, the data associated with these digital objects must be standardised so that it is easily accessible, distributed to the greatest number of people, and archived in the best conditions on long term basis, and the associated studies are reproducible. This study proposes ideas for defining metadata and paradata connected with digital objects, specifically 3D models. Above all, it evaluates existing data standards in the field of natural collections, such as nomenclature codes (Zoological and Plants), the Darwin Core, ABCD, and LIDO data standards, as well as the FAIR and CARE principles that apply to such data. To that purpose, this work proposes methods for standardising the data created by digital objects in biological collections and, by extension, for 3D digital documentation of cultural resources. The DFG project "Research & Responsibility. Virtual access to fossils and archival material from the Tendaguru expedition" at the Museum für Naturkunde in Berlin, is an excellent case study for this, as it encompasses more than 100 years of data-meta-paradata collection starting from the historic paleontological excavations (1909–1913) to the current digitization.

Keywords: Metadata · Paradata · Numerical object · 3D model · ABCD standard · Darwin Core · LIDO standard · FAIR principles · CARE principles · Tendaguru Expedition

1 Introduction

Since October 2023, the project "Research & Responsibility. Virtual access to fossils and archival material from the Tendaguru expedition", funded by the Deutsche Forschungsgemeinschaft, is being conducted at the Museum für Naturkunde in Berlin and can serve

M. Ioannides et al. (Eds.): 3D Research Challenges in Cultural Heritage V, LNCS 15190, pp. 89–102, 2025.
https://doi.org/10.1007/978-3-031-78590-0_8

as an excellent case study to understand and illustrate the intersections that exist between data, metadata, and paradata.

The concept of paradata is derived from statistics, which is the discipline that studies phenomena through data collection, processing, analysis, interpretation of results, and presentation in order to make this data understandable to everybody [19]. In this paper, we will investigate how to apply this concept to "object data".

Our work can prove to be useful in suggesting ways to standardise the metadata and paradata generated by digital objects in biological collections and by extension for the digital 3D documentation in cultural heritage.

2 Paradata: What is it and What for?

2.1 A Brief History

The term paradata is a very recent one, having appeared in the literature since the mid-1980s only rarely, to describe "data about the process by which the data was collected". It was not until the 2000s that the concept was democratised and used a little more frequently in printed sources [27] (see Fig. 1). However, its use remains anecdotal compared to the term "metadata" which, although also relatively recent, has been accepted since the late 70s [27] (see Fig. 2).

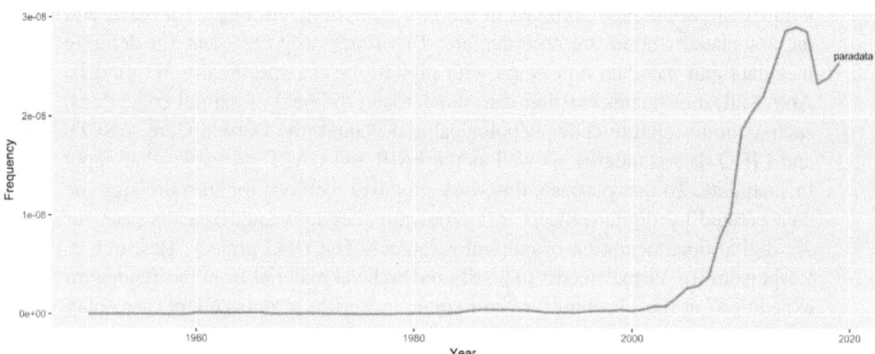

Fig. 1. Occurrences of the word "paradata" in printed sources between 1950 and 2019 according to Google Books Ngram Viewer (as of May 2024). The horizontal axis shows the year of publication of the works in the corpus, and the vertical axis shows the frequency of occurrence of the ngrams in the corpus [3, 27, 28].

It was with the advent of computer-assisted personal interviewing (CAPI) that the notion of process data was introduced. The initial purpose of collecting this data was to detect and correct system or interviewer errors. Their usefulness in improving survey processes was quickly demonstrated [7]. It was then that the concept of paradata was born. Today, the collection of paradata serves a wide range of purposes, from studying improvement and correction to studying predictions [18].

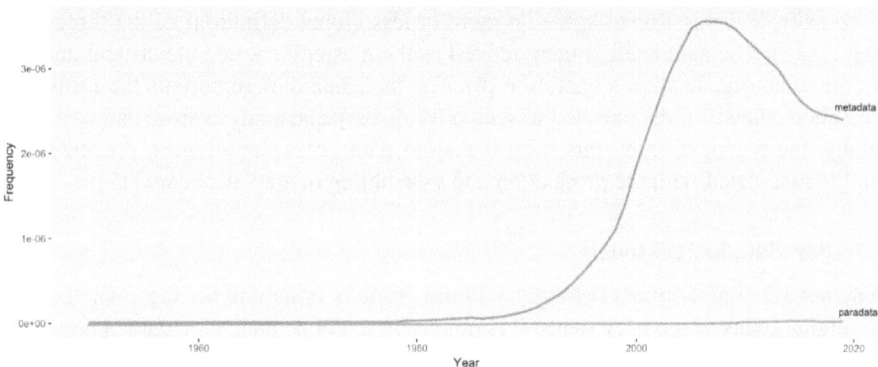

Fig. 2. Occurrences of the words "metadata" and "paradata" in printed sources between 1900 and 2019 according to Google Books Ngram Viewer (as of May 2024). The horizontal axis shows the year of publication of the works in the corpus, and the vertical axis shows the frequency of occurrence of the ngrams in the corpus [3, 27, 28].

2.2 Definition(S)

Even today, the distinction between the concepts data, metadata and paradata is not well defined and there are no standards generally used by all federal statistical agencies [17]. Depending on the source, their respective definitions vary (see Fig. 3). So, before the term paradata appeared, it was easy to define data as the data used for statistical analysis, and metadata as the data that defines and describes other data and processes. Paradata is therefore a specific category of metadata, and has been added to process data, data relating to the tools involved in data production and use [17]. Other sources also use the terms structural metadata, reference metadata and paradata, which are micro-levels of details about collection processes [24].

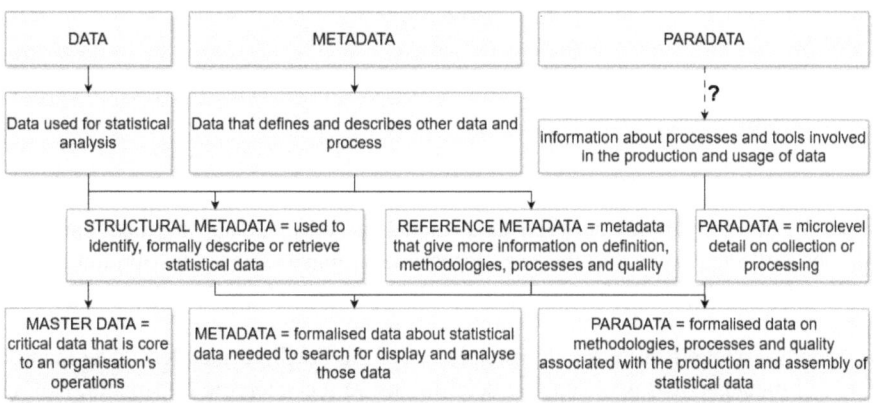

Fig. 3. Some examples of terms definitions "data", "metadata" and "paradata" in the statistical analysis fields, over time and, according to different sources [6, 17, 24].

Finally, it is possible to agree on more or less global definitions of the three terms (see Fig. 3). The data itself is then defined as the master data, i.e., the critical data that is core to an organisation´s operation [6]. The metadata then represents the formalised data about statistical data needed to search for display and analyse those data [17]. And finally, the paradata represents the formalised data on methodologies, processes and quality associated with the production and assembling of statistical data [17].

2.3 Paradata in 3D Models

Whether 3D digital objects belong to cultural property or natural heritage, whether they are digital twins or memory twins, it is important to define data, metadata and paradata for these 3D objects in general.

In our research, we have chosen to define the data, metadata and paradata of the generated 3D objects as follows (see Fig. 4):

- data are the 3D digital objects themselves and all associated documents,
- metadata is the data that defines each 3D object, such as its taxonomic name, the identifier of the physical specimen of which it is the digital model, its format, size, etc.,
- paradata is data relating to the 3D digital object's creation process, such as the software used, the person who created the object, the person who modified it, the place where it was made, the material used, etc.

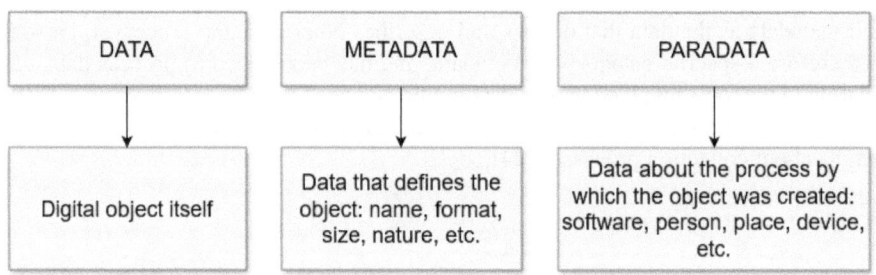

Fig. 4. Data, metadata and paradata definitions we choose to use in this paper for 3D objects in cultural heritage.

Although there is as yet no consensus on the definition of what exactly paradata is, nor on the boundaries between data, metadata and paradata; this data exists and must be collected to enable the use, accessibility, management, distribution, archiving, interoperability and reproducibility of 3D objects, and for this we need to define standards.

Finally, we can bear in mind principle 7.3 of the Seville Principles: "The incorporation of metadata and paradata is crucial to ensure the scientific transparency of any virtual [heritage] project. Paradata and metadata should be clear, concise and easily available. In addition, they should provide as much information as possible. The scientific community [whether archaeological or biological] should contribute with international standardisation of metadata and paradata" [13].

3   Data Management in Natural Collections

In the field of natural collections, hitherto no distinction between metadata and paradata was made. As a rule, we refer to all data derived from or closely and sometimes remotely related to physical collection objects as data. We use the term metadata to identify data derived from collection objects.

Objects in natural collections can take multiple forms. They can be zoological and botanical collection specimens put out on herbarium plates, pins, preserved in alcohol or on thin slides, complete or partial specimens, or specimens divided into distinct parts of the body, as is common with mammals, where the bones and skin are preserved separately. We can also find fossils, casts, and even living beings. They may also be aural or visual observations. Physical artefacts come from museum collections, observations come from field campaigns, but there is also an increasing amount of data from citizen science (studies in the fields of science, social science, and many other disciplines that involve participants from the general population, amateur or nonprofessional researchers, or individuals). Added to this diversity of collection occurrences is the myriad of digital objects that can be derived from them, such as in situ and in vivo photographs, videos, sound recordings, films, and of course 3D models.

These occurrences are not only various, but also quite numerous. For insect collections alone, the Muséum national d'Histoire naturelle in Paris is expected to have around 35 million specimens [9], and the Museum für Naturkunde in Berlin has over 15 million recorded specimens [26].

So, even if the uses themselves are not standardised, we're talking about the living. To communicate knowledge about the living, the scientific community has had to define standards and guidelines for taxonomy, as well as the data itself.

3.1   Codes, Standards and Principles in Natural Collections

Historians of natural sciences take Linne's work as a starting point for the classification of living things in the mid-18th century [20]. He is responsible for the binomial name in Latin that we use today to refer to all living organisms [21]. However, the standardisation of these taxonomic names began in the nineteenth century with the first version of the International Code of Nomenclature for algae, fungi, and plants (ICNafp) initiated in 1867 [2]. This code indicates the collection of recommendations and guidelines that specify how scientific names for plants and other species "traditionally considered as plants"—such as fungi and cyanobacteria—should be generated and attributed to these organisms [30]. Then, in 1958, the first version of the International Code of Zoological Nomenclature (ICZN), which defines and lays down the rules for the development and priority of scientific names for animal organisms [14], was published.

It was not until 2001 that data standardisation was introduced. The purpose of Darwin Core (DwC) is to offer a reliable, uniform reference for exchanging data regarding biological diversity (last version in 2009). The Biodiversity Information Standards (TDWG), a non-profit scientific and educational organisation that works to promote open standards for the exchange of biodiversity data and facilitate biodiversity informatics, is responsible for developing and maintaining a broader vocabulary and technical specifications that include the terms included in the DwC standard [31]. A significant attempt

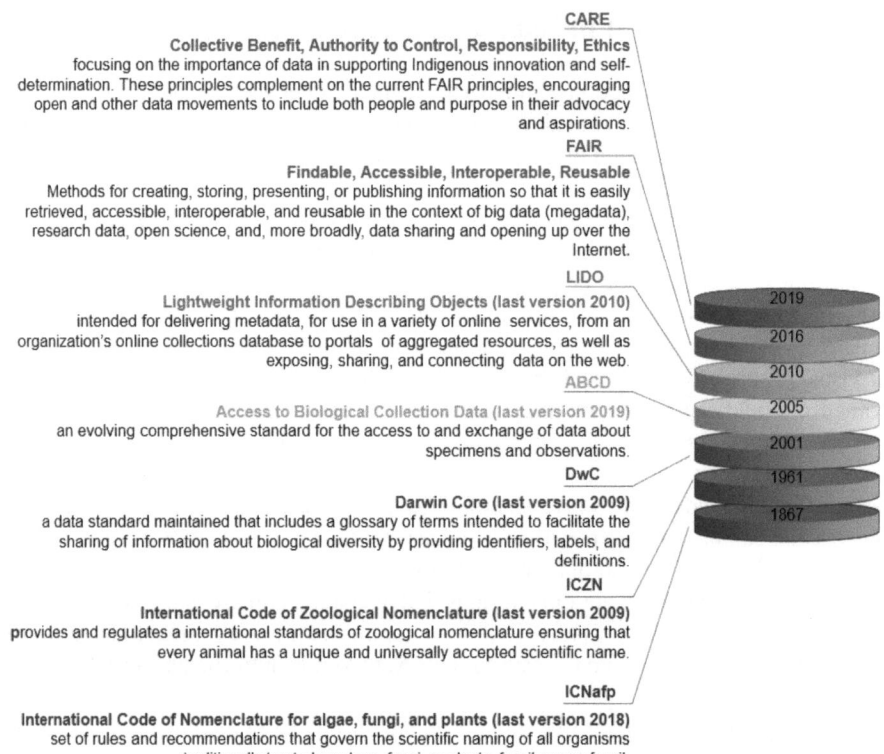

CARE
Collective Benefit, Authority to Control, Responsibility, Ethics
focusing on the importance of data in supporting Indigenous innovation and self-determination. These principles complement on the current FAIR principles, encouraging open and other data movements to include both people and purpose in their advocacy and aspirations.

FAIR
Findable, Accessible, Interoperable, Reusable
Methods for creating, storing, presenting, or publishing information so that it is easily retrieved, accessible, interoperable, and reusable in the context of big data (megadata), research data, open science, and, more broadly, data sharing and opening up over the Internet.

LIDO
Lightweight Information Describing Objects (last version 2010)
intended for delivering metadata, for use in a variety of online services, from an organization's online collections database to portals of aggregated resources, as well as exposing, sharing, and connecting data on the web.

ABCD
Access to Biological Collection Data (last version 2019)
an evolving comprehensive standard for the access to and exchange of data about specimens and observations.

DwC
Darwin Core (last version 2009)
a data standard maintained that includes a glossary of terms intended to facilitate the sharing of information about biological diversity by providing identifiers, labels, and definitions.

ICZN
International Code of Zoological Nomenclature (last version 2009)
provides and regulates a international standards of zoological nomenclature ensuring that every animal has a unique and universally accepted scientific name.

ICNafp
International Code of Nomenclature for algae, fungi, and plants (last version 2018)
set of rules and recommendations that govern the scientific naming of all organisms traditionally treated as algae, fungi, or plants, fossil or non-fossil.

Fig. 5. Lists of standards produced over time to standardise data from biological collections since their first versions to their last versions [1, 4, 5, 14, 30–32].

at standardising was made in 2005 with the ABCD Standard (most recent version 2019). In order to give the natural history collection community a unified approach, the ABCD Schema was created with the goal of being comprehensive. It was intended to define the semantics of all elements, accept detailed information when it was available, and develop a proto-ontology that would eventually lead to a collection ontology [1]. The Lightweight Information Describing Objects (LIDO) schema was introduced in 2008 with the goal of delivering metadata for use in a variety of online services, ranging from an organisation's online collections database to portals of aggregated resources, as well as exposing, sharing, and connecting data on the web [5]. LIDO's strength rests in its capacity to support all types of descriptive information on museum objects. It is applicable to a wide range of items, including art, architecture, cultural history, technological history, and natural history.

A list of principles for open data projects was developed in 2016. Because scientists increasingly rely on computational support to deal with data, which continuously expand in volume, complexity, and speed of data creation, the FAIR principles (Findable, Accessible, Interoperable, and Reusable) place an emphasis on the ability of computational systems to locate, retrieve, collaborate, and utilise data with little or no assistance from humans [32]. In addition to the FAIR principles, the CARE Principles for Indigenous

Data Governance (Collective Benefit, Authority to Control, Responsibility, Ethics) were added in 2019. These guidelines are meant to direct open data initiatives that support the rights and interests of Indigenous Peoples [4]. In light of the United Nations Declaration on the Rights of Indigenous Peoples and Indigenous data sovereignty, it delineates collective rights pertaining to open data.

3.2 Biodiversity Occurrence Repositories

All of these standards are quite useful for biodiversity occurrence repositories. Although it is impossible to list all repositories, the three most essential ones are the Global Biodiversity Information Facility (GBIF), the Biological Collection Access Service (BioCASe), and the Integrated Digitized Biocollections (iDigBio). They adhere to the ABDC, Darwin Core, and LIDO standards, as well as the FAIR and CARE principles, when processing data. Their importance is undeniable, since they allow all natural collection organisations to share their data freely in open access on solid, intuitive platforms [29]. The goal is to make global biodiversity data freely and universally accessible on the Internet via data portals and web services [11].

GBIF was established in 2001. It is an international organisation with the mission to provide web services that enable users to access scientific data on biodiversity over the Internet. Scientific name information and global distribution data for fungi, animals, plants, and microbes are the main features of the GBIF portal. In order to promote sustainable development, the GBIF aims to make biodiversity data globally open access [29]. BioCASe jointly operated with GBIF, is a global network of primary biodiversity repositories. It links information from huge observation databases to specimen data from botanical/zoological gardens, research institutions, and natural history collections worldwide [11]. Finally, in 2011, iDigBio debuted. It is one of iDigBio's tasks to create a national infrastructure that supports the ADBC (Advancing Digitization of Biodiversity Collections) vision by supervising the execution of digitization standards and best practices and planning for the long-term viability of the United States national digitisation work [15]. Just to give one example, on May 14, 2024, GBIF had 2,935,999,188 occurrences, which would not be conceivable without data standards (see Fig. 5).

4 The German Tendaguru Expedition Project in a Few Words

The German Tendaguru Expedition from 1909 to 1913 to Southeastern Tanzania, then part of the German colony Deutsch-Ostafrika, was led by members of the Museum für Naturkunde Berlin with the aim to excavate dinosaur bones from the Late Jurassic Period (150 Ma). During this period the Museum für Naturkunde in Berlin extracted several thousand fossil and extant specimens from diverse biological groups in the area around the landmark hill Tendaguru. The excavations were mostly conducted by local workers under violent colonial conditions [12]. In October 2023, the new DFG project "Research & Responsibility. Virtual access to fossils and archival material from the German Tendaguru expedition" started at the MfN focussing on more than 1000 single bones plus 2 skeletal mounts of two dinosaurs from the Tendaguru collection: the sauropod

Giraffatitan brancai (Janensch, 1914) and the ornithopod *Dysalotosaurus lettowvorbecki* Virchow, 1919. More than 1000 dinosaur bones are currently digitised in 3D and the archival documents in 2D, and it is planned to bring together all the data relating to the collection objects, the associated scientific work and the historical information in a data-driven, contextualised research environment. By following the FAIR and CARE principles, efforts will be made to make it accessible to diverse users in a transparent way. This will be done by connecting decolonial frameworks for collecting, processing, and visualisation of this data. Therefore, all diverse digitisation procedures, data infrastructures, and semantic processing adopted for data, metadata and paradata will be made part of the research platform.

The project is currently in its early phase of development; however, it offers a valuable case study in the definition of paradata, metadata and data in the documentation of 2D/3D digital heritage, thereby, in applying the data-metadata-paradata concept to a suite of collection data. Indeed, between the start of the excavations in 1909 and the current digitisation, more than 100 years of data-meta-para-data are associated with it. Data could be susceptible to invisibility, destruction or inaccessibility because of diverse historical, geo/political or societal factors such as changes in the ruling bodies, (neo)colonial power structures as well as global crises such as pandemics or environmental degradation. This project therefore represents a real challenge, as the data will come from a biological specimen database (Specify), an archive database (Actapro) and two repositories (EasyDB and Morphosource). Each of these tools contains data, metadata and paradata relating to the objects in the collections, the scientific work and the historical context which will be semantically integrated into the research environment through an ontological approach.

The data from the physical objects in the collection consists of casts from these fossils, thin sections, photographs of fossils and labels, 3D surface models and CT scans and, of course, all the data relating to their acquisition and storage. Data relating to scientific work includes the bibliography of publications, as well as the 3D surface models and CT scans and its results. Finally, the data relating to the historical and colonial context of the Tendaguru expedition consists of field books and sketchbooks, journals, documentary photographs, financial documents and correspondences mainly set up by the three German scientists who were present at the excavation site at Tendaguru, as well as the labels associated with the fossils that were written at the time. There are therefore complex relationships between these kinds of data. Depending on the nature of the medium and/or the context in which they were extracted, or the question we wish to answer, they may be considered as data, metadata or paradata.

5   Digitisation and Computerisation Protocol for the German Tendaguru Expedition Project

For the project, we have defined a robust protocol for digitising the objects and computerising the associated data in order to ensure that it is resilient and sustainable over time. To ensure that we have created and backed up all the essential and recommended files to follow best practices in the methodology, we have followed the guidelines outlined by Mallison and Wings [22]; Davies *et al.* [8], Falkingham *et al.* [10] and Moore *et al.* [23].

5.1 What is the Best Digitization Technique for Each Object?

The first steps in a digitisation protocol consist of the recognition and evaluation of the collection and the basic external characteristics of each specimen. These steps will help to increase the efficiency of the process. These characteristics can include: (i) the size of the specimen; (ii) topological complexity (e.g., presence of laminae, ridges, pits, fossae, etc.); (iii) preservation and general accessibility of the specimen, etc.

The first screening can be done based on the **size of the specimen**. Medium to large specimens (from ca. 5 cm to more than 1 m) are perfect objects for manual Structure from Motion (SfM) photogrammetry. If speed is sought throughout the digitisation process, structured light scanners (e.g., Artec 3D scanners) are the best device for digitisation if the specimen has a simple topology. If the object is small (from 2 to 5 cm), the user can opt for higher resolution scanners (Artec Space Spider) or SfM photogrammetry using a specific set-up: background of a homogeneous standard colour (black or white, depending on the colour of the specimen), turntable and a camera on a tripod.

The **topological complexity of the specimen** is also a factor in the choice of digitisation technique, and here the semi-autonomous photogrammetric station CultArm 3D (Fraunhofer-IGD) is one of the best options. Fossils with a very complex topology and medium size, such as cranial material and vertebrae, are perfect objects to digitise with the CultArm 3D, as the software has an algorithm that helps to evaluate the areas that need more photographs to reconstruct their topology. This contributes to more automatically and confidently capturing the surface of the specimen, avoiding holes in the mesh. This robotic arm is also capable of capturing challenging surface materials (e.g., reflective or very dark surfaces). The main limitation is the time taken to capture each specimen, which can range from 45 min to 2 h depending on the size and complexity of the object.

Accessibility and preservation of the specimen are two other factors to be taken into account. If the fossil is fragile, its handling should be minimised, so techniques in which the user is the one who moves around it are the most suitable (i.e., manual SfM photogrammetry or scanners). This applies similarly to fossils that are not mobile, e.g., in exhibition mounts or under protective glass cover. In the special case that the object is in a display glass case, the structured light scanner cannot give optimal results or is a more challenging technique, it is better to rely on manual SfM photogrammetry with polarising filters.

Computed tomography is the mandatory option when the internal volumes are needed, in contrast to the other methods, volumetric data are generated by this technique. As computed tomography is time-consuming and costly, it is used only for specific purposes, such as to capture the 3D morphology of small fossils (e.g. teeth, size below 2 cm), or specific research questions like fossil preparation protocols, but it is not generally used for the majority of the specimens of the collection.

5.2 Storage of the Data-Meta-paradata

For each digitised object, we keep the RAW files that we store over the long term in the Zuse Institute Berlin [33] repository. Additionally, we create and make accessible simplified 3D models in Morphosource with their associated data-meta-paradata [25], which are easier to work with and download than the high resolution 3D models. For every 3D object and its modified versions, we keep a certain amount of data based on the ABCD schema who already proposes some standard for digital objects [1] and on the expertise of the members of our teams, listed in the Table 1, in a.txt file that can easily be transformed into an.xml file if required. If applicable, we also keep the project reports, as generated by the various software programs.

Table 1. Suggestion of data to be stored for standardisation of metadata and paradata of 3D models

Data category	Property name	Property definition
Metadata	ID	Unique identifier of the 3D object
	ID of containing collection	Identifier of the object used to make the 3D object
	Subject part	Quick description of the object
	Type	Type of 3D object (Volumetric, Surface, Texture)
	Type of twin	Digital twin or Memory twin
	Sub-type	Final type of the 3D object as it will be stored in the repository
	Method	Method used to make the 3D object
	Number of pictures	Number of images used to make the 3D object
	File format	Format of attached file(s)
	Counter	Number of files attached to the folder
	Total files size	Total size of 3D object and attached files
	3D model size	Size of the 3D object
	Resolution	apply on CT data size of a voxel and resolution of the surface 3D
	Unit	Unit of the mesh (is the mesh in mm, cm, m, inch...)
	Licence	Creative Commons (CC) Licence
Paradata	Taxon	Taxon in background
	Explanation	Short explanation of why one method was chosen over another for creating the 3D model
	URL	If you want to link the object to a web page or similar
	Capture Equipment	Devices used to make the 3D object
	Lens model	Model of the lens used (if any)

(*continued*)

Table 1. (*continued*)

Data category	Property name	Property definition
	Software name	Software used to make the 3D object or modified 3D object
	Software version	Version of the software
	Recording environment	Name of the structure where the 3D model was made
	Multimedia context	Name of the project
	Remarks	Additional information about the 3D object
	Creator	Name of the person who produced the 3D model and carried out the simplification
	Date created	Date when the 3D object was created
	Date modification	Date when the modified 3D object was created

6 Conclusion

The concept of paradata raises many interesting challenges and emphasises the difficulty of managing data related with digital objects in cultural heritage fields.

Firstly, it is crucial to note that it is challenging to apply the concept of paradata on objects from natural collections. In fact, when we apply the definitions of "data", "metadata", and "paradata" to natural collection objects, the objects themselves constitute the data, the metadata is all the characteristics that identify the object (e.g., the associated taxon, the description of the object, the number of parts, its nature, its size, or the state of the object), and the paradata is all the rest of the data (i.e., the linked data about the field and geography on which the object was collected, information on the people who worked on and with the object, information on the place of storage or exhibition of the object, etc.), which accounts for 80–90% of the data. When it comes to digital collections, the concept of "data" vanishes since it refers to physical objects, and we lose one of the three levels of differentiation in the data.

Second, the approach can be entirely different when it comes to the cultural heritage field, especially when it comes to 3D models reconstruction of large human constructions (such buildings, boats, or other significant engineering works). As a matter of fact, 3D items are not related to actual objects in a collection. In other words, 3D things become "collectors' items" due to their interest and status as memory or digital twins. The terms "data", "metadata", and "paradata" acquire their complete significance in this regard. Data is what makes up 3D objects, which include polygons, images, metashapes, etc. Metadata is information about the object's identity, and paradata is information about the processes involved in creating the object, such as the circumstances under which the physical object that served as its original source was discovered, the process of creating the object, the circumstances under which it was stored, and so forth.

Thirdly, even if defining the boundaries between data, metadata and paradata remains complicated the important things to regard are:

1. to preserve all data, no matter into which category it belongs, and
2. to present it in a format that can be understood/read both by human users and machines.

To do this, we need to take into account the standards that have been developed to date and apply them to all 3D objects in order to ensure maximum interoperability. Finally, it is necessary to determine the characteristics of 3D data for which standardisation has not yet been established, as is the situation with the Tendaguru fossils. In this example, we need to consider the historical significance of the items found in a strong colonial historical context and then add it to the meta-paradata acquisition process [16].

By collecting the different data qualities and apply a model for data-metadata-paradata capture to a case-study as presented above, we hope to provide the basis for more research on the data-metadata-paradata issue and to encourage others to scrutinise their data-landscape with regard to these issues.

Acknowledgements. We warmly thank Dr. Marinos Ioannides and all the organizers of the Webinar "Paradata, metadata and data for 2D/3D documentation" for inviting us and allowing us to present our workWe would like to thank the Fraunhofer-IGD and all team members for additional input and discussion: Campbell A., Hennies M., and Mahlow K. We are also very grateful to everyone who has helped to enrich the Tendaguru project with their input: Botton-Divet L., Lederle M., Petersen M., von Mering S., Schurian B., Schuster F., Westwig E., and Wolff E.

The project is funded by the Deutsche Forschungsgemeinschaft (DFG, German Research Foundation) - Project number 511945957 (SCHW-1452/19-1).

References

1. Access to Biological Collection Data task group: Access to Biological Collection Data (ABCD). Biodiversity Information Standards (TDWG) (2007)
2. de Candolle, A.: Lois de la nomenclature botanique. V. Masson et fils, Paris (1867). https://doi.org/10.5962/bhl.title.139042
3. Carmody, S.: ngramr: retrieve and Plot Google n-Gram Data (2023). https://CRAN.R-project.org/package=ngramr
4. Carroll, S., Garba, I., Figueroa-Rodriguez, O., Holbrook, J., Lovett, R., Materechera, S., et al.: The CARE principles for Indigenous data governance. Data Sci. J. **19**, 1–12 (2020). https://doi.org/10.5334/dsj-2020-043
5. Coburn, E., Light, R., McKenna, G., Stein, R., Vitzthum, A.: LIDO - lightweight information describing objects version 1.0. International Council of Museums, CIDOC (2010)
6. Cooper, D.: What is the Difference Between Master Data and Metadata?. https://www.stibosystems.com/blog/what-is-the-difference-between-master-data-and-metadata. Accessed 15 May 2024
7. Couper, M.P.: Birth and diffusion of the concept of paradata. Adv. Soc. Res. **18**, 14–26 (2017)
8. Davies, T.G., et al.: Open data and digital morphology. Proc. Roy. Soc. B: Biol. Sci. **284**, 20170194 (2017). https://doi.org/10.1098/rspb.2017.0194
9. Dusoulier, F.: Le récolement des collections entomologiques. La Lettre de l'OCIM. Musées, Patrimoine et Culture scientifiques et techniques (2014). https://doi.org/10.4000/ocim.1375
10. Falkingham, P.L., et al.: A standard protocol for documenting modern and fossil ichnological data. Palaeontology **61**, 469–480 (2018). https://doi.org/10.1111/pala.12373

11. Glöckler, F., Hoffmann, J., Theeten, F.: The BioCASe Monitor Service - A tool for monitoring progress and quality of data provision through distributed data networks. BDJ. **1**(e968), e968 (2013). https://doi.org/10.3897/BDJ.1.e968

12. Heumann, I., Stoecker, H., Tamborini, M., Vennen, M.: Dinosaurierfragmente: Zur Geschichte der Tendaguru-Expedition und ihrer Objekte, 1906–2018. Wallstein Verlag (2018)

13. ICOMOS General Assembly, 19th: Principles of Seville. International Principles of virtual Archaeoloy. New Delhi (2017)

14. International Commission on Zoological Nomenclature, and International Union of Biological Sciences: International code of zoological nomenclature = Code international de nomenclature zoologique. International Trust for Zoological Nomenclature, c/o Natural History Museum, London (1999). https://doi.org/10.5962/bhl.title.50608

15. iDigBio: About iDigBio | iDigBio. https://www.idigbio.org/about-idigbio. Accessed 21 May 2024

16. Kaiser, K., et al.: Promises of mass digitisation and the colonial realities of natural history collections, vol. 11, pp. 13–25 (2023)

17. Karr, A.F.: Metadata and paradata: information collection and potential initiatives. National Institute of Statistical Sciences, Institute of Education Sciences National Center for Education Statistics (2010)

18. Kreuter, F., Casas-Cordero, C.: Paradata. Rat für Sozial- und Wirtschaftsdaten (RatSWD), Berlin (2010)

19. Larousse, É.: Définitions : statistique - Dictionnaire de français Larousse. https://www.larousse.fr/dictionnaires/francais/statistique/74516. Accessed 22 May 2024

20. von Linné, C.: Caroli Linnaei, Sveci, Doctoris Medicinae systema naturae, sive, Regna tria naturae systematice proposita per classes, ordines, genera, & species. Apud Theodorum Haak: Ex Typographia Joannis Wilhelmi de Groot, Lugduni Batavorum, Leiden, The Netherlands (1735). https://doi.org/10.5962/bhl.title.877

21. von Linné, C., Salvius, L.: Caroli Linnaei...Systema naturae per regna tria naturae :secundum classes, ordines, genera, species, cum characteribus, differentiis, synonymis, locis. Impensis Direct. Laurentii Salvii, Holmiae (1758). https://doi.org/10.5962/bhl.title.542

22. Mallison, H., Wings, O.: Photogrammetry in paleontology - a practical guide. J. Paleontol. Tech. **12**, 1–31 (2014)

23. Moore, J., Rountrey, A., Kettler, H.S.: 3D data creation to curation: community standards for 3D data preservation. Association of College & Research Libraries (2022)

24. Moris, F.: Thoughts on Inter-operable metadata for data quality, transparency, and reproducibility. CNSTAT Panel Study on Transparency and Reproducibility of Federal Statistics for NCSES (2019)

25. MorphoSource: MorphoSource. https://www.morphosource.org/. Accessed 16 May 2024

26. Museum für Naturkunde Berlin: digitize!. https://www.museumfuernaturkunde.berlin/en/press/press-releases/digitize. Accessed 15 May 2024

27. Ngram Viewer: Google Books Ngram Viewer. https://books.google.com/ngrams. Accessed 15 May 2024

28. R Core Team: R: A language and environment for statistical computing (2023). https://www.R-project.org/

29. Robertson, T., Döring, M., Guralnick, R., Bloom, D., Wieczorek, J., Braak, K., et al.: The GBIF integrated publishing toolkit: facilitating the efficient publishing of biodiversity data on the internet. PLoS ONE **9**, e102623 (2014). https://doi.org/10.1371/journal.pone.0102623

30. Turland, N.J., et al.: International Code of Nomenclature for algae, fungi, and plants (Shenzhen Code) adopted by the Nineteenth International Botanical Congress Shenzhen, China, July 2017. Koeltz Botanical Books (2018)

31. Wieczorek, J., Bloom, D., Guralnick, R., Blum, S., Döring, M., Giovanni, R., et al.: Darwin core: an evolving community-developed biodiversity data standard. PLoS ONE **7**(1), 1–8 (2012). https://doi.org/10.1371/journal.pone.0029715

32. Wilkinson, M.D., et al.: The FAIR guiding principles for scientific data management and stewardship. Sci. Data. **3**, 160018 (2016). https://doi.org/10.1038/sdata.2016.18

33. Zuse Institut Berlin: Home I zib.de. https://www.zib.de/. Accessed 16 May 2024

IDOVIR – A New Infrastructure for Documenting Paradata and Metadata of Virtual Reconstructions

Marc Grellert[1]([✉])[ID], Markus Wacker[2][ID], Jonas Bruschke[2][ID], Daniel Beck[1,3][ID], and Wolfgang Stille[1,3][ID]

[1] TU Darmstadt, Karolinenplatz 5, 64289 Darmstadt, Germany
`grellert@dg.tu-darmstadt.de`
[2] HTW Dresden, Friedrich-List-Platz 1, 01069 Dresden, Germany
{`markus.wacker,jonas.bruschke`}`@htw-dresden.de`
[3] hessian.AI, Landwehrstr. 50A, 64293 Darmstadt, Germany
{`daniel.beck,wolfgang.stille`}`@hessian.ai`

Abstract. In the context of source-based virtual reconstructions and its underlying decision-making processes (paradata), there has been a long-time demand for documenting why a reconstruction was executed in a certain way, and presenting it in a comprehensible and public manner. Lacking documentation leads to a loss of knowledge and that the scientific nature of a reconstruction won't be guaranteed anymore. Based on earlier prototypes, TU Darmstadt and HTW Dresden developed IDOVIR (Infrastructure for Documentation of Virtual Reconstructions) which enables the documentation of this kind of paradata and metadata, and, at the same time, supports communication during the reconstruction phase. The tool can be used free of charge and independently by registering via ORCID. The core of IDOVIR is the division of an entity into different spatial areas and time periods to which multiple variants can be assigned. Each variant contains the triple of 1) the representation of the reconstruction (2D or 3D), 2) the sources used, and 3) a textual argumentation that explains how the reconstruction has been inferred from the sources. For long-term storage and availability, IDOVIR is hosted by the University and State Library Darmstadt.

Keywords: Source-based virtual reconstruction · Paradata · Documentation of decisions

1 Introduction

Hypothetical, source-based virtual reconstructions have become an established tool for communication and research in the context of architectural and urban research. The documentation and evaluation of reconstruction processes are important elements for the transparency, assessment, and recognition of reconstruction solutions. Such documentation, including the decision-making processes in reconstructions, has been demanded and theoretically formulated for

M. Ioannides et al. (Eds.): 3D Research Challenges in Cultural Heritage V, LNCS 15190, pp. 103–114, 2025.
https://doi.org/10.1007/978-3-031-78590-0_9

some time [7,16]. Research results should be comprehensible, traceable, permanent and openly accessible. In addition, the documentation of paradata is so important because it is the only way to ensure scientific rigor – scientific in the sense that if sources and arguments are open, other scientists can come to the same conclusion if they follow the interpretations and arguments. At the same time, when documenting the paradata, it is possible to continue working effectively on the reconstruction at a later date if the initial situation has changed, for example if new sources have been discovered or sources are now interpreted differently. Nevertheless, it sadly can be stated that this has often been an exception to date, and there is a risk of losing the knowledge implicitly embedded in reconstructions [18,21]. Several reasons can be cited for this unfortunate state of affairs: Still today, documentation is generally neither explicitly demanded by the funding bodies, nor are additional funds made available for it. Thus, it is mostly left to the individuals and institutions who create reconstructions to finance a documentation with their own resources.

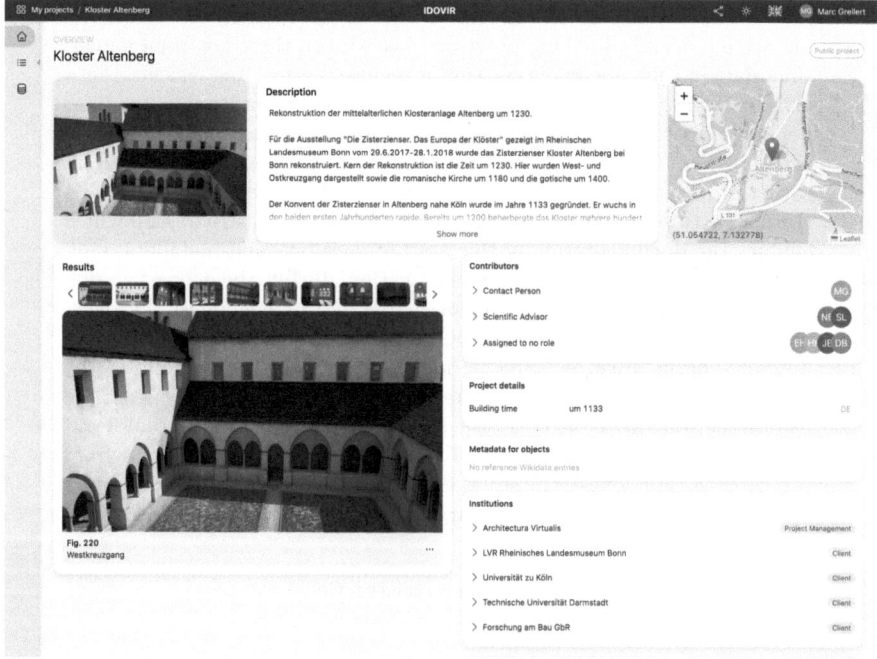

Fig. 1. Graphical user interface of IDOVIR with a project's overview including description, localization, contributors, and a selection of images.

While the London Charter and Seville Principles define what should be documented, they do not declare how it should be documented. Hence, there is not only a missing universal agreement on how to structure, file, and convey the gathered knowledge, but there is also a lack of established tools to support this work. In order to foster documentation, this work should be accomplished in such a way that users will recognize a clear added value in its reusability and ideally perceive it as facilitating the reconstruction process through intelligent software support instead of merely seeing it as extra work or a cumbersome bureaucratic formality. The infrastructure IDOVIR (Fig. 1) is set out to provide a practical tool for easy documentation which eventually leads to an established documentation standard.

2   Related Work

At the latest since the EPOCH Research Agenda 2004–2008 [2], the subject of documenting 3D reconstructions has come into focus. One result of that four-year research project was the London Charter [7], which remains decisive for subsequent theoretical considerations and their practical implementation. For some years now, there have been tentative attempts in the academic community to meet the challenge posed by the lack of documentation with concrete proposals for solutions. Demetrescu & Fanini [6] and Wacker & Bruschke [21] provide a good summary of these. A first draft for a systematic documentation tool was developed by Pletinckx [19] in the form of a web-based tool built on Wiki technology. The aim was to systematically document sources, their interpretation, the formulation of hypothesis, and the resulting visualizations. To ensure data exchange, metadata standards came into increasing consideration.

One standard that received particular attention in the field of 3D digital reconstructions is the CIDOC Conceptual Reference Model (CIDOC CRM) [3], an ontology in the field of cultural heritage that was originally designed for use in museums. Despite various extensions, for example for digital objects [8], there remains a degree of ambivalence in the way that certain kinds of information are linked. Moreover, the input and retrieval of data can be far from intuitive. Nevertheless, there are projects that put effort into integrating CIDOC CRM in 3D reconstructions. A web-based prototype, in which both, the sources and their provenance with the reasoning behind the reconstruction decisions, were linked to a 3D model, was developed by Guillem, Zarnic & Bruseker [11]. WissKI (https://wiss-ki.eu) is a system that uses Semantic Web technologies to build on CIDOC CRM and also allows for the integration of various vocabularies and thesauri. It is primarily intended for institutions and the documentation of collections and archival holdings.

Also under discussion as a basis for the documentation of 3D reconstruction is the use of Building Information Modeling (BIM), stemming from the construction industry [15,17]. MonArch [20], a documentation system that is geared towards the field of building research, seeks to implement and advance the integration of BIM. However, this system focuses on recording existing buildings instead of hypothetical architecture.

Coming from archaeology, Demetrescu [5] takes a completely different approach: here, virtual reconstruction is seen as an extension of the findings during excavations. To also allow for the documentation of virtual elements and sources, the methods and tools typically used in archaeology, especially stratigraphy and the Harris matrix, are expanded accordingly. A prototype of an interactive tool for the visualization and exploration of data in connection with 3D models has already been developed by Demetrescu & Fanini [6].

In conclusion, we can state that many practitioners addressed specific aspects of documentation. Dealing with data and paradata, the degree of uncertainty associated with fragmentary or otherwise incomplete source material is of particular interest that can be interpreted in a wide range of ways. Various metrics have been developed, among them that of the Level of Hypothesis [12] or a classification that takes account of a source's information content, ambiguity and need for interpretation [1]. The question of visualizing the different levels of uncertainty and reliability directly on the model has also been discussed in several publications [13,14].

3   A New Documentation Approach

In order to meet the demand for documentation of research results in a practical sense, two prototype web applications (ScieDoc [10] and DokuVis [4]) were developed at the TU Darmstadt, Digital Design Unit and at the HTW Dresden, respectively. They have now been brought together in the development of the online tool IDOVIR (Infrastructure for Documentation of Virtual Reconstructions) funded by the DFG (German Research Foundation) in the first phase.

The tool provides a freely accessible, free-of charge and user-friendly platform with only 20 min of familiarization time (https://idovir.com). Reconstructions are documented with the triple *sources*, *reconstructions* and *decisions* quickly and easily. By this, they become comprehensively accessible. The documentation is done in such a way that the decisions as to why a reconstruction was created in the present way, which sources it is based on, which other variants were considered, but also which conceivable variants were rejected and why (comprehensible documentation of negative results), are documented and made accessible via the Internet. At the same time, IDOVIR supports the communication of those involved in the genesis of a reconstruction and is intended to help structure the creation of the reconstruction in a meaningful way.

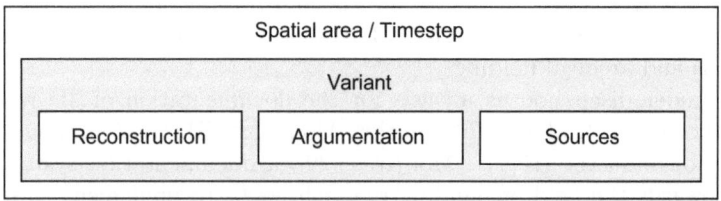

Fig. 2. The core documentation concept includes a spatio-temporal hierarchy in which each element can have multiple variants consisting of the reconstruction, the sources and the argumentation (RAM triple).

3.1 Spatio-Temporal Structure and Variants

The core documentation concept is based on the reconstruction-argumentation method (RAM) developed at the TU Darmstadt (Fig. 2). After starting a new project with some general information including project description, involved users, used software, geolocation, etc. (Fig. 1), the main first structural step is that the user sets up a subdivision of the buildings or urban complexes that are to be reconstructed into different spatial areas and time periods. Users are free to choose their own designations, subdivisions, and hierarchies in a tree structure (cf. Fig. 3, structure on the left hand side). IDOVIR makes it very easy to configure, expand, and change this structure as required.

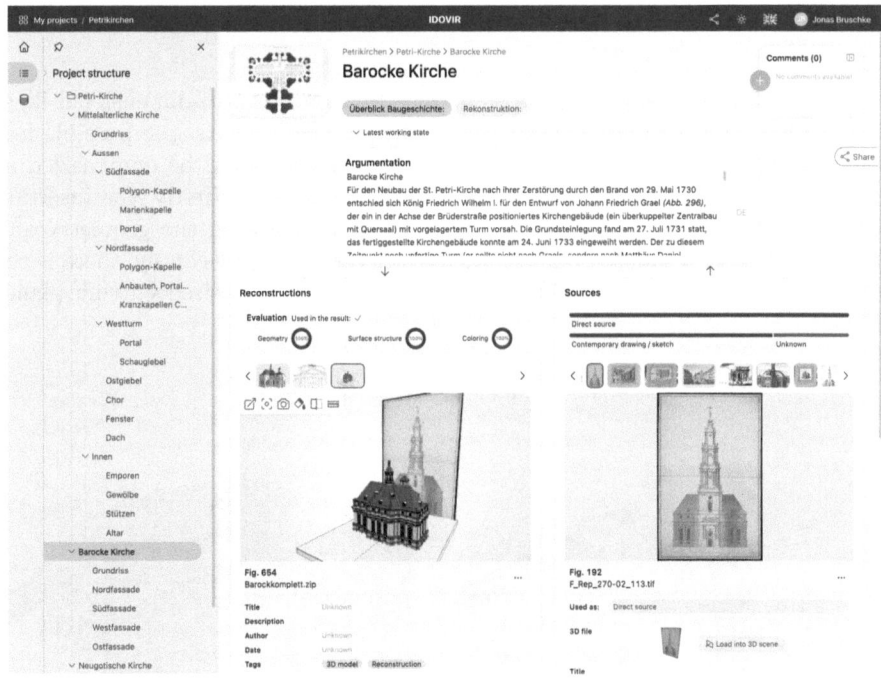

Fig. 3. The core documentation interface of IDOVIR: the triple of reconstruction – sources – argumentation on the right hand side accompanied by the navigational structure on the left hand side.

In the next step, for each spatial area or time period the triple *sources*, *reconstructions* and *decisions* can be defined. This leads to a structural element and constitutes the semantic knowledge of the origin of the data (paradata). Each of these structural elements is represented by 1) representations of the reconstruction (renderings, 3D models), 2) references, e.g. images of the sources used, and 3) a textual argumentation explaining how the reconstruction was inferred from the sources. The sources and reconstructions of each structural element are kept in a separate collection and can easily be accessed, edited, and referenced from every substructure of the project.

For each structural element, it is possible to lay out several variants with a RAM triple. The category of variants is subordinate to the structural levels of areas/time periods. The decision to incorporate variations within the hierarchical structure stems from the observation that architectural reconstructions rarely result in a single, unambiguous version of a building or complex. To this end, it is important to record the underlying discourse in its entirety. This means that further plausible variants, as well as those that may have been rejected, should be recorded and documented. If new findings change the factors that had previously led to the rejection of a variant, it is possible to refer back to those earlier discussions.

3.2   3D Model Support

While it is easy to illustrate reconstructions by means of two-dimensional illustrations based on renderings of the respective model variants, the possible features for 3D models are more complex. Two options should be emphasized as exploration/evaluation features of the loaded 3D models: Firstly, the insertion of plans that can be moved parallel to the model, allowing the geometry and source used to be validated against each other (cf. Fig. 3). Secondly, there is the option of slicing the loaded models and displaying any desired cutting planes (Fig. 4).

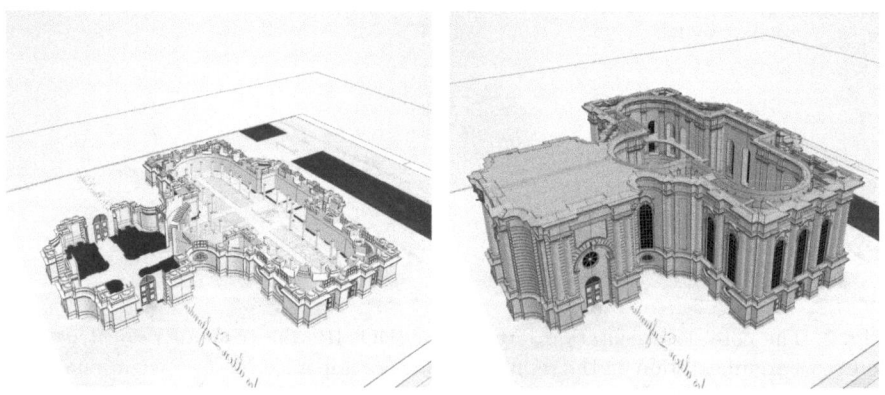

Fig. 4. 3D models can be sliced in order to better gain insights into the interiors and its relation to the sources.

Also the representation of variants in reconstructions by means of 3D models is more challenging than with two-dimensional illustrations. Using 3D models may entail uploading many similar states. Here, it might be more practical to represent the individual areas and their respective variants in the documentation in the form of partial models. In combination, these partial models of the different areas then yield a specific variant of the overall model. For the presentation of further variants, the partial models can be removed and substituted as required. Thought through to its logical conclusion, this suggests that it may make sense (for this and other reasons) to have the same structure in the documentation and the model, i.e., the designation and structure of the areas in the documentation correspond to those in the modeling software. This would also make it possible in the future to import the layer structure from the modeling software into IDOVIR and to automatically generate or update the structure of the areas and time frames – an additional incentive to lay down a sensible layer structure in the modeling software, which does not always happen in practice.

3.3 Communication

The collected data is most valuable if it can be applied and reused in (other) projects – one of the aspects of the FAIR principles. Moreover the involved community should have discussions about the interpretation and conclusions presented. Hence, the data is not a fixed collection but should discussed and negotiated. As stated above, it may appear that new findings change the argumentation and led to new variants or even the revival of a rejected one. To this end, IDOVIR provides communication features such as specific comments (source, argumentation, respectively reconstruction review/criticism). They can be added to each variant of a structural element and can be enriched with own source references. Comments can be replied to, creating a 2-level hierarchy. A notification or overview of new comments is about to be integrated.

Another important aim of IDOVIR, and for data and paradata in particular, is the easy accessibility and readability. To this end, we provide an export into PDF and DOCX format to provide a way of saving and passing on the project documentation or a version of the documentation independently of IDOVIR. A concept for the structure and layout of a sample document was developed, which served as a template for the implementation.

3.4 Evaluation of Reconstruction Results

A reconstruction process almost always entails the interpretation and evaluation of sources to provide a starting point for the creation of a (hypothetical) model. The plausibility of the reconstruction result depends not only on the informational value and nature of the sources used but also on subjective, conscious or unconscious decision-making processes, such as, for example, stylistic or aesthetic preferences. The evaluation of plausibility can therefore never be purely objective. Nevertheless, a subjective evaluation of a reconstruction can contribute to the assessment of the plausibility of the results or partial results. How such an assessment can be made and communicated has already been subject of several studies that also include various structuring and communication strategies [1,12–14]. Undoubtedly, a classification of the sources used and their use in the project is essential for the assessment and evaluation of the reconstructions.

In IDOVIR, the evaluation consists of three categories. It combines the option of self-evaluation with regard to the (subjective) assessment of the plausibility of the reconstruction with an (objective) classification of the sources used. Corresponding to the structural division into areas, the evaluation refers to a single area of a reconstruction. The first two categories refer to the sources used. In the first category, a used source is classified according to its type. The following classification scheme is based on a collaboration with Fabrizio Apollonio [9]. The idea behind this classification of sources is to capture its relationship to an object. It is divided into four main groups: 1) the source is an architectural survey, 2) it shows a design, 3) it is a contemporary description or depiction, or 4) it is a non-contemporary interpretation:

- Architectural surveys
    - Laser scan and/or SfM of architectural remains
    - Survey drawing
    - Photography
    - Excavation plan
- Designs
    - Drawing carried out
    - Drawing
    - Marquette caried out
    - Marquette
- Contemporary description or depiction
    - Contemporary Marquette
    - Contemporary drawing/sketch/painting
    - Contemporary map
    - Contemporary relief/seal/coin/medal
    - Contemporary written/oral description
- Non-contemporary interpretation
    - Drawn reconstruction
    - Reconstruction model
    - Non-contemporary map
    - Non-contemporary relief/seal/coin/medal
    - Written/oral interpretation

Here, the classification is usually unambiguous and made by the user while uploading the source. Since sources are supplied and made available for the entire project via a global directory, the type of source always remains the same. The automatic evaluation then shows which type of source occurs with which percentage frequency in the reconstruction of the corresponding area. The representation is shown in a bar chart (Fig. 5, top).

The second category establishes the relation of the source to the reconstruction. It indicates whether the source describes the reconstructed object itself or whether the source represents (merely) an analogy. The following subdivision is proposed here:

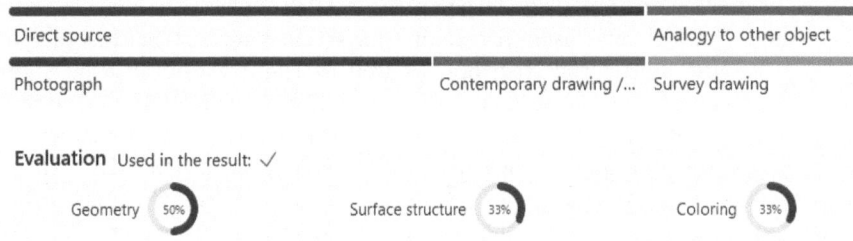

Fig. 5. Graphical summary of the classification of sources according to type and relationship to the reconstruction (top) and the evaluation of the reconstruction (bottom).

- Direct source
- Analogy to the object
- Analogy to another building
- Analogy to a constructive/technical system
- Analogy to an idea

The third category is an assessment by the user of the plausibility of the reconstruction of an area subdivided into:

- Geometry
- Surface structure
- Coloring

It is possible to enter a rating for each of these three subsets. The user may take a default setting, which refers to the degree to which an object is handed-down and is structured as follows:

- 1 Hypothetical – nothing handed-down
- 2 Little handed-down
- 3 Some handed-down
- 4 Much handed-down
- 5 Very good/completely handed-down

However, users are free to select both the name and the evaluation grades themselves, for example purely numerically (e.g. 1–5 or less or more). The evaluation is represented by a pie chart, in which the portion of the circle that is filled in rises with the user's confidence in the plausibility of the reconstruction (Fig. 5, bottom).

4   First Experiences and Outlook

The applicability, readiness, and usefulness of the new tool were tested with existing and new projects. The testing of new projects provided insights into the handling of IDOVIR and profitable impulses for further development. These include the documentation in the Department of Digital Design of the TU Darmstadt, where IDOVIR was used in teaching for student reconstructions of synagogues destroyed during the Nazi era, as well as the extensive use in a joint research project of the Department of Digital Design with the Berlin State Office for the Preservation of Monuments and the Museum of Prehistory and Early History in Berlin on churches on Berlin's Petriplatz. In 2023, IDOVIR was also tested by students from several countries as part of the Erasmus project CoVHer, and experiences were reflected back in Mainz in September 2023. This allowed further suggestions to be incorporated into the development and future direction of IDOVIR. The response was extremely encouraging. The students emphasized the intuitive and easy-to-understand method of documenting their reconstruction results and stated that the tool helped them to structure their project. In September 2023, Bob Martens (TU Vienna, Institute of Architecture and Design) switched the documentation of his virtual reconstructions in the context of student theses from the previous tool ScieDoc to IDOVIR.

Since January 2023, IDOVIR has been used to document modeling projects in teaching at the HTW Dresden. Students reconstructed buildings from selected sources of the plan collection of the State Office for the Preservation of Monuments in Saxony. IDOVIR was used to document and assess the status of the work. On the one hand, IDOVIR could be used profitably for students who still have little modeling experience and could thus help to structure the content of reconstruction projects. On the other hand, the low-threshold use and the short training period in IDOVIR could be verified. This teaching assignment showed that the IDOVIR concepts have proven themselves valid and are ready for use. In some areas, it was possible to gain helpful feedback and hints on improvement of features and simplification of work processes, which will be incorporated into further development and the follow-up application. A master's thesis on the usability and redesign of the user interface has taken a very close look at the workflows and has proven the redesign to be clearer and easier to understand for users.

To make documentation even more efficient, time-saving and intuitive, future developments of IDOVIR will focus on enhancing workflows and communication functions. A crucial aspect will be the refinement of the correlation and comparison capabilities between sources and reconstruction outcomes. This should provide an important basis for discussions and evaluations and at the same time facilitate the identification of inconsistencies in the sources and the detection of contradictions in the reconstruction solutions. This should be made possible by a kind of light table (canvas) on which several sources or reconstruction views (2D or 3D) can be flexibly arranged without losing any metadata links and while maintaining the ability to access the corresponding entries.

Acknowledgments. The research upon which this paper is based has received funding from the DFG (German Research Foundation), grant identifier 460771453.

Disclosure of Interests. The authors have no competing interests to declare that are relevant to the content of this article.

References

1. Apollonio, F.I., Fallavollita, F., Foschi, R.: The critical digital model for the study of unbuilt architecture. In: Niebling, F., Münster, S., Messemer, H. (eds.) UHDL 2019. CCIS, vol. 1501, pp. 3–24. Springer, Cham (2021). https://doi.org/10.1007/978-3-030-93186-5_1

2. Arnold, D., Geser, G.: Epoch research agenda for the applications of ICT to cultural heritage – full report. Brighton (2008)

3. Bekiari, C., Bruseker, G., Doerr, M., Ore, C.E., Stead, S., Velios, A.: Definition of the CIDOC conceptual reference model v7.1.1. The CIDOC Conceptual Reference Model Special Interest Group (2021). https://doi.org/10.26225/FDZH-X261

4. Bruschke, J., Wacker, M.: Simplifying documentation of digital reconstruction processes. In: Münster, S., Pfarr-Harfst, M., Kuroczyński, P., Ioannides, M. (eds.) 3D Research Challenges in Cultural Heritage II. LNCS, vol. 10025, pp. 256–271. Springer, Cham (2016). https://doi.org/10.1007/978-3-319-47647-6_12

5. Demetrescu, E.: Archaeological stratigraphy as a formal language for virtual reconstruction. Theory and practice. J. Archaeol. Sci. **57**, 42–55 (2015). https://doi.org/10.1016/j.jas.2015.02.004

6. Demetrescu, E., Fanini, B.: A white-box framework to oversee archaeological virtual reconstructions in space and time: methods and tools. J. Archaeol. Sci. Rep. **14**, 500–514 (2017). https://doi.org/10.1016/j.jasrep.2017.06.034

7. Denard, H.: Implementing best practice in cultural heritage visualisation: the London charter. In: Corsi, C., Slapšak, B., Vermeulen, F. (eds.) Good Practice in Archaeological Diagnostics. NSA, pp. 255–268. Springer, Cham (2013). https://doi.org/10.1007/978-3-319-01784-6_15

8. Doerr, M., Theodoridou, M.: CRMdig: a generic digital provenance model for scientific observation. In: TaPP 2011, 3rd USENIX Workshop on the Theory and Practice of Provenance (2011)

9. Grellert, M., Apollonio, F.I., Martens, B., Nußbaum, N.: Working experiences with the reconstruction argumentation method (RAM) – scientific documentation for virtual reconstruction. In: Proceedings of the 23rd International Conference on Cultual Heritage and New Technologies (CHNT 23) (2018)

10. Grellert, M., Pfarr-Harfst, M.: Die Rekonstruktion-Argument-Methode – Minimaler Dokumentationsstandard im Kontext digitaler Rekonstruktionen. In: Kuroczyński, P., Pfarr-Harfst, M., Münster, S. (eds.) Der Modelle Tugend 2.0: Digitale 3D-Rekonstruktion als virtueller Raum der architekturhistorischen Forschung, pp. 264–280. arthistoricum.net, Heidelberg (2019). https://doi.org/10.11588/arthistoricum.515

11. Guillem, A., Zarnic, R., Bruseker, G.: Building an argumentation platform for 3D reconstruction using CIDOC-CRM and Drupal. In: 2015 Digital Heritage, vol. 2, pp. 383–386. IEEE (2015). https://doi.org/10.1109/DigitalHeritage.2015.7419529

12. Hauck, O., Kuroczyński, P.: Cultural Heritage Markup Language – How to record and preserve 3D assests of digital reconstruction. In: Proceedings of the 19th International Conference on Cultural Heritage and New Technologies (CHNT 19) (2014)

13. Heeb, N., Christen, J.: Strategien zur Vermittlung von Fakt, Hypothese und Fiktion in der digitalen Architektur-Rekonstruktion. In: Kuroczyński, P., Pfarr-Harfst, M., Münster, S. (eds.) Der Modelle Tugend 2.0: Digitale 3D-Rekonstruktion als virtueller Raum der architekturhistorischen Forschung, pp. 226–254. arthistoricum.net, Heidelberg (2019). https://doi.org/10.11588/arthistoricum.515.c7570

14. Kensek, K.M., Swartz Dodd, L., Cipolla, N.: Fantastic reconstructions or reconstructions of the fantastic? Tracking and presenting ambiguity, alternatives, and documentation in virtual worlds. Autom. Constr. **13**(2), 175–186 (2004). https://doi.org/10.1016/j.autcon.2003.09.010

15. Kuroczyński, P., Brandt, J., Jara, K., Große, P.: Historic building information modeling (hBIM) und linked data – Neue Zugänge zum Forschungsgegenstand objektorientierter Fächer. In: Sahle, P. (ed.) DHd 2019 Digital Humanities: multimedial & multimodal. Konferenzabstracts, pp. 138–141 (2019)

16. Bendicho, V.M.L.-M.: International guidelines for virtual archaeology: the Seville principles. In: Corsi, C., Slapšak, B., Vermeulen, F. (eds.) Good Practice in Archaeological Diagnostics. NSA, pp. 269–283. Springer, Cham (2013). https://doi.org/10.1007/978-3-319-01784-6_16

17. Martens, B., Peter, H.: Virtuelle Rekonstruktion –BIM als Rahmenbedingung für eine langfristige Nutzung von 3D-Gebäudemodellen. In: Kuroczyński, P., Pfarr-Harfst, M., Münster, S. (eds.) Der Modelle Tugend 2.0: Digitale 3D-Rekonstruktion als virtueller Raum der architekturhistorischen Forschung, pp. 313–328. arthistoricum.net, Heidelberg (2019). https://doi.org/10.11588/arthistoricum.515

18. Münster, S.: Interdisziplinäre Kooperation bei der Erstellung geschichtswissenschaftlicher 3D-Modelle. Springer, Wiesbaden (2016). https://doi.org/10.1007/978-3-658-13857-8

19. Pletinckx, D.: How to make sustainable visualizations of the past: An EPOCH common infrastructure tool for interpretation management. In: Bentkowska-Kafel, A., Denard, H., Baker, D. (eds.) Paradata and Transparency in Virtual Heritage, pp. 203–244. Ashgate Publishing, Farnham (2012)

20. Stenzer, A., Ehrlinger, C., Schmid, M.: Ansätze zur semantischen 3D-Repräsentation von Bauwerken in Datenbanken. In: Kuroczyński, P., Pfarr-Harfst, M., Münster, S. (eds.) Der Modelle Tugend 2.0: Digitale 3D-Rekonstruktion als virtueller Raum der architekturhistorischen Forschung, pp. 1–390. arthistoricum.net, Heidelberg (2019). https://doi.org/10.11588/arthistoricum.515

21. Wacker, M., Bruschke, J.: Dokumentation von Digitalen Rekonstruktionsprojekten. In: Kuroczyński, P., Pfarr-Harfst, M., Münster, S. (eds.) Der Modelle Tugend 2.0: Digitale 3D-Rekonstruktion als virtueller Raum der architekturhistorischen Forschung, pp. 282–294. Computing in Art and Architecture, arthistoricum.net, Heidelberg (2019). https://doi.org/10.11588/arthistoricum.515.c7574

Documentation and Publication of Hypothetical Virtual 3D Reconstructions in the CoVHer Project

Igor Piotr Bajena[1,2(✉)] ⓘ, Fabrizio Ivan Apollonio[1] ⓘ, Karol Argasiński[2,3] ⓘ,
Federico Fallavollita[1] ⓘ, Riccardo Foschi[1] ⓘ, Jakub Franczuk[3] ⓘ,
Krzysztof Koszewski[3] ⓘ, Piotr Kuroczyński[2] ⓘ, and Jan Lutteroth[2] ⓘ

[1] Department of Architecture, University of Bologna, Bologna, Italy
{igorpiotr.bajena,fabrizio.apollonio,federico.fallavollita,
riccardo.foschi}@unibo.it
[2] Institute of Architecture, Hochschule Mainz, Mainz, Germany
{piotr.kuroczynski,jan.lutteroth}@hs-mainz.de
[3] Faculty of Architecture, Warsaw University of Technology, Warsaw, Poland
{karol.argasinski.dokt,jakub.franczuk,
krzysztof.koszewski}@pw.edu.pl

Abstract. The CoVHer Erasmus+ project addresses the long-standing lack of standardisation in hypothetical virtual 3D reconstruction and modelling in architectural heritage research. It aims to develop best practices for the 3D reconstruction of lost or never-built architectural heritage, enhancing research quality, transparency, and reusability. The collaborative effort includes contributions from five European universities and two private companies, focusing on architecture, archaeology, digital humanities, and art history. The presented workflow of documentation is the result of the joint effort in extensions of the approaches of the Scientific Reference Model (SRM) and Critical Digital Model (CDM), which strive for faithful reconstruction, documenting all decisions and inferences and advocate open licensing and use of non-proprietary formats to promote accessibility and reusability. The developed methodology aims to provide tools for the scientific evaluation of hypothetical reconstructions and support data exchange between researchers.

Keywords: hypothetical virtual 3D reconstruction · lost and never-built architectural heritage · computer-based visualisation

1 Introduction

Virtual 3D reconstruction and 3D modelling in architectural heritage research have lacked standardisation for many years. Significant theoretical issues and unresolved challenges persist, particularly regarding the documentation of procedures, decision-making processes, methods employed, and results sharing. Despite well-known theoretical guidelines [1, 2], the academic community involved in virtual 3D reconstructions has yet to reach a consensus on a unified standard for scholarly approved 3D models.

© The Author(s) 2025
M. Ioannides et al. (Eds.): 3D Research Challenges in Cultural Heritage V, LNCS 15190, pp. 115–126, 2025.
https://doi.org/10.1007/978-3-031-78590-0_10

The CoVHer Erasmus+ project[1] aims to address these issues by developing and promoting best practices for the hypothetical virtual 3D reconstruction of lost or never-built architectural heritage. This research presents a methodology to improve the quality, transparency, and reusability of 3D models. This collaborative effort includes contributions from various disciplines, including architecture, archaeology, digital humanities, and art history.

The method developed is based on the principles of the Critical Digital Model (CDM) and Scientific Reference Model (SRM). The CDM aims to reconstruct objects of study as faithfully as possible to the original author's intent at a specific moment, documenting all subjective choices, additions, and inferences [3]. The SRM can be considered as the predecessor of CDM. It is a clearly described methodology, explaining step by step how to prepare and structure the project of the reconstruction, tearing attention to the aspect of using data exchange formats and open access repositories for sharing and re-using the results [4]. By using these methodologies as foundations, the CoVHer project emphasises the need for an appropriate rigour of work in terms of structured data acquisition, semantic enrichment of the 3D model, assessment of the scientific value and sustainable data sharing.

2   Data Acquisition: Capturing the Process

The data acquisition process is critical to accurately and reliably reconstruct lost or hypothetical architectural heritage. This process involves collaboration with other scientific disciplines, each with its own standards and methods, which has made a single standard for data acquisition impractical until now. The European CoVHer project outlines methodologies and best practices to ensure scientific integrity and transparency in data collection and acquisition.

Proper documentation, including metadata and paradata, is essential for transparency and future research. Metadata details the sources, dates, accuracy, and significance of data points, while paradata records decision-making processes, assumptions, uncertainties, and limitations during reconstruction. Scientific research and archaeological discoveries, as well as original architectural drawings, constitute the documentary sources incorporated to enhance the accuracy and authenticity of the reconstruction.

Advanced digital techniques, [5] such as 3D scanning, photogrammetry and laser imaging, capture detailed data, which undergo critical analysis and verification to ensure accuracy and reliability. All that data needs thorough critical analysis and verification to assess its accuracy and reliability [1].

This involves identifying and addressing uncertainties and inconsistencies in the data to enhance the overall reliability of the reconstruction. [3] Evaluating the precision and correctness of the data collected from various sources and clearly documenting the assumptions, uncertainties, and limitations encountered during the data acquisition process provide context and transparency.

The CoVHer project aims to set clear objectives, adopt rigorous methodologies, and ensure comprehensive documentation through metadata and paradata. This structured

---

[1] Project Number: 2021–1-IT02-KA220-HED-000031190. More information about project is available on the website https://covher.eu/, last accessed 2024/07/27.

approach facilitates comparison between virtual reconstructions and progress in the field. An example from the AFRIPAL[2] project, focusing on the city of Mustis in Proconsular Africa, illustrates the reality-based data acquisition framework. The project's data collection follows the principles of CDM and SRM and the Integrated Digitally Enabled Environment (IDEE), [6] enabling digital data processing, analysis, storage and sharing. The following case shows how, at the data-capturing stage, the information that forms the basis for the Informative Model (IM) was entered into the Raw Model (RM). The organisation of data acquisition was based on the following framework presented in Table 1.

Table 1. Framework for the organisation of data acquisition

Scope and data sources	Objectives	Recipients
• Photogrammetric models of individual details and objects • LiDAR 3D scans • Geodetic surveys • Archaeological surveys • Archive images	• Archaeological and architectural documentation • Virtual 3D reconstruction in BIM with attributed information, data, and sources • Virtual anastylosis of scanned elements • Publication of results – informative virtual tour • Archaeological and architectural documentation	• Professionals • Laypersons

On-site data collection utilized a Network-Attached Storage (NAS) system, with files uploaded and archived daily. The data organization involved coordinating existing and new systems. An excavation plan was created using an orthophoto map from a Unmanned Aerial Vehicle (UAV) and geodetic survey points, subdivided into a 10x10 meter grid with marked structures (Fig. 1a), facilitating collaboration among researchers and simplifying analogue data collection. Due to limited excavation time and weather, correct naming (Fig. 1b) of digital files and paper documentation was crucial.

Photographs for documentation and photogrammetry included an in-camera prefix (e.g., C2_B5_L2_number) for systematic naming. Post-organization used this prefix as a

---

[2] The archaeological work was conducted under the project "(Reading) African Palimpsest: The dynamics of urban and rural communities of Numidian and Roman Mustis (AFRIPAL)," a grant from the National Science Centre (NCN), no. 2020/37/B/HS3/00348. The directors of the project are Jamel Hajji (Institut National du Patrimoine) and Tomasz Waliszewski (University of Warsaw).

keyword in IPTC metadata[3] managed by a script in ExifTool[4], saving time by automating the process for approximately 33,000 photographs.

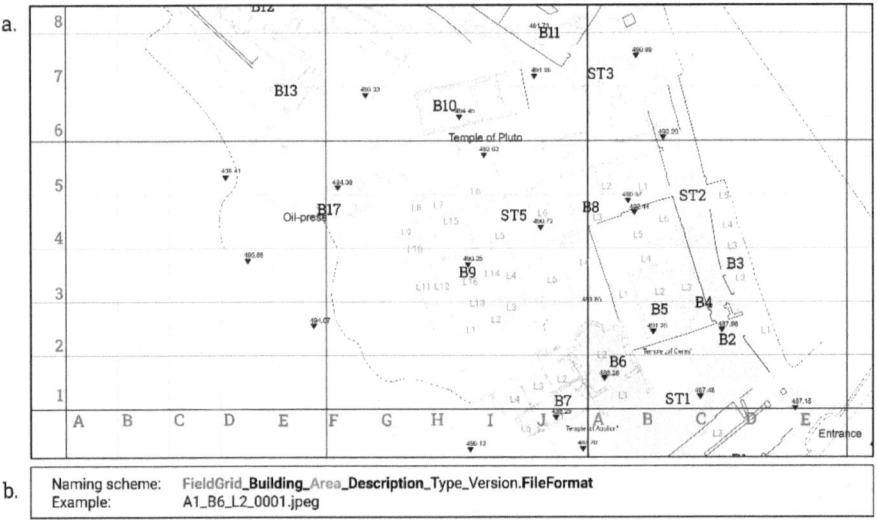

Fig. 1. a: Excavation plan with 10 m × 10 m grid, building and area labels. Drawing by Magdalena Antos. **b:** Naming scheme for files (bold ones required)

Systematic naming enabled filtering of images in cataloguing software (e.g., Adobe Lightroom Classic) by specific areas or structures. Additional keywords, such as indexes of architectural elements, were added to classified images, which were then used to create photogrammetric models. The same process tagged archive images, previous photographs, and LiDAR scans, following manual data verification and interpretation. It was preceded by manual verification and interpretation of the data in BulkRenameUtility[5].

3   Semantic Enrichment of 3D Models

The beginning of the development of a hypothetical virtual 3D reconstruction is the preparation of the semantic segmentation of the model into elements that can be given a specific meaning. Semantic segmentation is the essence of working with heritage assets because it is the culturally encoded meaning that gives a physical object its historical value. It is then the clue of the digitalization process to maintain object's significance

---

[3] International Press Telecommunications Council. (2024). *IPTC Photo Metadata Standard* (Version 1.4). Retrieved from https://iptc.org/standards/photo-metadata/, last accessed 2024/07/24.

[4] Harvey, P. (2024). *ExifTool* (Version 12.58) [Software]. Available from https://exiftool.org/, last accessed 2024/07/24.

[5] TGRMN Software. (2024). *Bulk Rename Utility* (Version 3.4.3) [Software]. Available from https://www.bulkrenameutility.co.uk/, last accessed 2024/07/24.

through such semantic enrichment. Without semantic segmentation and enrichment, we only have raw models that are of limited use in the scientific field. This leads to a data classification that should be determined to integrate the relevant Levels of Geometry (LoG) and Information (LoI). The use of Building Information Modelling (BIM) allows for the definition of such information within the Level of Information Need standard. [7] This encompasses not only the aforementioned LoG and LoI coefficients but also the analysis of the purpose of the data (Why?), the timing of its delivery (When?), the responsible party (Who?), and the specifics of its delivery (How and What?) (Fig. 2).

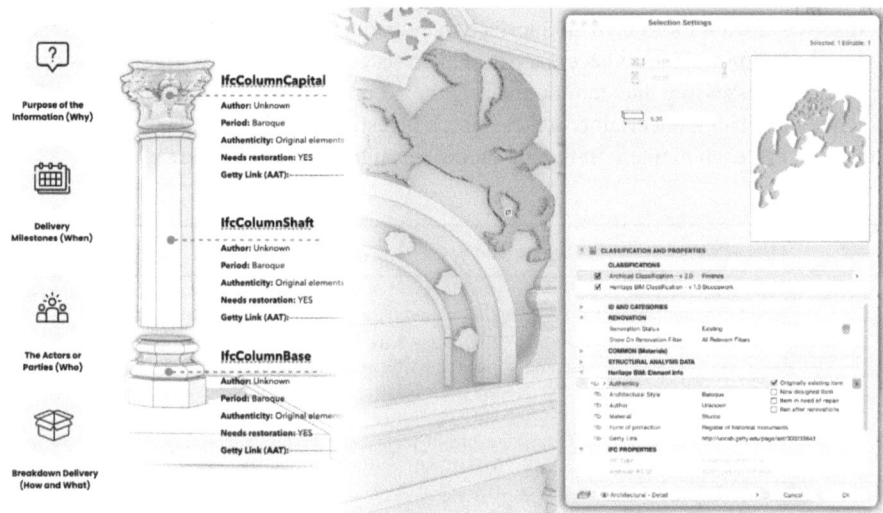

Fig. 2. Level of Information Need and classification assessment in BIM software of choice – Graphisoft Archicad.

To ensure correct data interpretation and its accessibility to researchers, it is essential to use interoperable data formats. OpenBIM standards, part of BIM, facilitate direct communication and data exchange through taxonomies and ontologies in building SMART data dictionaries (bSDD). The recommended format for exchanging model data is the Industry Foundation Classes (IFC) format, which ensures interoperability and consistency among different platforms and stakeholders.

Effective models require meticulous geometric and semantic segmentation. Geometric segmentation represents spatial relationships of heritage assets, while semantic segmentation adds meaning to elements, contextualising and naming them. Semantic enrichment involves integrating comprehensive metadata and paradata into 3D models, including attributes like material properties, historical context, and state of conservation and the level of uncertainty. This detailed information aids heritage interpretation, management, and risk reduction.

Integrating model data with metadata and paradata enhances the precision and efficiency of creating virtual reconstruction models. These 3D models can incorporate complex geometries of individual building elements and detailed semantic data provided by experts, resulting in more accurate and informative virtual reconstructions [8].

4   Scientific Value Evaluation: Knowledge Representation in Terms of Levels of Uncertainty

Semantically segmented and enriched 3D models are knowledge representations by themselves and are more than an interface to embedded knowledge. Proper documentation and dissemination are necessary to make this embedded knowledge accessible. A key aspect is assessing and communicating the reconstruction's uncertainty. One effective method is using uncertainty scales, which investigate and visually communicate the uncertainty of each element in the 3D model through false-colour views.

Colour Code			Uncertainty	Description
	1	1	lowest uncertainty (~0 to 14% uncertain[1])	The analysed feature[2] of the 3D model is derived mainly from good quality **reality-based data**, which reaches the target LoD[3].
1.5	2	2	low uncertainty (~14 to 28% uncertain)	Reliable conjecture based mainly on clear and accurate **direct[4] / primary[5] sources**, which reach the target LoD. When reality-based data is unavailable, available but unusable, or not reaching the target LoD.
		3	average-low uncertainty (~28 to 43% uncertain)	Conjecture based mainly on **indirect/secondary sources**, by the **SAME AUTHOR/S**, which reach the target LoD. Or logic deduction/selection of variants. When **direct/primary sources are available**, but minimally unclear, damaged, inconsistent, inaccurate, or not reaching the target LoD.
3.5				
4.5		4	average uncertainty (~43 to 57% uncertain)	Conjecture based mainly on **indirect/secondary** sources by **DIFFERENT AUTHOR/S** (or unknown authors), which reach the target LoD. When **direct/primary sources are available**, but minimally unclear, damaged, inconsistent, inaccurate, or not reaching the target LoD.
		5	average-high uncertainty (~57 to 71% uncertain)	Conjecture based mainly on **indirect/secondary sources** by the **SAME AUTHOR/S**, which reach the target LoD. When **direct/primary sources are not available** or unusable.
5.5		6	high uncertainty (~71 to 86% uncertain)	Conjecture based mainly on **indirect/secondary** sources by **DIFFERENT AUTHOR/S** (or unknown authors), which reach the target LoD. When **direct/primary sources are not available** or unusable.
7	7	7	highest uncertainty (~86 to 100% uncertain)	Conjecture based mainly on personal knowledge due to missing or **unreferenced sources**.
\	\	\	abstention	not relevant, not considered, left unsolved, missing data and missing conjecture (it does not count for the calculation of the average uncertainty)

Fig. 3. Source-based CDM scale of uncertainty

Various scales for assessing and visualizing uncertainty in 3D reconstructions exist [9–11], each with different descriptions, granularity, and colours. These scales sometimes extend into multidimensional matrices (e.g., extended matrix[6] [12]). Despite the recognition of the importance of uncertainty assessment and visualisation, a shared standard approach is lacking due to the need for tailored scales for specific projects, which compromises comparability across projects.

The CoVHer Erasmus+ project developed good practices to create new scales of uncertainty that are reusable, exhaustive, unambiguous, and objective. These principles ensure the scales' reusability in similar contexts, completeness, lack of overlap, and user-independence. The scale developed for the CDM [3] was improved and extensively tested in the CoVHer project, proving effective for assessing hypothetical reconstructions of lost or never-built architecture (see Fig. 3). [13] Additionally, a new methodology for mathematically quantifying average global uncertainty was introduced.

The methodology introduces two mathematical formulations to quantify uncertainty in a clear, synthetic, transparent and user-independent manner. These formulas yield a single percentage value by averaging the uncertainties of each element, weighted by their volume and possibly a user-assigned relevance factor. This provides a concise summary of uncertainty assessment, useful for quick comparisons of hypothetical reconstructive models in 3D web-based repositories. However, these synthetic measures should complement, not replace, false-colour visualisation.

The formulas are Average Uncertainty weighted on the Volume (AU_V) and Average Uncertainty weighted on the Volume and Relevance (AU_VR). It is important to note that higher uncertainty in hypothetical reconstructions does not imply lower scientific value; well-documented high-uncertainty models can enhance understanding by critically integrating diverse sources and advancing scientific discourse.

5 Publication of the Results: Open Infrastructure for Virtual 3D Reconstruction

The scientific community still perceives 3D models as a tool for visualisation in the form of renderings, but not as a result worth of a 3D publication in the sense of sharing the 3D model. 3D data is often unavailable, and when data is published, it is not prepared for reuse or verification. Therefore, the CoVHer project adopts the SRM approach by designating proper data publication as a determinant for research transparency. The data publication package should consist of three parts: documentation of the modelling, analysis and decision-making (**paradata**), a 3D model prepared for reuse in an open data exchange format (**3D data**), and an appropriate package of contextual information about the published 3D resource (**metadata**) [4].

5.1 Paradata

Virtual 3D reconstructions are a multi-stage process. In addition to the mentioned earlier documentation of data acquisition and evaluation of uncertainty, considerable relevance

---

[6] Extended Matrix - Glossary, https://www.extendedmatrix.org/discover/glossary, last accessed 2024/07/24.

is also attributed to the analysis of historical source materials. Documenting the decisions made at work can be time-consuming and requires appropriate structuring. Therefore, the Reconstruction-Argumentation Method (RAM) [14] is used within the platform IDOVIR[7]. This method is based on a pre-determined semantic division of the object and assigns sources and argumentations to identified elements. The IDOVIR guarantees consistency with predefined templates and the rapid generation of paradata packages. These packages include the visualisation of the sources in combination with their interpretation alongside the argumentation. The metadata provides the necessary copyrights and serves as scientific citations but can also be marked hidden if the copyright is not clarified. This step is still necessary, even though the EU copyright law is changing. [15] The latest updates of the IDOVIR also include bibliographic input, enhancing the traceability of decision-making based on various authors.

5.2 3D Data

Publication of 3D data is challenging due to the lack of standardised formats and the variety of modelling techniques and software. Creating a reusable 3D file that integrates easily with other data requires following specific rules. Guidelines in this matter for data on the web were developed as a 5-star deployment scheme for Linked Open Data[8]. Those assumptions can be translated towards 3D data.

The minimum required in terms of data publication to gain one star is to make the file available under an open licence (OL). Two stars can be achieved if our model has structure (MS), which, in the case of models, can be applied by use of structure in the model layers. Three stars requires file conversion to one of the neutral formats (NF). Four stars require the attachment of a set of structural elements properties (SEP) of the model, and five stars require the addition of a link to external data repositories to provide context to the information and creation of a Linked Open Model (LOM) [4].

Achieving four stars on this scale requires open, structured formats that preserve the semantics of the objects. Formats that meet these requirements include IFC and City Geography Markup Language (CityGML). Both formats successfully stored information on virtual 3D reconstruction during courses with architecture students who tested the formats as part of an elective class on the virtual reconstruction of wooden synagogues [16].

5.3 Metadata

Despite many metadata schemas for cultural heritage objects, no solution has been found for the hypothetical 3D reconstruction of cultural heritage. Current 3D repositories either omit issues related to research uncertainties or do not address them comprehensively. [17] The problem is related to the heterogeneous nature of 3D reconstructions. They are digital products requiring technical specifications and copyright declarations, typically provided in commercial repositories oriented for data reuse. Additionally, 3D models are used to visualise history, which many cultural heritage repositories prioritise over technological

---

[7] https://idovir.com/, last accessed 2024/07/24.

[8] https://5stardata.info/en/, last accessed 2024/07/24.

aspects. Furthermore, 3D models are part of research, with metadata usually found only in specialised virtual research environments (VRE) [18].

The CoVHer project addresses these challenges by presenting a documentation scheme combining all these aspects in a new web-based open-access repository according to the SRM approach. Developed within the framework of the VRE WissKI[9], it provides triplestore storage using the CIDOC CRM-referenced application ontology of OntPreHer3D[10], oriented towards creating data deposits in the repository. It is a further development of OntSciDoc3D ontology, which was tailored for documentation in VRE. [19] The system uses five main documentation units: people, organisations, projects, heritage objects and virtual reconstructions. Users create semantic relationships between those units during data input. Entities are referenced through identifiers pointing to controlled vocabularies and authority files to reduce data ambiguity. In the end, ontologically encoded metadata, supported by controlled vocabularies and a package of 3D files and paradata, allows the creation of comprehensive scientific documentation of 3D models (Fig. 4). This publication supports future model reuse for applications like 3D printing or virtual reality. The interoperability of 3D file formats provides a solid foundation for creating derivatives aimed at disseminating lost architectural heritage, with reference to relevant documentation.

6 Conclusion

This study presents the current methodology for working with hypothetical virtual 3D reconstructions of lost or never-built architectural heritage developed as a combined interdisciplinary effort by the CoVHer project. The method follows the guidelines of the London Charter and the Seville Principles, shaping a practical (or applicable) way of publishing hypothetical 3D models while preserving the transparency of the reconstruction process and guaranteeing easy access to the research data through precise documentation, self-assessment of the model's level of uncertainty and the accessibility of the research data within a semantic data repository, ontologically tailored to the needs of hypothetical virtual 3D reconstructions. The methodology encourages the creation of paradata through documentation, enriches the research object with metadata, and provides access to the research data through standardised exchange file formats. Thus enabling the assessment of its scientific value. The authors are convinced that the proposed methodology - if followed conscientiously - will lead to a significant rethinking that could establish 3D model-based hypothetical research as a key discipline in the field of cultural heritage. Based on the experiences throughout the workshops, the CoVHer project is testing and establishing a general curriculum on hypothetical 3D reconstructions that is rooted in the concepts of the proposed methodology and aims for the promotion of scientific practices in various disciplines that deal with cultural heritage.

---

[9] WissKI is a free and open virtual research environment for managing scholarly data and provides benefits of semantic web technology. It works in Drupal content management framework, Available from: https://wiss-ki.eu/, last accessed 2024/07/27.

[10] Development of OntPreHer3D ontology can be followed on: https://github.com/igorbajena/Ont PreHer3D/, last accessed 2024/07/27.

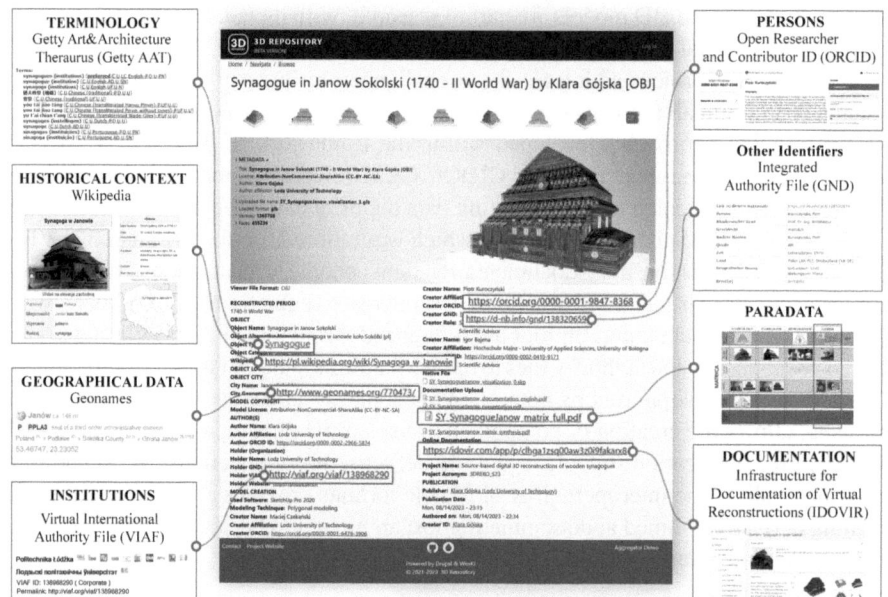

Fig. 4. Cross-referencing of context data on the example of virtual 3D reconstruction of the synagogue in Janów Sokolski by Klara Gójska and Maciej Czekański. Entry created during the seminar about virtual 3D reconstruction of wooden synagogues

Acknowledgments. The study was funded by the European Commission in the Erasmus+ program (2021–1-IT02-KA220-HED-000031190). We would also like to express our thanks to project partners from Universitat Autònoma de Barcelona (Juan A. Barceló and Evdoxia Tzerpou), Universidade do Porto (Clara Pimenta do Vale), La Tempesta (Marc Hernández Güell and Paul Guiu) and IGSD (Mark Fichtner) actively contributing to the development of the CoVHer curriculum, of which the presented methodology is a part, and technical support.

Disclosure of Interests. The authors have no competing interests to declare that are relevant to the content of this article.

References

1. London Charter. https://londoncharter.org/introduction.html. Accessed 28 July 2024
2. Principles of Seville. http://sevilleprinciples.com/. Accessed 28 July 2024
3. Apollonio, F.I., Fallavollita, F., Foschi, R.: The Critical Digital Model for the Study of Unbuilt Architecture. In: Research and Education in Urban History in the Age of Digital Libraries, pp. 3–24. Springer, Cham (2021)
4. Kuroczyński, P., Apollonio, F.I., Bajena, I.P., Cazzaro, I.: Scientific Reference Model – Defining Standards, Methodology and Implementation of Serious 3D Models in Archaeology, Art and Architectural History. Int. Arch. Photogramm. Remote Sens. Spat. Inf. Sci. **XLVIII-M-2–2023**, 895–902 (2023)

5. Li, Z., Liu, J., Dong, Y., Hou, M., Wang, X.: From data acquisition to digital reconstruction: virtual restoration of the Great Wall's Nine Eyes Watchtower. Built Herit. **8**, 22 (2024)
6. Plume, J.: Integrated digitally-enabled environment: the internet of places. In: AGI foresight report 2020, pp. 207–209. Association for Geographic Information (2020)
7. International Organization for Standardization.: Building information modelling—Level of information need (ISO 7817-1:2024) (2024)
8. Argasiński, K., Kuroczyński, P.: Preservation through digitization - standardization in documentation of build cultural heritage using capturing reality techniques and heritage/historic BIM methodology. Int. Arch. Photogramm. Remote Sens. Spat. Inf. Sci. **XLVIII-M-2–2023**, 87–94 (2023)
9. Apollonio, F.I.: Classification schemes for visualization of uncertainty in digital hypothetical reconstruction. In: Münster, S., Pfarr-Harfst, M., Kuroczyński, P., Ioannides, M. (eds.) 3D Research Challenges in Cultural Heritage II. LNCS, vol. 10025, pp. 119–135. Springer, Cham (2016)
10. Project Byzantium 1200, Case of Portus Theodosiacus. https://www.byzantium1200.com/port_t.html. Accessed 24 July 2024
11. Ortiz-Cordero, R., León Pastor, E., Hidalgo Fernández, R.E.: Proposal for the improvement and modification in the scale of evidence for virtual reconstruction of the cultural heritage: a first approach in the mosque-cathedral and the fluvial landscape of Cordoba. J. Cult. Herit. **30**, 10–15 (2018)
12. Demetrescu, E., Ferdani, D.: From field archaeology to virtual reconstruction: a five steps method using the extended matrix. Appl. Sci. **11**, 5206 (2021)
13. Apollonio, F.I., Fallavollita, F., Foschi, R., Smurra, R.: Multi-feature uncertainty analysis for urban-scale hypothetical 3D reconstructions: piazza delle erbe case study. Heritage **7**, 476–498 (2024)
14. Pfarr-Harfst, M., Grellert, M.: The reconstruction – argumentation method. In: Ioannides, M., et al. (eds.) Digital Heritage. Progress in Cultural Heritage: Documentation, Preservation, and Protection, pp. 39–49. Springer, Cham (2016)
15. Directive (EU) 2019/790 of the European Parliament and of the Council of 17 April 2019 on copyright and related rights in the Digital Single Market and amending Directives 96/9/EC and 2001/29/EC. https://eur-lex.europa.eu/eli/dir/2019/790/oj. Accessed 24 July 2024
16. Bajena, I., Kuroczyński, P.: Development of the methodology and infrastructure for digital 3D reconstruction. In: Proceedings of (IN)TANGIBLE HERITAGE(S) A Conference on Technology, Culture and Design. AMPS Conference Proceedings Series, Canterbury, pp. 72–83 (2023)
17. Bajena, I., Kuroczyński, P.: Metadata for 3D digital heritage models. In the search of a common ground. In: Münster, S., Pattee, A., Kröber, C., and Niebling, F. (eds.) Research and Education in Urban History in the Age of Digital Libraries, pp. 45–64. Springer, Cham (2023)
18. Kuroczyński, P., Bajena, I., Große, P., Jara, K., Wnęk, K.: Digital reconstruction of the new synagogue in breslau: new approaches to object-oriented research. In: Niebling, F., Münster, S., Messemer, H. (eds.) Research and Education in Urban History in the Age of Digital Libraries, pp. 25–45. Springer, Cham (2021)
19. Kuroczyński, P., Große, P.: OntSciDoc3D – ontology for scientific documentation of source-based 3D reconstruction of architecture. In: Abstracts of the 25th International Conference on Cultural Heritage and New Technologies. CHNT 25, Vienna (2020)

A Metadata/Paradata Design Framework for Historic BIM

Maurice Murphy[1]([✉]), Petra Krajacic[1], Eimear Meegan[2], Rebecca O. Reilly[2],
Garrett Keenaghan[3], Alain Chenaux[3], Rafael Fernandes Dionizio[4],
and Eloisa DezenKempter[4]

[1] Virtual Lab Dublin, Dublin, Ireland
morris.murphy@TUDublin.ie
[2] Discovery Programme Ireland, Dublin, Ireland
{eimearmeegan,rebeccaoreilly}@discoveryprogramme.ie
[3] Technological University of Dublin, Dublin, Ireland
{garrett.keenaghan,alain.chenaux}@TUDublin.ie
[4] State University of Campinas, São Paulo, Brazil
r200299@dac.unicamp.br, eloisak@unicamp.br

Abstract. In this paper a systematic examination of metadata/paradata is presented to support the creation and reuse of digital heritage data as a means of engaging in some way with the experience of past material cultural discourse. The contextual and procedural information generated throughout Historic Building Information Modelling (HBIM) workflows are presented through a series of case studies. The three phases of data capture, modelling and knowledge dissemination for HBIM workflows are reflected in the presented case studies. The first case study illustrate how metadata is recorded automatically by the terrestrial and aerial laser scanning instruments and software, whereas it is necessary to document paradata. Case study 2, shows how shape grammar libraries of architectural elements and procedural modelling both contained metadata within the HBIM software platforms. Again, there is a need to document the paradata using both graphic and text format, proving the need for standards and guidelines for HBIM. Finally, additional software platforms were reviewed to ensure survival of metadata (geometry, geolocation and other semantic attributes) when the virtual model is disseminated outside of HBIM in this case using Heritage GIS. The HBIM design framework is presented as a set of Data Cards, a standardised documentation to record key information about datasets, allowing for enhanced reuse of the data recorded in such a way as to contribute more meaningfully to the consideration of the many and various ways of living in the past.

1 Introduction

Metadata provides information about other data, on the other hand paradata specifically describes the process by which the data was collected, including the conditions under which the data was gathered. In the context of digital 3D modelling and virtual representation of the built heritage a design for a paradata framework is an essential appendage. A design for a framework requires initially the identification of suitable metrics and

M. Ioannides et al. (Eds.): 3D Research Challenges in Cultural Heritage V, LNCS 15190, pp. 127–138, 2025.
https://doi.org/10.1007/978-3-031-78590-0_11

project requirements and secondly the protocols and procedures to implement these metrics. Appropriate metrics for a HBIM framework may include for example correctly described workflows in data acquisition (current and historic), 3D modelling and dissemination methods. The project requirements must be incorporated to demonstrate how accuracy and authenticity is measured and achieved and to illustrate the project goal and deliverables. File protocols will define how to specify defined access to all data such as IFCs (Industry Foundation Class) in addition to the sustainability and quality of data and its preservation approaches. The Framework for Historic BIM is best expressed as set of procedures which set out options for the accompanying paradata access and presentation. The final part of this paper proposes documenting paradata using data cards, the format can range from text to graphic records.

1.1 Interrogating Paradata

In the area of archaeological and cultural heritage research, there is widespread consensus that paradata refers to data concerning the processes that underly information phenomena. Similarly, it is broadly agreed that the documentation of such processes serves to provide much needed transparency in support of data reuse scenarios. Beyond this, however, there is considerably less agreement as regards the precise nature of the data types and formats involved, or indeed the way in which it can and should be used. As a research concept, it is closely associated with that of provenance in that it concerns the recording of contextual details in relation to data capture or collection. Both concepts serve to align data creators, manipulators and users. In a recent scoping review of scholarly publications concerning the characteristics and use of paradata, the following conclusions were reached [6]:

- Paradata is concerned with past practice and is most often understood in terms of processes or a series of sequential, goal-oriented actions, whether they be mental or physical or whether they involve technological or other methodological applications.
- Paradata exists only in relation to the research output it describes and with which it has a symbiotic or mutually sustaining relationship, with the former ensuring, through various re-use scenarios, the continued usefulness of the latter, which itself serves to make sense of the former, likewise ensuring its continued usefulness.
- Paradata creation is driven by those responsible for the development of the research output it describes, allowing them to achieve a level of transparency in terms of the interpretive process that sit behind the data presented to a broad range of user groups, both expert and non-expert, for reuse.

The documentation, records or information that comprise paradata can be structured or unstructured, purposefully or accidentally recorded, embedded or stand-alone. They can be manually or automatically generated, taking both analogue and digital forms that range from the handwritten contents of site and lab notebooks to the born digital data classes that are automatically populated in computer-aided processing [6, 7].

2   Metadata/Paradata Design Framework for HBIM – Methodology

Historic or Heritage BIM is best described as a solution to build a digital or memory twin and or a virtual representation of a heritage object, structure or environment. Interactive parametric objects representing architectural elements are constructed from historic data, these elements (including detail behind the scan surface) are accurately mapped onto a point cloud or image-based survey to create a Historic Building Information Model (HBIM). The HBIM can be used not only as a visualisation tool but equally importantly as a tool for conservation and engineering analysis for historic structures and objects. The Technological University Dublin (formally the Dublin Institute of Technology) developed the original concepts for HBIM using digitally remotely sensed data as mapping system to plot designed parametric library of architectural objects creating an intelligent virtual digital twin of a structure or object [1–5]. A metadata/paradata design framework is best identified from previous HBIM case studies *by examining the completed projects.* This can then determine how project requirements of accuracy and authenticity are achieved, including the project goal and deliverables. The review of past HBIM case studies is described in this section, this retrospective review will assist the development of a HBIM framework for the documentation of paradata/metadata. There are three phases to HBIM workflows, the first is data capture using remote sensing and digital surveying tools such as photogrammetry and laser scanning. The second phase has two sub sections, the first is digital curation whereby historic related data such as drawings, text and other media are stored and associated with both the digital survey data and later the Historic Building Information Model. The second sub-section of phase two involves mapping the digital survey data with 3D architectural elements from libraries. The objects are semantically enriched to behave as intelligent objects and brought together to form either a digital or memory twin of a heritage object or structure. Finally, the virtual model is disseminated as HBIM or wider dissemination through Game Engine Platforms or Heritage GIS.

2.1   Case Studies – Data Capture

A case study illustrating a sample of the laser scan survey and recording of the interiors of Russborough House, an Irish Neo-Classical Building is presented here. The Entrance Hall, the Saloon and the Main Staircase were identified as the rooms of most note at present by head of Collections and Conservation of Russborough House. There is no existing scan data for Russborough House therefore this survey will also exist as a survey and record of these parts of the structure to assist with future conservation. Virtual Historic Dublin, the second case study described in this section, which encompasses a design and prototype for an Historic Building Information Model of the historic centre of Dublin. Historic town centres encapsulate collective history of the society, and their buildings, environments, and objects, each tell a story that has been a subject of global efforts in digital documentation, virtual modelling, and archiving [7, 8]. The development of the Virtual Historic City Dublin was based on the dataset acquired from the 2008 and the 2015 Aerial Laser and Photogrammetry Survey of Dublin City. This initiative combined existing historical 2D mapping dataset, with particular focus on aerial and terrestrial laser scanning as well as image-based survey [9] (Figs. 1 and 2).

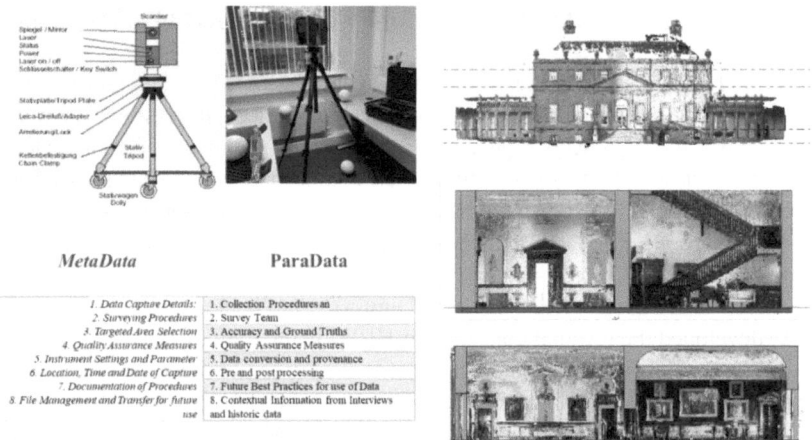

Fig. 1. Identifying Metadata/Paradata from Case Study, Laser Scan Survey interior of Russborough House Irish Neo-Classical Building.

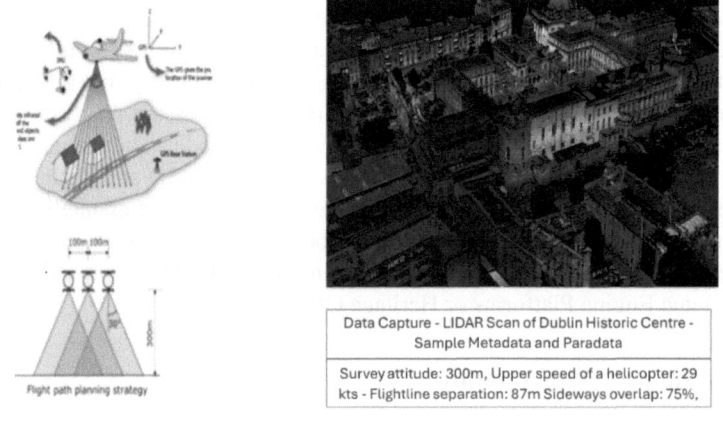

Fig. 2. Identify Metadata/Paradata from Case Study Virtual Historic City Dublin

Metadata includes information about the equipment used for data capture, for example the laser scanning instrument and its associated software and hardware to illustrate the range of the technology used. Metadata includes information on scan parameters, resolution settings, and color inclusion to enhance data quality and fidelity during the laser scanning process. Metadata records the specific date when the data was captured, providing a temporal context for the dataset. Metadata may encompass details about file management practices, such as formatting SD cards, copying scan data to external devices, and ensuring data integrity during transfer and storage.

Paradata. Contextual information may also include insights from interviews with conservation experts and technical advisors, who provide guidance and expertise related to the project's objectives. Standards for accuracy are examined to decide on resolution, registration targets to ensure accurate alignment and stitching of scans, particularly in narrow or complex architectural spaces such as doorways and staircases. Quality assurance measures for data collection are adhered to, optimizing scan quality and coverage, aiming to capture comprehensive data for modeling and conservation purposes. Documentation should record the step-by-step procedures followed during data capture, including the use of registration targets (spheres) and scanning methodologies employed to ensure comprehensive coverage of the selected areas. In the case of Virtual Historic Dublin, the paradata describes a comprehensive dataset gathered through high-density aerial remote sensing covering a 2 km^2 area of Dublin, Ireland. The survey was conducted at an average altitude of 300 m and comprised aerial laser scanning (ALS) data from 41 flight paths presented as a 3D point cloud and 3D full waveform ALS data. The location storage, quality, processing workflows and file protocols for the collected data are documented alongside Level of Detail, and Accuracy to ensure the provenance and sustainability of the data.

2.2   Case Study 2, HBIM Virtual Historic Dublin

As described in the previous section Virtual Historic Dublin is a design and prototype for an Historic Building Information Model of the historic center of Dublin. Essentially our approach to HBIM combines parametric, feature-based, shape grammars and procedural modelling. This approach to modelling would benefit from documentation of the paradata illustrating the additional intelligence introduced into the elements of a model and elements of automation within the workflow. Parametric modelling stores all object's parameters such as geometry, position and textures. Whereas feature-based modelling facilitates basic objects as windows and doors to carry an information of their role and relation to other objects within the building/structure. For example, a window object in a HBIM model does not only represent a physical opening but conveys parametric data about its dimensions, materials, and spatial relationship with other elements. The parametric and feature based objects can be stored as libraries for re-use.

Shape grammar theory evolves from computer graphic science whereby BIM, GIS or 3D CAD software recognises the evolution of basic shapes to more developed shapes as a set of rules that the software recognises to automate the development of a 3D object. Classical Orders and Architectural Rules are ideally suited to algorithmic expression. Described as generative shape grammars the architectural elements use the principles of classical architecture for their construction in HBIM. These rules are documented in historic architectural text from Vitruvius to Renaissance architectural treatises onto 18th century architectural pattern books.

Procedural modelling approaches uses a sequence of generation instructions, algorithms, and rules to automatically produce 3D geometries for modelling existing buildings from remotely sensed data. To generate a high-quality 3D model of existing buildings, two procedural approaches are required. The first includes a meticulous process of converting point cloud data into semantic building model, while second procedural approach offers a semi-automated solution, wherein the required geometry is initially generated automatically and then manually refined to align with specific survey data and alongside developed procedural rules generate various building facades and outer fabric. Subsequently procedural rules are then applied which facilitates semi-automatic generation and automatically integrate building components. Like parametric objects the rules can be applied to various scenarios of similar architectural types. There is also an absence of standardised methods for representing objects and information for HBIM and its obvious that transparent documentation of the modelling methods enables future users to understand and replicate the workflows and procedures effectively. The use of guidelines and standards for documenting metadata and paradata for HBIM workflows will help guide and establish best practices [12–15] (Fig. 3).

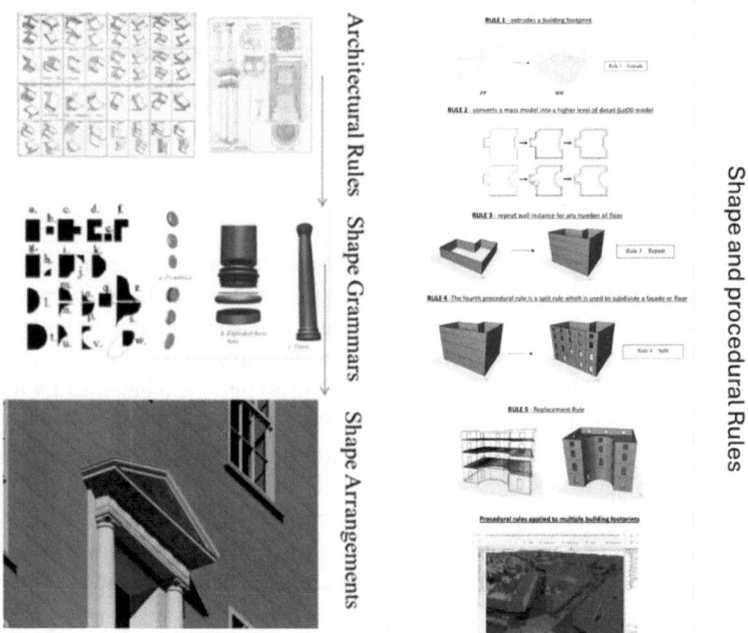

Fig. 3. Case Study HBIM Virtual Historic City Dublin, A Modelling Standard Is Necessary - Shape grammar and procedural modelling informs metadata/paradata documentation, in the case of procedural modelling, graphic illustration can be used to identify paradata.

2.3   Case Study 3, Dissemination HBIM to HGIS Preserving Metadata

The focus of this Case Study is the modern architecture designed by Oscar Niemeyer, built in 1944, located in Belo Horizonte, Minas Gerais, Brazil. The modern ensemble is modelled in LOD 400 based on 3D scanning data through terrestrial laser scanner, drone scanning for photogrammetry, and Revit software is used for HBIM modelling based on point cloud. HBIM data is exported in IFC format and integrated into a geographic database using data integration software. The HBIM model is then integrated into a 3D scene in ArcGIS Pro along with HGIS data for conservation analysis and visualisation [16].

Liu et al. concluded in their 2017 study that there are still no automated methods for integrating BIM data into GIS [17, 18], nevertheless, utilizing the latest technology from ESRI, ArcGIS Pro it is possible for HBIM/HGIS integration. In ArcGIS the HBIM/Industry Foundation Class (IFC) model was inserted into ArcGIS. Despite all the buildings in the Pampulha ensemble being georeferenced, the scale and geo-referencing were distorted and appeared empty, devoid of any HBIM data or metadata. ArcGIS recognized the IFC model solely as a singular geometry. The utilization of an integrative data software, such as Safe Software FME (Feature Manipulation Engine), enables effective visualization of BIM data and metadata for GIS without data loss. For this purpose, HBIM data needs to be converted and integrated into a compatible 3D GIS format, suitable formats such as CityGML, Shapefile, and Geodatabas, in this case Geodatabase format, which is native to ArcGIS Pro, offering better interoperability with the software compared to CityGML format was used [19]. FME is an engine that supports an array of data types and formats, Excel, CSV, XML, and databases, as well as various types of mapping formats including GIS, CAD, BIM, and many more. Data Inspector FME extension and the Workbench FME extension was used in this study. Integrating HBIM data into GIS requires inspecting each metadata to ensure all HBIM data are within the GIS domain. Thus, the Data Inspector serves as a semi-automated data inspection tool to ensure HBIM data are not missing or empty.

The Industry Foundation Classes (IFC) is a CAD data exchange data schema describing (AEC) architectural, engineering and construction industry data for use across BIM platforms. For instance, in the Revit environment, when selecting a component such as a wall, it comes with predefined parameters like body, axis, id, among others. When these data are exported to IFC, the IFC standard restructures Revit's BIM data to the IFC information standard. Therefore, Revit parameters that are now IFC standard will have classes, and their subclasses will be empty, for example, the IFC Project class subclass "axis" without any data. These data need to be inspected and cleared before being sent to the Workbench, as during the data integration in the Workbench, data with "empty" metadata hinder data conversion, resulting in a GIS file with missing data. This can disrupt data reading performed by ArcGIS. Hence, to avoid interoperability issues, it's essential to validate, check, and calibrate HBIM data through the Data Inspector.

The IFC model exported in IFC4 format with the "shared coordinates" function. With the IFC model open in the Data Inspector, a table is displayed, showing all IFC information standards. In the Data Inspector's 3D function, it is possible to select each component of the building and check its IFC data and metadata. The Data Inspector allows data inspection, displaying the data contained in the IFC model in tables. Through filters of the IFC standards, it is possible to visualize missing data and metadata. The Georeferencing function and shared coordinates were checked to ensure that when inserting the HBIM model into ArcGIS, it is at the exact georeferenced point. ArcGIS does not allow moving the model without losing data. Georeferencing data can be validated through metadata (Fig. 4).

After verifying data and metadata in data inspector, the IFC model is imported into the Workbench FME software. At this stage, the software prompts you to define

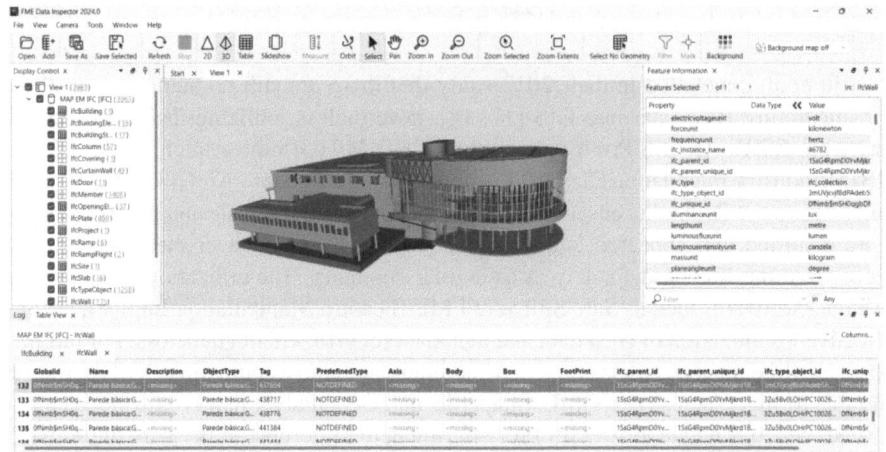

Fig. 4. Pampulha Art Museum model visualized in the Data Inspector FME with missing axis, body, and description information.

the final integration format. The Workbench restructures the data visually, based on the illustration of classes and subclasses. Therefore, initially, it's necessary to define the final data writing format so that the input (reader feature) and output (writer feature) data are visually represented. Based on pre-defined settings established during file import, FME restructures the data based on reader features (input) and writer features (output), allowing visualization of the IFC information standards. For example, in the case of the IFC Column standard, a Geometry Filter is inserted into its workspace. Through subclasses, it's possible to quantitatively visualize the data contained in the IFC Column. At this stage, it's possible to exclude subclasses that do not contain data, such as examples of the subclass code, axis, box, and description. Then, in the Writer Feature function, FME automates the writing of IFC data into the Geodatabase format.

The Geodatabase format essentially divides the data into geometric, point, textual, linear, polygonal, and surface data. In this way, each IFC standard is rewritten based on the Geodatabase standard. For example, the IFCColumn standard in the Geodatabase will be rewritten as 'IFCColumn class' with subclasses IFCColumnGeometry, IFCColumn-Point, IFCColumnText, IFCColumnLine, IFCColumnPolygon, and IFCColumnSurface. After verifying the data in the Workbench, the Run function, rewrites the IFC data to Geodatabase format. After approximately 30 min, the conversion is successfully completed. Figure 5 illustrates the information standards in the Workbench and their data and metadata [16–20].

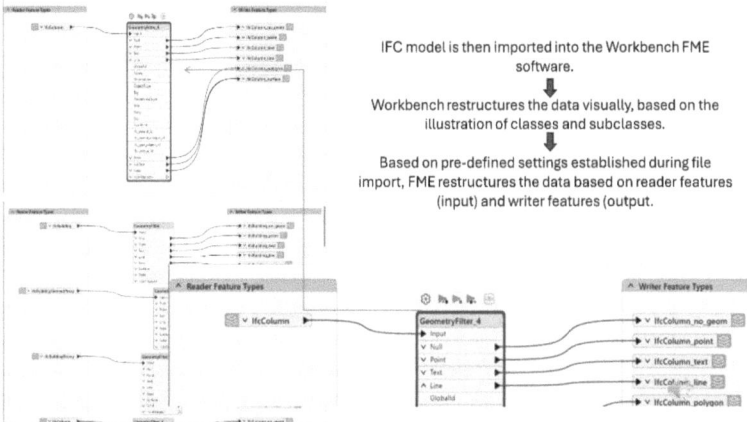

IFC model is then imported into the Workbench FME software.

Workbench restructures the data visually, based on the illustration of classes and subclasses.

Based on pre-defined settings established during file import, FME restructures the data based on reader features (input) and writer features (output).

Fig. 5. IFC model is imported into the Workbench FME software, to define the final integration format restructuring the data visually, based on the illustration of classes and subclasses.

3 Future Work - Data Cards

Integrating paradata into HBIM workflow design improves transparency, and its integration and interpretation is essential in leading to possibilities to automate paradata analysis and dissemination. In the field of Artificial Intelligence (AI), Pushkarna et al. [21], explore the concept of "Data Cards" as a structured approach to dataset documentation, aimed at enhancing understanding and trust in AI. Data Cards serve as comprehensive and standardised documentation that encapsulates key information about datasets, enabling researchers, developers, and users to make informed decisions about data usage in AI. Inspired by the concept of model cards, Data Cards aim to enhance transparency and facilitate informed decision-making in AI research and deployment. Data Cards include vital components such as dataset overview, data statistics, data quality measures, privacy considerations, and potential use cases. Data card can be integrated into HBIM development workflows and perhaps standardised to facilitate collaboration, knowledge sharing, and ethical decision-making like the initiatives in AI. There are three phases to HBIM workflows Data acquisition, Modelling and Dissemination, which are the main divisions in the elements required for recording and documenting paradata for HBIM. Paradata is concerned with past practice and processes for HBIM, these are represented by the Technology, Software used and the Time Period. It exists only in relation to the research output, best described as its Project Goal. Paradata is driven by those responsible for its development which details the Organisation and people responsible. Finally, if it achieves a level of transparency for reuse the following elements should be documented, Accuracy, Authenticity, Organisation, Data Access, Provenance, Quality and Health and Safety. As a point of entry, a matrix is constructed with the y axis divided into the elements of Data Capture, Modelling and Dissemination and the x axis divided into the elements of Process, Output, People Responsible, Re-use and Transparency resulting in the use of both axis headings are used to document the data cards (see Fig. 6, below).

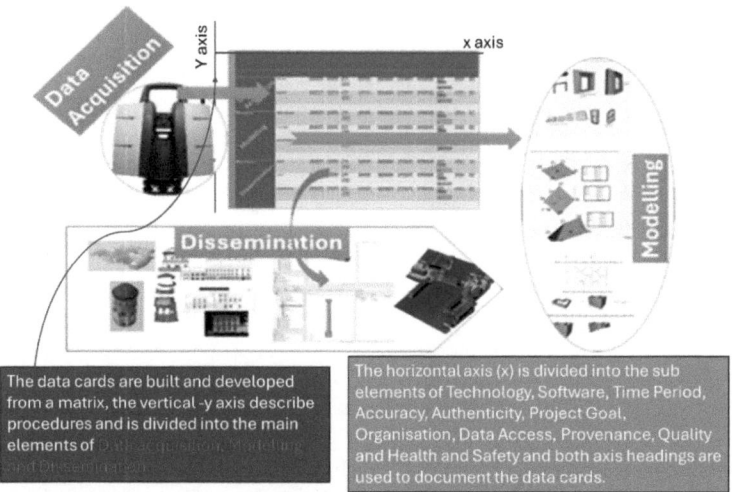

Fig. 6. A HBIM framework design for documenting meta/paradata using data cards

4   Conclusion – A HBIM Design Framework

By its nature, and as its name suggests, the study of the material cultural record, involves, to varying degrees, a documentary approach which layers or interweaves description with interpretation of the evidence. Bentkowska-Kafel, Denard and Baker's, definition of paradata as "information about human processes of understanding and interpretation of data objects" [7]. In the case of the broader field of digital heritage, the alignment of metrics which underpin visualisation strategies with the interpretive process, would serve to support the creation of research outputs, allowing for enhanced reuse of the data recorded in such a way as to contribute more meaningfully to the consideration of the many and various ways of living in the past.

In this paper a systematic examination of metadata/paradata included within the procedural information generated throughout the HBIM workflows was presented through a series of case studies. The three phases of data capture, modelling and knowledge dissemination for HBIM workflows were presented in the case studies. The first case studies illustrated how metadata was recorded automatically by the terrestrial and aerial laser scanning instruments and software whereas it is necessary to document paradata. Case study 2, shows how shape grammar libraries of architectural elements and procedural modelling is used to map these libraries onto the structured survey data both contained metadata within the HBIM software platforms. Again, there is a need to document the paradata using both graphic and text format, proving the need for standards and guidelines for HBIM, specifying how libraries and mapping systems are established. Finally, additional software platforms were reviewed to ensure survival of metadata (geometry, geolocation and other semantic attributes) when the virtual model is disseminated outside of HBIM in this case using Heritage GIS.

Acknowledgements. The projects described in this paper were supported by Technological University of Dublin, Discovery Programme Ireland, CIMS Carleton University Ottawa and the Office of Public Works Ireland.

Disclosure of Interests. The authors have no competing interests to declare that are relevant to the content of this article.

References

1. Murphy, M., McGovern, E., Pavia, S.: Historic building information modelling (HBIM). Struct. Surv. **27**(4), 311–327 (2009)
2. Murphy, M., McGovern, E., Pavia, S.: Historic Building Information Modelling – adding intelligence to laser and image-based surveys of European classical architecture. ISPRS J. Photogramm. Remote Sens. **76**, 89–102 (2013)
3. Murphy, M., et al.: Developing historic building information modelling guidelines and procedures for architectural heritage in Ireland. Int. Arch. Photogramm. Remote Sens. Spatial Inf. Sci. **XLII-2/W5**, 539–546 (2017). https://doi.org/10.5194/isprs-archives-XLII-2-W5-539-2017
4. Fai, S., Graham, K., Duckworth, T., Wood, N., Attar, R.: Building information modeling and heritage documentation. Paper Presented to CIPA 2011 Conference Proceedings: XXIIIrd International CIPA Symposium (2011)
5. Oreni, D., Brumana, Della Torre, R., Banfi, S., Barazzetti, F., Previtali, M.: Survey turned into HBIM: the restoration and the work involved concerning the Basilica di Collemaggio after the earthquake (L'Aquila). ISPRS Ann. Photogramm. Remote Sens. Spatial Inf. Sci. **II-5**, 267–273 (2014)
6. Sköld, O., Börjesson, L., Huvila, I.: Interrogating paradata. In: Proceedings of the 11th International Conference on Conceptions of Library and Information Science, Oslo Metropolitan University (2022)
7. Bentkowska-Kafel, A., Denard, H., Baker, D.: Paradata and transparency in virtual heritage Print Book. Ashgate, Farnham (2012)
8. Chenaux, A., Murphy, M., Pavia, S.: A review of 3D GIS for use in creating virtual historic Dublin. 3D Virtual Reconstruction and Visualisation of Complex Architectures, pp. 249–253 (2019). https://doi.org/10.5194/isprs-archives-XLII-2-W9-249-201
9. Murphy, M., Pavia, S., Cahill, J., Lenihan, S., Corns, A.: An initial design framework for virtual historic Dublin. Int. Arch. Photogram. Remote Sens. Spat. Inf. Sci. **42**(2), 901–907 (2019)
10. Laefer, D.F., Vu Vo, A., Abuwarda, S., Trungo-Hong, L., Gharibi, H.: Aerial laser and photogrammetry survey of Dublin City collection record. New York University. Centre for Urban Science and Progress (2015). https://doi.org/10.17609/N8MQ0N. https://archive.nyu.edu/handle/2451/38684. Accessed 10.04.2024
11. Dore, C., Murphy, M.: Integration of historic building information modeling and 3D GIS for recording and managing cultural heritage sites. In: 18th International Conference on Virtual Systems and Multimedia: Virtual Systems in the Information Society, 2–5 September 2012, Milan, Italy, pp. 369–376 (2012)
12. Fai, S., Rafeiro, J.: Establishing an appropriate level of detail (LOD) for a building information model (BIM) – west block, Parliament Hill, Ottawa, Canada. In: ISPRS Annals of the Photogrammetry, Remote Sensing and Spatial Information Sciences. Presented at the ISPRS Technical Commission V Symposium, June 23–25, 2014, Italy, vol. II-5 (2014)

13. Dore, C., Murphy, M., MsCarthy, S., Breechin, F., Casidy, C., Dirix, E.: Structural simulation and conservation analysis-historic building information model (HBIM). Int. Arch. Photogramm. Remote Sens. Spatial Inf. Sci. **XL-5/W4**, 351–357 (2015). https://doi.org/10.5194/isprsarchivesXL-5-W4-351-2015

14. Murphy, M., et al.: Shape grammar libraries of european classical architectural elements for historic BIM. In: 28th Symposium "Great Learning & Digital Emotion", pp. 479–486 (2021). https://doi.org/10.6194/isprs-archives-XLVI-M-1-2021-479-2021

15. Brumana, R., Banfi, F., Cantini, L., Previtali, M., Della Torre, S.: HBIM level of detail-geometry-accuracy and survey analysis for architectural preservation. In: The International Archives of the Photogrammetry, Remote Sensing and Spatial Information Sciences, Volume XLII-2/W11. Presented at GEORES 2019 – 2nd International Conference of Geomatics and Restoration, 8–10 May 2019, Italy (2019)

16. Dionizio, R.F., DezenKempte, E.: Multi-scale digital documentation of cultural heritage: HBIM/HGIS approach. State University of Campinas, São Paulo, Brazil (2024)

17. Liu, X., Wang, X., Wright, G., Cheng, J.C., Li, X., Liu, R.: A state-of-the-art review on the integration of Building Information Modeling (BIM) and geographic information system (GIS). ISPRS Int. J. Geo-Inf. **6**(2), 53 (2017)

18. Vacca, G., Quaquero, E.: BIM-3D GIS: an integrated system for the knowledge process of the buildings. J. Spat. Sci. **65**(2), 193–208 (2020)

19. Vacca, G., Quaquero, E., Pili, D., Brandolini, M.: GIS-HBIM integration for the management of historical buildings. Int. Arch. Photogramm. Remote. Sens. Spat. Inf. Sci. **42**, 1129–1135 (2018)

20. Volk, R., Stengel, J., Schultmann, F.: Building Information Modeling (BIM) for existing buildings—literature review and future needs. Autom. Constr. **38**, 109–127 (2014)

21. Pushkarna, M., Zaldivar, A., Kjartansson, O.: Data cards: purposeful and transparent dataset documentation for responsible AI. FAccT 2022: 2022 ACM Conference on Fairness, Accountability, and Transparency (2022)

Toward a Trustable Digitisation of Built Heritage: The Role of Paradata

Pedro Luengo[1]([⊠]) [ID], Gerardo Boto Varela[2] [ID], Sergio Coll Pla[3] [ID],
Agustí Costa Jover[3] [ID], Albert Samper Sosa[3] [ID], and David Vivó Codina[2] [ID]

[1] Universidad de Sevilla, Seville, Spain
`pedroluengo@us.es`
[2] Universidad de Gerona, Girona, Spain
`{gerardo.boto,david.vivo}@udg.edu`
[3] Universitat Rovira i Virgili, Tarragona, Spain
`{sergio.coll,agusti.costa,albert.samper}@urv.cat`

Abstract. Recent development of built heritage digitisation has not included required interest on scientific control tool. Without such information, such efforts can be useless for later reuse of digital models. Paradata were developed with this purpose but discussion about its content remained limited. This paper aims to provide a first specific set for digital three-dimensional models of built heritage based on other experiences and previous fieldwork. It includes works developed with photogrammetry, 3D scanning and at a lesser extent manual CAD reconstruction. Thanks to these series of paradata it would be possible not only to document the scientific process behind the digitisation of heritage, but also to provide data for further research.

Keywords: paradata · 3D scanning · photogrammetry · architectural history · architectural simulations

1 Introduction

Academics, private organisations, and enthusiasts have contributed in the last years to the increasing digitisation of monuments. The availability of various tools and their growing accessibility to the general public have fuelled this trend. However, only a limited amount of research has been conducted on the reliability of 3D models. To address this, recent international charters have recommended the development and use of shareable data, which remain underutilized. Therefore, this study aimed to establish a specific and shareable set of paradata for the digitisation of built heritage. Metadata and paradata serve distinct purposes in the context of art and research. Metadata pertain to information about the artwork itself, while paradata document the research process involved in achieving such results. This will provide both scientific and amateur users confidence in the accuracy of the model, enable the identification and correction of recurring errors, and serve as a research tool. To achieve this goal, this study draws on extensive experience from traditional heritage databases. It has been observed that this information is

M. Ioannides et al. (Eds.): 3D Research Challenges in Cultural Heritage V, LNCS 15190, pp. 139–150, 2025.
https://doi.org/10.1007/978-3-031-78590-0_12

not merely a collection of data about the processes but rather a valuable tool for the proper development of the database. Therefore, data that are unlikely to be relevant in the future should be avoided. Consequently, contrary to popular belief, the number of fields of paradata and the possibilities of including free text should be minimized as much as possible. This proposal emphasizes three aspects of the digitisation process. Firstly, the team should participate in the entire process, providing a normalized list of names. Secondly, it is essential to document the digitisation context, including the exact date of fieldwork, number of photographs or scanner positions, general temperature of the site, equipment list, and software used. Thirdly, the post-production stages must be documented, particularly the manual intervention of the technician and the final calibration of the results to create trustworthy models. Paradata must include this information as a crucial element.

The objective of this proposal is to evaluate our set of paradata set by comparing it with information from comparable platforms, including SketchFab, OpenHeritage, 3D-Heritage, or Virtual Heritage just to mention a few of them. Following this cross-analysis, the new proposal will be communicated to the managers of these projects, with the aim of establishing common fields. Only through this standard can a future migration to a shared European database or platform be possible, and confidence in the accuracy of these works can be ensured.

1.1 State of the Art and Its Limitations

While the significance of paradata in archaeological endeavours has been widely discussed (Sköld et al., 2022), the discourse often encompasses both the archaeological process and the digital development process, which may not be entirely beneficial. Although conclusions from the former can be applicable to the latter, each area necessitates its own specific considerations. As Baker (2012) highlights, any digital representation of a cultural artefact is not a replica, but rather a representation of the original piece. Thus, a comprehensive description of the tools and techniques employed in its creation can enhance its reliability and validity. In line with this thinking, the London Charter (2009) emphasized the importance of paradata as the human processes involved in the understanding and interpretation of data objects.

The absence of paradata on well-known digital platforms like Google Open Heritage is notable. On the contrary, some information can be found on selected models hosted at SketchFab, such as the Château de Versailles (n.d.) for instance, which offers a rich profile dedicated to architectural heritage and furniture. Although the model information provides details such as image formats, size, number of triangles, and vertices, it fails to explain the technical process developed by Google Art&Culture professionals. Similarly, Virtual Heritage (n.d.) [pl. Wirtualne Dziedzictwo] offers a small table with information about the building but does not address the issue of paradata. Upon visiting the digital model on SketchFab, such as the Assumption of the Blessed Virgin Mary Church, the lack of paradata becomes apparent. Other similar platforms also exhibit analogous problems. For example, 3D-heritage provides information about the owner of the model, the team which digitised it, the number of polygons, and the level of accuracy, but the technical process remains unexplained. However, among all the analysed platforms, the deepest group of paradata is provided by Open Heritage (n.d.). It includes information about the contributors, the equipment used, the size of such files, the dates of the works, licenses, funders, or DOI. Such information contributes to the robustness of the model but could be improved by facilitating more information about the physical context of the cultural item and a better hierarchy of information.

1.2   The Eternal Discussion About the Aim of (Heterous) Paradata

Paradata was initially developed in 1998 with the primary aim of documenting case management information, and to a lesser extent, detecting and correcting system errors. The author (Couper, 2010: 394) subsequently highlighted the potential for this to be used in the second aspect, although this was largely overlooked. Over time, this concept has been adapted to the humanities, including archaeology and art history, although its original intent has evolved. As Havemann (2012:161–162) noted, the storage of meaningful paradata can help assess the authenticity of cultural data. While the initial purpose of paradata involved detecting errors and reinforcing the robustness of results, recent studies, such as Sköld et al. (2022), have identified its main intentions as documentation, record-keeping, and information provision. The detection of errors, and the possibilities of reuse of the model, appear to have taken a secondary role. The use of paradata can offer robustness to research, enabling evaluation and assessment while facilitating cross-boundary communication. However, it is not designed to address systemic errors within a team or tool. In the case of digital models, paradata focuses on the credibility of visual results rather than other aspects such as how digital twins could be affected by common failures or how they could be modified for further scientific use. Börjesson-Sköld-Huvila (2020:195) further discussed the various methods for managing paradata, which include free texts, video diaries, and formal modelling of intellectual processes.

Despite the diverse range of options available, Huvila (2022) pointed out the unequal attention given to the significance of paradata and its limited incorporation in most datasets. One possible reason for this trend could be the customary role assigned to paradata. If the effort invested in creating them is solely focused on documenting the process, their advantages would be severely restricted. Conversely, paradata offers a much broader scope of potential applications. As previously mentioned, paradata can be a valuable tool for identifying errors and facilitating the sharing of models among researchers, not only for visualising outcomes, but also for reusing digital files. Among other possibilities, if a team's specific equipment is determined to have an issue, it would be feasible to promptly pinpoint and rectify all digitised models that were created using this tool. In this sense, the accessibility of paradata would be readily available to all users, while its editing would be the responsibility of the researchers who maintain the platform. Therefore, it is essential to elucidate the implications of paradata for specific digitisation methods utilized in built heritage, specifically Computer-Aided Design (CAD), photogrammetry, LiDAR, and 3D scanning.

1.3   Paradata for CAD, Photogrammetry, LiDAR and 3D Scans

Previous research on paradata and cultural heritage has primarily focused on its extensive potential, while the specific challenges of architectural cases necessitate special attention, particularly with the advent of HBIM (Brusaporci et. al., 2018; Maiezza, 2019).

Remarkably, it is difficult to find a proposal for a standard for this type of paradata of digital models (Niccolucci, Felicetti, Amico, D'Andrea, 2013:867), even in recent contributions to the field, such as the 3D-Icons project (Corns, 2013) or other academic reviews (Opgenhaffen et al., 2024). According to recent findings, such as those from project VIGIE 2020/654, the relationship between the perception of quality and the acquisition of paradata appears to be lacking in substance. In parallel, mapping and implementing paradata have a long tradition in archaeological sites, preserved buildings, and historical structures. For instance, paradata can be utilized as a valuable tool to extract knowledge from archaeological processes (Börjesson et al., 2022). However, the scientific development documented here is the traditional one, not the digital and its own set of challenges. After the integration of digital tools, these early solutions were enhanced with computer-assisted tools. In this case, the genuineness of the cultural item to be digitised is not a crucial factor to consider, as the historical background of the item must be documented and incorporated as metadata. For instance, CAD software allows a researcher to express an interpretation of a site. In this case, the level of automatic processing was relatively low, and human intervention was high. Although this method can produce highly accurate results, additional control is required. In terms of the overall robustness of the results, photogrammetry and LiDAR provide a second level. Current software offerings enable a largely automatic process, with the option for manual adjustments. Typically, there is limited information provided about cloud correspondence, with technicians relying on visual interpretation to produce convincing models. Automation can be enhanced if metadata is included in captions to provide georeferenced positioning information, as is common in aerial photogrammetry. It is essential to verify this information with supplementary tests, such as manual measurements. The field of heritage studies is increasingly utilizing three-dimensional scans, including both manual and fixed scans. Manual intervention is less common in this process, but a lack of context control can result in misinterpretations by the software. For instance, changes in artificial or natural light can impact photogrammetry and scans, making subsequent assembly challenging.

2   A (First) Proposal

While discussions have been centred around the London Charter's conclusions, relatively few platforms have established their own paradata set. Therefore, it is necessary to discuss specific selections of fields, including their reasons and technical specifications, and subsequently test them on actual platforms. Only through this process will it be possible to develop a common paradata framework that can subsequently be utilized as research data. In this context, this article suggests a collection of paradata, which are categorized into several aspects, with a focus on system error management and the subsequent utilisation of models (Tables 1, 2 and 3).

Table 1. Proposed for Fieldwork Group Paradata Fields.

Item	Technical characteristics	Description	Reason	Importance to robustness
Author (normalised)	NL	A selection of technicians who took part during the entire process, including their roles	Technical failures are often recurrent, and a normalized list can be useful in identifying these issues	L
Date and time of the shots	C	Information about the date of the fieldwork	Besides serving to offer historical data for future analysis, it may also be employed to showcase shifts in structure	M
Duration of the fieldwork (hours)	N	Evaluation of the entire duration of the shots	A limited duration of fieldwork can result in minimal modifications to the structure and conditions	M
Temperature during the shots	N	Ambient temperature including sun and shadow	A limited amount of time spent on fieldwork can result in minimal alterations to the structure and conditions	M
Lux at extreme points	N	Lux measurements of sun-exposed and dark spaces during the digitisation	Specially photogrammetry but also scanning can be affected by the light exposure	
Map of the shots	JPG	A map locating the shots/positions	A technician can comprehend the difficulties that arise from a flawed design in the context of position election. Furthermore, the significance of the distance of the shots may vary based on the intended application of the model	H
Equipment	N	Selection of equipment	Systemic errors by specific equipment can be more easily identified	M

(*continued*)

Table 1. (*continued*)

Item	Technical characteristics	Description	Reason	Importance to robustness
Method	NL	Select which technique was/were used: Photogrammetry, LiDAR, manual or extant 3D Scanner, manual CAD, etc	The chosen method entailed a series of potential risks and an uncertain level of dependability for the outcomes	H
Number of shots	N	Number of shots used both for photogrammetry or 3D scanning (positions)	The quantity of shots may provide insight into the calibre of the fieldwork	L
Georeferenced shots	Y/N	Confirm if it was possible to provide information about the georeference of the shots/positions	The feasibility of the model is influenced by the georeferencing of shots/positions	H
Photography	Y/N	Confirm if it was possible to provide photography from positions	This has little impact on feasibility but provide much information for further simulations	L
Thermal Imaging	Y/N	Confirm if it was possible to provide thermal imaging from positions	This has little impact on feasibility but provide much information for further simulations	L
Calibration measurements	ChL	A selection of procedures to be lately used for calibration such as manual/laser measurement, light, or acoustic tests, etc	The calibration process enhances the robustness of the model while simultaneously offering additional insights into the cultural item in question	H
Total digitisation	LS	Define if the selected item was digitised completely, including entourage, all visible external sides and interior, or it is a partial model	A model may necessitate manual reconstruction for additional examination	L

(*continued*)

Table 1. (*continued*)

Item	Technical characteristics	Description	Reason	Importance to robustness
Risky materials	ChL	A selection of materials which can affect the correct application of the tool such as mirrors or metals	The reflection of certain materials can have an impact on the accurate interpretation of data by the scanner or camera	M

Table 2. Proposed for Lab Processes Group Paradata Fields.

Item	Technical characteristics	Description	Reason	Importance to robustness
Software used	NL	Identify every software required during the process from a normalised list	All software has its technical limitations, which are specified in the user's guide, and systemic errors, which are typically identified later. It is essential to take these factors into account in order to effectively manage future failures	M
Migration process	NL	Define the different extensions used by the model from the register to the provided version	Migration is a usual procedure but it usually implies changes in the geometric structure	H
Number of faces	N	Define the number of faces included	The number of faces is a very relevant information when the model is going to be used by a simulator based on Python	M
Initial resolution (N of points/cm^3)	N	Provide information about the resolution of the initial digitisation	At times, the resolution may be insufficient, necessitating a straightforward model. On other occasions, the final file may be a streamlined version of a more complex digitisation process. Comprehending these aspects is essential for assessing the potential of the file	H

(*continued*)

Table 2. (*continued*)

Item	Technical characteristics	Description	Reason	Importance to robustness
Simplification technique	Y/N	Define which procedure was selected to simplify/reduce the number of faces or the resolution	In certain instances, the starting resolution may be low, resulting in the use of a basic model. Conversely, in other situations, the final file may be a streamlined version of a more comprehensive digitisation process. Understanding these aspects is crucial for assessing the potential of the file	H
Final resolution (N of points/cm^3)	N	Provide information about the resolution of the final	In certain situations, the initial resolution may be low, resulting in a straightforward model, while in other instances, the final file may be a streamlined version of a master digitisation. Understanding these possibilities is crucial in assessing the capabilities of the file	H
Average of coincidence percentage	N	During the register process, the software usually provides information of the percentage of coincidence between two point-clouds. Provide maximum and minimum	Defining maximum and minimum of these data would contribute to understand the model properly	H
Available formats	ChL	Specify the formats of the digital model (ie. OBJ, DXF, DXF, PLY, etc.)	Only so it is possible to understand if the model is useful for the researcher interested in transferring it into simulators	L

(*continued*)

Table 2. (*continued*)

Item	Technical characteristics	Description	Reason	Importance to robustness
Final weight/s	N	Specify the number of GBs/TBs	Only so it is possible to understand if the model is useful for the researcher interested in transferring it into simulators, or it might be reduced	L
Multiple layers	Y/N	Indicate if the model is overlapping different layers at the same points	Including information of several chronological stages (i. e. before/after restorations) is likely irrelevant for the robustness of the model but it is pertinent for later digital interpretation	M
Manual intervention/corrections	LS	Indicate if any manual intervention was used, from a complete manual reconstruction (CAD) to a pure automatic process	Purely automatic process usually reproduces systematic errors which are likely to modify. Manual processes would require of further description of the decision-making process	H

Table 3. Proposed for Rights Group Paradata Fields.

Item	Technical characteristics	Description	Reason	Importance to robustness
Owner of the reproduction rights	NL	Indicate the institution/technician who owns the reproduction rights of the model, taken from a normalised list	Without this information other colleagues would not be allowed to use the file legally	L

(*continued*)

Table 3. (*continued*)

Item	Technical characteristics	Description	Reason	Importance to robustness
Type of license (CC)	NL	Indicate which Creative Common license is defined	This data allows users to take advantage of the file properly	L
Acknowledgement	NL	Indicate the (research) project which developed the file	Apart from identifying possible systemic errors, it is a requirement by most of calls	L
DOI	URL	Indicate the hosting and URL where the file is located	Hosting can be affected by different preservation challenges, being so a way of identifying them easily	L

* NL, normalized list; C, calendar; N, number; ChL, checklist; LS = Linear scale; L, low; M = Medium; H = High

3 Conclusion

As recent studies by Huvila and others have highlighted, the significance of paradata is crucial for contemporary heritage science, yet it remains an underdeveloped field with limited examples. While discussions have centred on employing archaeological practices to achieve this goal, there has been scant attention given to the documentation of technical issues arising from the digitalisation process. Moreover, most efforts to integrate archaeological knowledge and digital technique specifications have been aimed at bolstering the credibility of results, rather than as a means to identify systemic shortcomings, assess quality preliminarily, or explore possibilities for reuse in other software with different objectives. To address this gap, a preliminary set of paradata is proposed here, designed to cover the full range of fieldwork to lab work, and including information on ownership, which were previously alluded to or required by other paradata sets. The aim is not to document the process in detail, but to provide a standard framework that can be filled in. Using a common set of paradata can help foster trust in the final models. On the contrary, generic descriptions typically emphasize the unique features of each model or item, making it challenging to make broader decisions in the future to maintain their validity. The objective of the proposal is to serve as a valuable resource for scientific data analysis, rather than merely functioning as a concluding visualisation of the piece. By avoiding free-text entries in favour of normalized or checklist formats and promoting the use of numbers and scales, all results can be compiled using a common analytical tool, which is much more complex if descriptions and reports are included without proper paradata. Incorporating information about fieldwork and laboratory processes will facilitate the identification of model production issues across various contexts. Moreover, emphasizing the significance of proper rights management for the file will encourage responsible behaviour among its owners and contribute to its effective reuse.

Acknowledgements. This research was supported by the Spanish Ministry of Science as part of the proposal titled *"Smart Built Heritage. Del registro a la simulación digital para inmuebles medievales y modernos"* (TED2021-129148B-I00).

Disclosure of Interests. The authors have no competing interests to declare that are relevant to the content of this article.

References

Baker, D.: Defining paradata in heritage visualisation. In: Paradata and Transparency in Virtual Heritage, pp. 163–175. Routledge (2016)

Börjesson, L., Sköld, O., Huvila, I.: Paradata in documentation standards and recommendations for digital archaeological visualisations. Digit. Cult. Soc. **6**(2), 191–220 (2020)

Börjesson, L., et al.: Re-purposing excavation database content as paradata: an explorative analysis of paradata identification challenges and opportunities. KULA **6**(3), 1–18 (2022)

Brusaporci, S., Maiezza, P., Tata, A.: A framework for architectural heritage HBIM semantisation and development. Int. Arch. Photogramm. Remote. Sens. Spat. Inf. Sci. **42**, 179–184 (2018)

Château de Versailles [@chateauversailles]. Profile [SketchFab profile]. SketchFab (n.d.). https://sketchfab.com/chateauversailles. Accessed 15 June 2024

Corns, A.: 3D-ICONS: D7.3-Guidelines and Case Studies (Final). Zenodo (2013). https://doi.org/10.5281/zenodo.1311797

Couper, M.P.: Usability evaluation of computer-assisted survey instruments. Soc. Sci. Comput. Rev. **18**(4) (2000). https://doi.org/10.1177/089443930001800402

Havemann, S.: Intricacies and potentials of collecting paradata in the 3D modelling workflow. Paradata. Intellec. Transp. Hist. Vis. Ashgate 154–162

Huvila, I.: Improving the usefulness of research data with better paradata. Open Inf. Sci. **6**(1), 28–48 (2022)

Maiezza, P.: As-built reliability in architectural HBIM modeling. Int. Arch. Photogramm. Remote. Sens. Spat. Inf. Sci. **42**, 461–466 (2019)

Niccolucci, F., Felicetti, A., Amico, N., D'Andrea, A.: Quality control in the production of 3D documentation of monuments. In: Built Heritage 2013 Monitoring Conservation Management, pp. 864–873. Politecnico di Milano, Milan (2013)

Open Heritage (n.d.). https://openheritage3D.org

Opgenhaffen, L., Jeffra, C., Hilditch, J.: Balancing data storage and user functionality: the 3D and archaeological data strategy of the tracing the potter's wheel knowledge hub. In: Hostettler, M., et al. (eds.) The 3 Dimensions of Digitalised Archaeology. State-of-the-Art, Data Management and Current Challenges in Archaeological 3D-Documentation, pp. 131–150. Springer, Cham (2024)

Sköld, O., Börjesson, L., Huvila, I.: Interrogating paradata. Inf. Res. **27** (2022)

The London Charter (2009). https://londoncharter.org/downloads.html
Virtual Heritage (n.d.). https://wirtualnedziedzictwo.pl/

Paradata to Reuse Holistic HBIM Quality Models in the SCAN-to-HBIM-to-VR Process. The Mausoleum of Cecilia Metella and the Castrum Caetani

Raffaella Brumana[1], Stefano Roascio[2], Dario Attico[1],
Maria Radoslavova Gerganova[1], and Nicola Genzano[1(✉)]

[1] Department of Architecture, Built Environment and Construction Engineering (ABC),
Politecnico di Milano, ABCLab-GIcarus, via Ponzio 31, 20133 Milan, Italy
`{raffaella.brumana,dario.attico,nicola.genzano}@polimi.it,`
`maria.gerganova@mail.polimi.it`
[2] PAAA - Parco Archeologico dell'Appia Antica (Ministero della Cultura - MIC), P.za delle
Finanze, 1, 00185 Rome, Italy
`stefano.roascio@cultura.gov.it`
`https://www.gicaruslab-dabc.it/`

Abstract. The multiplication of efforts to digitize complex architectural and archaeological heritage sites in the form of informative models increasingly requires to document survey and modelling methods through qualitative and quantitative parameters to ensure mutual trustworthiness and proper re-use for different purposes by the potential multiple users, as well as the citation of the contributors' data source (archaeologists, designers, conservators, civil engineers, geologists, XR-VR developers). The HBIM of the Mausoleum of Cecilia Metella and the Castrum Caetani (Rome, Italy), is part of the digitization of the PAAA (Parco Archeologico dell'Appia Antica, Archaeological Park of the Appian Way): it is emblematic for the complexity of the interconnections among users and contributors across the time. The article discusses needs and definition of Paradata for the re-use of holistic HBIM quality information models documenting the entire SCAN-to-HBIM-to-XR process, through diverse Levels of Development and Levels of Geometry (LODs100-600, LOGs100-600) from the surveys to the modelling phases including Virtual Reality experiences built on informative models, as well as remote environmental risk applications as part of long life management and monitoring. Being the models generated for different HBIM-USES and users, parameters that document the Grade of Accuracy of the Survey and of the Object Models generated in various times are identified. It is the case of the construction technologies associated to the transformation phases for potential future HBIM-uses, as for BIM-to-FEA and Seismic Vulnerability Plan exploitation, remote monitoring or XR (eXtended Reality) in a holistic process.

Keywords: Paradata · Informative models · HBIM · Stratigraphic Units · 3D quality models · Grade of Accuracy · GOAs · GOAm · GOAp · LOG · LOD · LOI · Construction Techniques · Parco Archeologico dell'Appia Antica · EMS · NHI · XR

© The Author(s) 2025
M. Ioannides et al. (Eds.): 3D Research Challenges in Cultural Heritage V, LNCS 15190, pp. 151–163, 2025.
https://doi.org/10.1007/978-3-031-78590-0_13

1 Introduction

The paper describes the design of Paradata within the HBIM 3D content models considered as a gear node attracting the knowledge generated, keeping memory for the future in a continuous process that accompany the long life of complexes as the case study. The research aims to create a common framework made by informative quality models updatable and re-usable across the time by different users obtained with multi-disciplinary contribution (i.e. archeologists, architects, geologists, engineers) and for different purposes, and users. The Archaeological Park of Appia Antica (PAAA, MiC – Ministry of Culture) together with the ABCLab-GIcarus of the Politecnico di Milano has undertaken an organic and systemic project of digitization of the larger urban Park in Europe including 10 km of the Appian Way [1], and its sites as Digital Twins, as the Roman Claudius-Anio Novus Aqueduct on the Fiscale Tower [2], the Cecilia Metella Mausoleum and the Castrum Caetani [3]. The Appian Way has submitted the candidacy for the World Heritage Site, now under the UNESCO nomination: PAAA is the coordinator of the activities of the Appian Way. The Appian Way (IV-III cen. BC) has been called "Regina Viarum" for its finest 'long durée' construction, its role in the strategic connection of Rome with Brundisium (South Italy) and the Magna Grecia, as a military and trade road, whose importance was enlightened by the presence of sepulchers and mausoleums such as the Mausoleum of Cecilia Metella erected as a funerary celebrating monument (30–20 BC) on the III Mile in Rome. The massive digitization in such wide contexts finds in Paradata a common framework to document the SCAN-to-HBIM-to-XR holistic processes to re-use models (Sect. 2). HBIM LODs-LOGs (100–600) Paradata are proposed to describe the Levels of Development and Geometry in the heritage domain (Sect. 3); LOD200 (surveying) and LOD300 (modeling) accuracies are proposed (Sect. 4.1) to guarantee correct re-use and circulation in the LOD400 (HBIM-Uses), and in LOD600 remote environmental monitoring and XR (Sect. 4.2–4).

2 Why Paradata: The Appian Way and Cecilia Metella Mausoleum Multi-scale Quality Data Model Re-use

According to dictionaries (i.e. IGI-Global), Paradata can be generically referred to the process by which the survey data are collected, a kind of metadata focused on the use of data: moreover it describes the transformation of data during their "inter-use" in participatory systems. Data models are often limited by the lack of information about the data making: Paradata can contribute to make data models findable, accessible, interoperable, and reusable supporting massive efforts of digitalization [4]. Researchers can play a key role in making their outputs aligned with open IPR and FAIR principles [5] as promoted by the EC (European Commission) on long-term 3D data re-use: on course new change and modification of presenting ready to be used/re-used 3D content (enriched with Paradata) carried out by Europeana re-present an added value for the proper circulation [6]. If we want to valorize the efforts given in 3D model construction to circulate culture generated and to generate new knowledge in the re-use, starting from Metadata schemas as CIDOC CRM-based model [7] and standards as W3C, we need Paradata describing the processes, here from surveys to the 3D content models, and supporting web-capturing Paradata to retrieve data models for the future researches. Data sharing among different actors (i.e., architects, archaeologists, engineers, geologists, multimedia experts, curators) requires the implementation of Paradata capable to describe the entire process gathering a multidisciplinary approach we summarize with the Scan-to-HBIM-to-XR process that an holistic HBIM framework can keep together as a gear connecting Surveying with the Design processes and Communications Actions. Based on the published results and findings of VIGIE 3D Study [8], the paper describes how explicit parameters documenting the Quality and Complexity of 3D Model [9] can be inherited by Paradata in the re-use of the 3D HBIM Informative Models addressed to different purposes and users. A set of parameters (#Paradata Parameters) that contribute to the definition of 3D quality model describing the complexity and uniqueness of cultural heritage are defined: grade of accuracies applied to the surveying phases up to the models scales (GoAs, GOAp, GOAm) are identified as a multiple switch gate to support different informative models with diverse HBIM LODs-LOGs. This case study is emblematic as it represents the context in which we work on complexes sites, including the planning of the surveys in several phases in term of priorities and temporally shifted funding tranches; the informative models can be addressed to diverse BIM-uses, as here the HBIM models enriched by construction technologies, with the aim to support the preservation and design projects as well as VR communication purposes. This requires a constant updating of the requirements demanded by the clients/users and of the results achieved by the producers.

3 Paradata Documenting Multi-purposes Holistic HBIM LODs-LOGs (100–600): Surveying, Planned Conservation, Remote Monitoring, and Multimedia Communication

This paragraph is aimed at defining the optimal workflow to collect, organize, document, manage and share a large amount of information models across the phases of documentation, intervention, monitoring, and communication: Paradata describing HBIM Levels of Developments (LODs) and of Geometry (LOGs) are proposed adapting the new-construction BIM LODs-LOGs definition to the complexity of Archeological and Architectural Heritage [8]: the progression of the Scan-to-HBIM-to-XR sharing process is supported by Paradata describing the diverse levels of development across the time (Fig. 1). Contents and purposes of the LODs-LOGs are exploited in Sect. 4.1–4.

4 SCAN-To-HBIM-to-XR Paradata

4.1 LOD200 and LOD 300: Paradata on Grade of Accuracy of Surveys (GOAs, GOAp) and Models (GoAm) Scales for Multi-actors' Purposes

Starting from surveys specifications, a set of parameters has been defined as Paradata to describe the survey accuracy, the methodologies, the tools, and the results achieved from the requirements as hereafter explained in the Mausoleum of Cecilia Metella and the Castrum Caetani (Table 1). The concept of scale and accuracy has been derived from the surveying and cartographic specifications defining for each scale (i.e., 1:100, 1:50, 1:20)

HBIM Level of Development (LOD) – process phases					
LOD 100 Pre-design	**LOD 200** Digital documentation	**LOD 300** As-found HBIM Model	**LOD 400** Conservation plans /Design	**LOD 500** Construction stage	**LOD 600** Facility Management
HBIM Level of Geometry (LOG)					
LOG 100	**LOG 200**	**LOG 300**	**LOG 400**	**LOG 500**	**LOG 600**
REPORTS **Historical reports/** Archives;	APPROPRIATE GEOMETRY	PRECISE GEOMETRY Scan-to-BIM Model	BIM USES **Preservation/Maintenance Plans/**	Conservation SITE	**As Built** (after interventions), **LLCM** (Life Cycle Management
Documents. Available drawing/ **Conceptual models**	**On-site** data acquisition, 3D **Survey** (i.e., LIDAR, Photogrammetry); Plans/Sections, Orthophoto/3D textured models; **Diagnostics**-NDT	Objects **As Found HBIM**	WBS/ computation, Design, **BIM-to-FEA, Energy Efficiency** Models	(as COSIM)	& Intervention Monitoring, **Environmental risk APP**), CDE, **WEB-VR/XR** Communication
Mausoleum of Cecilia Metella and Castrun Caetani - *Achieved LOGs*					
LOG100	**LOG200**	**LOG300**	**LOG400**	**LOG500**	**LOG600**
Archives documentation; historical reports; environmental geologic report.	3D surveying acquired for the portions of the first contract	HBIM 3D Object Models	Accessibility design plan for Multimedia purposes Construction techniques	Not planned	Risk Hazard Remote Monitoring, Services; Multimedia VR on informative models
LOGS to be planned					
On course data collection	Survey integration: Mausoleum portions, Tower; external Fronts on private property; NDT inspection, Cuniculi-Void check.	HBIM Updating with new surveys	BIM-to-FEA Vulnerability Seismic Plan on the 3D HBIM MODEL (to be planned on 2025)	Not planned	WEB-XR implementation on the HBIM reconstruction of the Mausoleum of Cecilia Metella

Fig. 1. The HBIM LODs and LOGs proposed Paradata achieved so far by the Cecilia Metella and Castrum Caetani, and the planned ones (courtesy of ABClab-GIcarus Brumana & Banfi ©)

the correspondent Graphic Error and Tolerance parameters (Fig. 2–3): once defined the accuracy required, the survey methods need to be chosen to satisfy such values consistent with the scales [10]. The choosing of scale models depends on the objectives and can be diversified within the same object: it becomes crucial to register Paradata: users need to know such information in the re-use (as in structural analysis).

GOAs (Grade of Accuracy of Surveys) parameters refer to the mean scale accuracy required by the contract specifications (G.E and T values), to the surveying methods and processes (i.e., the geodetic network, laser scans, photogrammetry). G.E. here ranges from GOAs20 (1:20 scale, 4 mm) on the façade on the Appian Way, and on the 3 Halls of the Castrum Caetani to support the accessibility design project and the VR communication, to the GOAs50 (1:50 scale, 10 mm) of the Mausoleum, or GOAs200 (the corner tower not part of the 1st survey campaign), (Table 1).

Table 1. Paradata documentation of survey requirements, methodology and outputs accuracies.

Surveying methods	Outputs and Restitutions	Survey accuracy	Model scales
Plano-altimetric Geodetic Network; GCP	11 Points (Total Station Leica T70); 65 GCP (Ground Control Points) for Scan Registry & SFM images	$\sigma = \pm 1$ mm $\sigma = \pm$ 1.5 mm	
Laser Scanner Faro Focus 3D	point clouds (with geodetic network and GCP data registry)	$\sigma = \pm 3$ mm	
Photogrammetric Blocks Orthophoto / 3D textured models	**GOAs20 1:20 (Main Façade, 3 Halls accessibility/Multimedia, Access court)** Ground Dimension Pixel (GDP) - Terrain Pixel Resolution. (GOAs200 for Lateral Fronts on private properties and Tower not yet surveyed /conceptual models).	GOAp20 (GDP) 2mm, 1:20 (Main Façade, 3 Halls fronts); GOAp50 5mm 1:50 (other fronts)	GOAm20 (3 Halls/ Main Facade) GOAm50 (Mausoleum)
Plans (horizontal sections)	**1:20 (2 Fireplace Halls, Lava Hall, Access court, Mausoleum Front)** Ground level, Underground, accessible cuniculi (1:50)	$\sigma = \pm 3$-5 mm GOAs20 (Halls)	GOAm20 (Halls) GOAm200 (Tower)
Vertical Profile and Sections	**1:20 (2 Fireplace Halls, Access court)** **internal walls profiles (GOAs20); external** profile on the private properties and out of plumbs to be surveyed.	$\sigma = \pm 3$ mm GOAs20 (Halls) GOAs50 (Mausoleum)	GOAm20 (Halls) GOAm50 (Mausoleum).
UAV/APR Flight - Mausoleum and Castrum facades	**1:50 (3D textured model, GDP RGB 5mm);** IRT flights for the Mausoleum cover to be planned to check evidence of the double walls of the drum.	GOAp20 (Halls) GOAp50 (Mausoleum).	GOAm20 (Halls) GOAm50 (Mausoleum).
NDT/other inspections	To be planned for the portions not accessible, i.e., inner consistency/voids		

Paradata document the punctual accuracies required for the surveys and on the models of each HBIM component in function of the objectives and planned activities (Fig. 2).

	GOAs Grade of Accuracy of Surveys	GOAs GE Graphic Error	GOAs Tolerance Value T=2÷3 G.E	GOAp GPR Grade of Accuracy	GOAm Grade of Accuracy HBIM Model G.E.; T
Façade/Halls 1:20	GOAs20	4 mm	8 ÷ 12 mm	2 mm	G.E. 4 mm; T 10 mm
Mausoleum 1:50	GOAs50	10 mm	20 ÷ 30 mm	5 mm	G.E.10 mm; T 25 mm

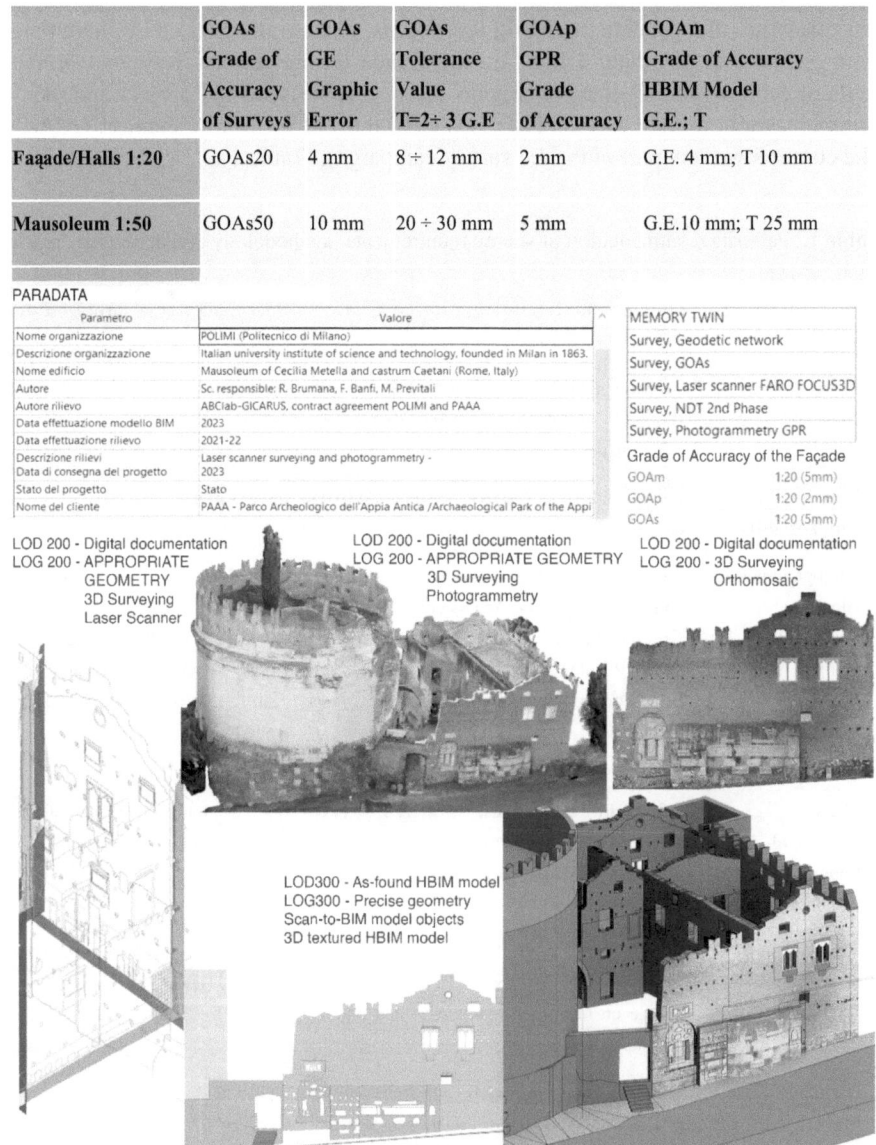

Fig. 2. Upper: Surveying (GOAs, GOAp) and HBIM modeling (GOAm) Paradata for the different scales. Centre: General Information embedded in the HBIM objects with the LODs/LOGs 200–300 achieved in the Façade (below); left: profiles (GOAs20, 5 mm); upper center: 3d textured model, GPR Pixel resolution and Orthophoto (GOAp20, 2 mm). Bottom - the HBIM Quality Model Paradata (GOAm20) obtained by the SCAN-to-HBIM process (left) textured by the Orthophotos (right), (courtesy of ABClab GIcarus, F. Banfi, R. Brumana, M.Gerganova ©).

Together with the GOAs, Fig. 2 illustrates the GOAp and GOAm as follows:

GOAp describes the GDP (Ground Dimension Pixel), geometric and radiometric, required by the photogrammetric blocks processing. Following the cartographic and architectural specification conventionally adopted for the different scales, it is defined as 1/2 Graphic Error (G.E.) (i.e., GOAp for the scale 1:50, 5 mm in the RGB range [10]).

GOAm (Grade of Accuracy of the Model) parameters refer to each object model, including the processing methods from cloud points to vector-generative to 3D models (as NURBS, Mesh, retopology), and the Automatic Validation System (AVS) documenting the achieved accuracy of models [9]: they can be more adherent to survey clouds in function of the needs and shapes complexity or simplified.

From a good survey it is possible to derive also simplified models, not vice versa!

Paradata describe the methodologies of data acquisition, data processing and modeling oriented to guarantee high-quality-high resolution 3D informative models capable to achieve HHBIM (Holistic HBIM) with the contributions of archaeologists, park curators, architects, engineers, designers, experts, professionals, multimedia developers and people, from the common baseline of the surveys, opened to re-use.

Paradata documented the quality achieved in the surveying (LOD-LOG200) and in the HBIM modeling phases (LOD-LOG300) on each HBIM object modelled on the generative profiles [11], (Fig. 2). HBIM LOG300 can generate different models with different accuracies. Paradata collection helps users to avoid misuses, as in the different BIM-Uses (LOD-400). For the same component (as a wall), we can require both complex models as for the BIM-to-FEA analysis on the most fragile structures than simplified model (as for the Energy Efficiency models) correspondent to different GOAm. Obviously, the GOAs adopted are the more restrictive in case of different needs.

In case of the Seismic Vulnerability Plan to be adopted in the next 2 years, an extension of the surveys on some portions (i.e., wall extrados, tower, shifting from GOAm200 to GOAm20) to check out of plumbs - as detected in the 3 surveyed Halls - will be required to increase the model's accuracy. Thus, we need to distinguish and update Paradata of the different campaigns surveys, as well as the ones to be done. GOAs/GOAm coherence is crucial to the reliability of the object models, as for BIM-to-FEA Finite Element Analysis, to understand the behavior of the fragile walls of the Caetani Castle weakened by roof lost connections; or of the heavy Mausoleum structure requiring further investigation and NDT to check the inner consistency, the presence of voids or *'cunicula'*.

4.2 LOD400 (HBIM-Uses): Toward HBIM Informative Multiple Uses-Models. Materials, Construction Technologies, and Transformation Phases

The HBIM Development phases managing the Conservation process and design are defined as HBIM-USES (LOD-LOG400) dealing with models with different accuracy depending on the sub-phases' requirements, and tools limitations. LOG400 refers to a multidisciplinary ecosystem where it becomes crucial to describe the different HBIM-USES. In this case, an informative model has been started in view of the Seismic Vulnerability Plan planned in the next two years, that will be carried out based on the surveys and on the 3D HBIM model to support the BIM-to-FEA analysis. Also, it will be integrated by environmental data and monitoring services available in this area, thus involving LOD-LOG600 (Sect. 4.3). Here it is presented the HBIM implementation with the construction phases that characterized the evolution of the whole complex over the centuries, reading the history of transformations by documenting the construction techniques associated to the different time periods: signs are partially still clearly visible, other just supposed at the level of indicia. Paradata have been integrated with the description of the materials adopted and the construction techniques starting from 3D textured models of each component with the support of the PAAA archeologists [12]: the historiographical and iconographic analysis with the on-site surveys and interpretation of the Stratigraphic Units (US) has set up the input of the HBIM information model, as part of the LOG400. As a result, several historical phases characterizing the complex have been documented, where possible, and related to a database (Fig. 3). Such database can be shared with its Paradata to compare other phases and USs from other HBIMs. Levels of Uncertainty are associated as Paradata to the phases, sometimes just hypothesized. The HBIM is conceived as a centralized source of information conveyed into the 3D object models of the archeological-architectural components, avoiding losing the knowledge achieved across the times, and supporting data circulation, as in the monitoring and communication LOGs600.

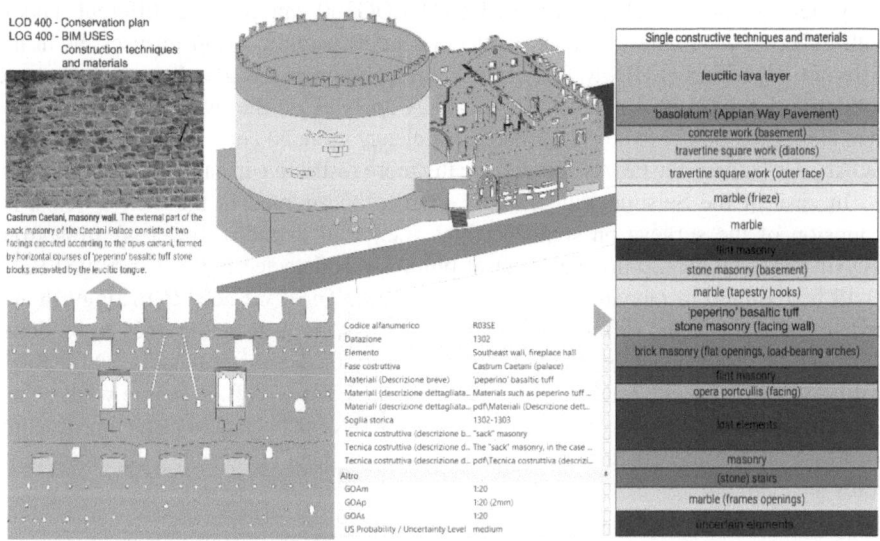

Fig. 3. The Cecilia Metella's HBIM construction phases (upper center, right), part of LOD400; the Castrum Caetani HBIM wall object Paradata (left and below): GOAs-GOAp-GOAm, and LOI with the stratigraphic units, construction technologies and materials (courtesy of ABClab-GIcarus R. Brumana, M.Gerganova, A.Landi, and PAAA S. Roascio ©).

HBIM objects colors (Fig. 3) correspond to the construction phases hypothesized and related to the information (the construction techniques, the supposed dating ranges), among which: Light Grey - The geomorphological setting layer of the volcanic eruption (around 260.000 B.C.) creating the basaltic rock layer upon which the Appian Way was realized in the section from Colli Albani to Rome (IV-III cen. B.C.), still viewable in the underground Lava Hall (whose 3D model has been used for the VR); Dark Grey - Materials from the Lava Volcanic layer, as the '*Basolatum*' Appian Way Pavement; Ocher tones - The Cecilia Metella's Mausoleum construction (30–20 B.C.), basement and drum; Pink - The Castrum Caetani (XIII-XIV cen.) built by Pope Boniface VIII the 'peperino' basaltic tuff bricks facing walls, again from the basaltic rocks; Dark pink -L. Canina and G. Valadier (XIX cen.) first 'open outdoor archeological museum' on the Appian way (with the façade access closed to keep on site the ancient remains); Purple: A. Munoz Open Museum intervention (1909–13).

4.3 Paradata Documenting LOD 600 - Remote Services and Applications for Environmental Risk Monitoring and Live Digital Twins' Services

LOD600 refers to the Long-Life Cycle Management and Monitoring (LLCM), today mostly remote accessed by Common Data Environment (CDE) [11]. Once the data models start remotely circulating, the reasons for which a 3D model was acquired in a certain context, with the required scale and accuracy, risk to be missed if not registered in the Paradata: Paradata can contribute to transfer data of the source model supporting their proper uses during the Memory Twins circulation where different actors can be involved also in the re-use process for further enrichment. Paradata at this level can include data on services at the environmental scale (Fig. 4) managed by digital twins that can be linked to the HBIM-USES nodes (Fig. 3), within an holistic multi-disciplinary approach: Structural Health Monitoring can easily find remote environmental services available on this area, as Digital Twins from Earth Observation or IOT based local data monitoring.

The Appian Way section from the Monti Albani to the Mausoleum of Cecilia Metella in Rome (III Mile) was built directly on the lava tongue of which remains traces in the Mausoleum Lava Room (in the basement) and in the documented Castrum Caetani Masonry HBIM walls. Available data such as the historical reconstruction of the volcanic area that classifies this volcano as dormant [13] fed up the LOD100 (Historical reports). Paradata on LOD600 (Remote data access), can document the Emergency Management Service (EMS), part of the Copernicus program, with a tradition in the data source and data processing description [14]; other services on risk map monitoring applications have been added at LOD600 in the HBIM's Paradata design. It is the case of the NHI-tool APP [15] based on satellite time series monitoring in the Monti Albani area with the Appian Way segment to Rome (Fig. 4).

The app, developed in GEE, allows users to select the investigated area and time window, here 2015–2024 within 20 km area, and to display the identified volcanic hotspots with an intensity range of the variations based on the NHI indices (i.e. Extreme-, High Intensity- and Mid-low pixels). The HBIM LOD600 includes the Paradata documentation of the NHI-tool, the Google Earth Engine (GEE) App, based on the NHI algorithm, providing information on active volcanoes at global scale, through the analysis of Sentinel 2 MSI (Multispectral Instrument) and Landsat 8/9 OLI/OLI2 (Operational Land Imager) daytime data. Google Earth Engine, whose catalogue is continuously updated at a rate of nearly 6000 scenes per day with a latency of about 24 h from scene acquisition, allows the analysis of large geospatial datasets. The NHI tool exploits features of GEE to support users with rapid visualization of thermal anomalies at volcanic areas and periods of interest, such as the Appian Way sites. In addition, the tool enables time series analyses of volcanic thermal anomalies, in terms of hotspot pixel number and total SWIR radiance. Paradata can play a role in growing culture toward the use of monitoring services, punctual and global, as part of the holistic HBIM in the heritage sites.

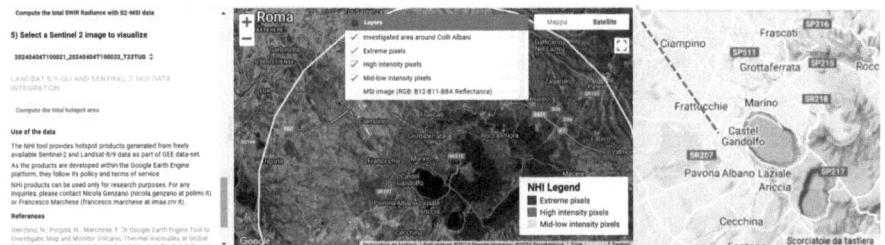

Fig. 4. Environmental scale Paradata design: the Colli Albani dormant volcanoes and the Appian Way section. The HBIM LOD-LOG600 remotely access services: the rGEE NHI application and legend (left-center) and a detail (right), (courtesy of ABClab-GIcarus, N. Genzano ©).

4.4 LOD 600-LOG600 Paradata on Informative Models Feeding VR

LOD600-LOG600 is here referred also to communication levels based on eXtended Reality, web XR/VR, fostering the achieved informative models content circulation, data sharing and re-use by curators-professionals-people (Fig. 5).

The transformation phases are progressively embedded into multi-scale informative models to support the Virtual Reality modeling with validated information by the PAAA curators. All the information inserted can be exported and shared as Paradata to support the LOD600, for the remote management, here for XR. The successful experience of the Multimedia virtual exhibition opened to the public on 22nd December 2023 [16], with n.10 Oculus Gears, demonstrated the growing role of implementing narratives on the transformations occurred across the centuries by mean of the informative models generated by the SCAN-to-BIM-to-XR process into web-XR experiences [17, 18]. The storyboard has been so far developed on the 3D HBIM of the 'Lava' Hall narrating the excavation and the '*Basolatum*' artefact for the Appian Way pavement and the 'Peperino' Tuff basaltic rocks used for the Castrum Caetani walls as showed in the Figs. 3 and 5. The increased numbers of the visitors attracting the public, mostly absent from the mausoleum before VR experience, testifies the potentials in circulating informative quality models and, once again, the needs of circulating proper information on the data source, including the surveys process and 3D data models authors.

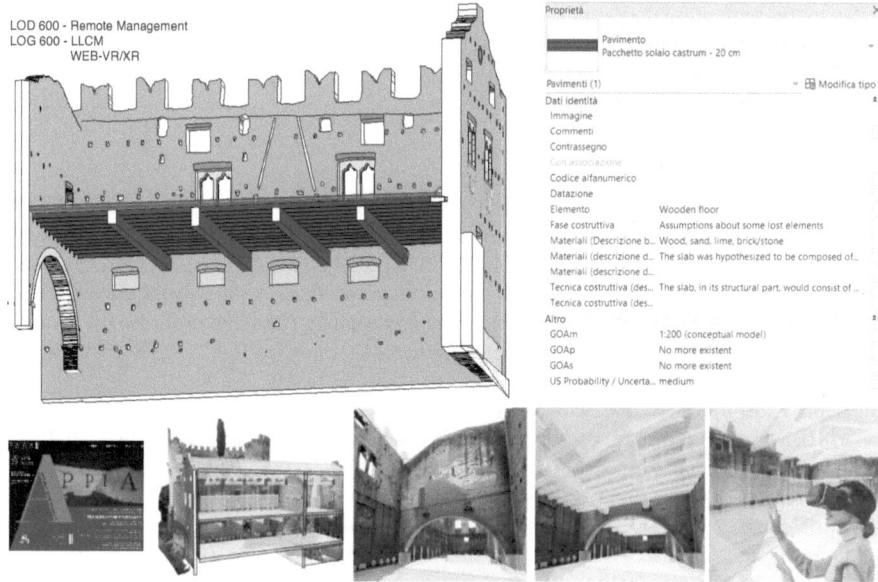

Fig. 5. Construction phases progressively embedded into informative models supporting Virtual Reality (LOG600): the HBIM 'Fireplace' Hall at the 1st floor (Upper). The reconstruction of the no longer existent wooden floor (GOAm 200) included in the HBIM Paradata. The immersive exhibition opened to public on Dec 2023 (Below), (Courtesy of ABClab-GIcarus and PAAA ©).

5   Conclusions

Paradata here implemented within HBIM can be easily kept updated, indexed, and exported into common platform and indexes. What we need is to define a common framework to co-develop languages, web-indexing, schemas, tools, and formats interoperability (i.e., CIDOC CRM, XML, IFC) to generate, retrieve, re-use and increment Paradata. Paradata contribute to the Documentation of the Heritage Architectural Archeological complex sites, Museum & Digital Archives, and Memory Twins, to the co-sharing of the informative models achieved among the multi-actors' communities involved into the SCAN-to-HBIM-to-XR processes, and not only, documenting survey and 3D models accuracies. Paradata can help growing a culture of data source citations rising awareness of recognizing holistic multidisciplinary efforts by all the experts and contributors responsible of the different data in the re-use circularity, as in the case of future vulnerability seismic analysis re-using the data models created, monitoring services, or the VR/XR experiences destined to be multiplied in the future being keeping memory of the data-sources.

Acknowledgments. The research have been carried out under the Consultancy Research Contracts among PAAA and ABClab-GIcarus (Sc. Resp. R. Brumana, F. Banfi, M. Previtali): our thanks to the PAAA Director Arch. S. Quilici; to Prof. A. Grimoldi, A.M. Landi, for the material analysis, F. Banfi, F. Roncoroni; and to M. Ioannides: this research is built on the results of EU

VIGIE2020/654 Study at the request of and financed by the EC (Coord. DHR Lab/UNESCO Chair on DCH, CUT, CY, POLIMI expert member).

References

1. Brumana, R., Quilici, S., Oliva, L., et al.: Multi-sensor HR mass data models toward multi-temporal-layered digital twins: maintenance, design and XR informed tour of the multi-stratified Appian Way (PAAA). Sensors **23**, 8556 (2023). https://doi.org/10.3390/s23208556

2. Banfi, F., Roascio S., et al.: Diachronic and synchronic analysis for knowledge creation: architectural representation geared to XR building archaeology (Claudius-Anio Novus aqueduct in Tor Fiscale, the Appia Antica Archaeological Park). Energies **15**(13), 4598 (2022) https://doi.org/10.3390/en15134598

3. Banfi, F., Brumana, R., Roascio, S., Previtali, M, et al.: 3D heritage reconstruction and scan-to-HBIM-to-XR project of the tomb of Caecilia Metella and Caetani Castle, Rome, Italy. Int. Arch. Photogramm. Remote Sens. Spatial Inf. Sci. **XLVI-2/W1-2022**, 49–56 (2022). https://doi.org/10.5194/isprs-archives-xlvi-2-w1-2022-49-2022

4. Börjesson, L., Sköld, O., Huvila, I.: Paradata in documentation standards and recommendations for digital archaeological visualizations. Digit. Cult. Soc. **6**(2), 191–220 (2020). https://doi.org/10.14361/dcs-2020-0210

5. Quantin, M., Tournon, S., Grimaus, V., Laroche, F., Granier, X.: Combining FAIR principles and long term archival of 3D data. In: ACM 3D Web Technology, pp.1–6 (2023)

6. Europeana Pro. https://pro.europeana.eu/post/how-the-5dculture-project-supports-the-reuse-of-archaeological-content-in-3d. Accessed 22072024

7. Niccolucci, F., Felicetti, A.: A CIDOC CRM-based model for the documentation of heritage sciences. In: DigitalHERITAGE, pp. 1–6 (2018)

8. VIGIE Study Study on quality in 3D digitisation of tangible cultural heritage

9. Brumana, R.: How to measure quality models? Digitization into informative models re-use | SpringerLink. In: 3D Research Challenges in Cultural Heritage III: Complexity and Quality in Digitisation, pp.77–102 (2023). Open Access, (LNCS, volume 13125), Eds, M. Ioannides, P. Patias

10. Brumana, R., Stanga, C., Banfi, F.: Models and scales for quality control: toward the definition of specifications (GOA-LOG) for the generation and re-use of HBIM object libraries in a common data environment. Appl. Geomat. **14**(Suppl 1), 151–179 (2022). https://doi.org/10.1007/s12518-020-00351-2

11. Brumana, R., Della Torre, S., Banfi, F., et. Al.: Generative HBIM-modeling to embody complexity. Surveying, preservation, site intervention. The Basilica di Collemaggio (L'Aquila). Appl Geomat I **10**(4), 545–567 (2018). https://doi.org/10.1007/s12518-018-0233-3

12. Roascio, S.: Il palinsesto materiale del complesso monumentale di Cecilia Metella/Castrum Caetani. In: Picchione A., Roascio S., et al. (eds.), Misurare la Terra, Roma, pp.49–64 (2021)

13. Marra, F.C., et al.: Monti Sabatini and Colli Albani: the dormant twin volcanoes at the gates of Rome. Sci. Rep. **10**, 8666 (2020). https://doi.org/10.1038/s41598-020-65394-2

14. "Copernicus Emergency Management Service" (EC JRC). Accessed 17 May 2024

15. Genzano, N., Pergola, N., Marchese, F.: A google earth engine tool to investigate, map and monitor volcanic thermal anomalies at global scale by means of mid-high spatial resolution satellite data. Remote Sens. **12**(19), 3232 (2020)

16. PAAA-Immersive digital exhibition (Cecilia Metella/Castrum Caetani) Accessed 17052024

17. Banfi F.: The evolution of interactivity, immersion and interoperability in HBIM: digital model uses, VR and AR for built cultural heritage. ISPRS Int. J. Geo-Inf. **10**(10), 685 (2021). https://doi.org/10.3390/ijgi10100685

18. Banfi, F., Dellù, E., et al.: Representing intangible cultural heritage of humanity: from the deep abyss of the past to digital twin and XR of the Neanderthal man and lamalunga cave. ISPRS **XLVIII-M-2-2023**, 171–181 (2023). https://doi.org/10.5194/isprs-archives-XLVIII-M-2-2023-171-2023

Three-Dimensional Reconstruction of an Egyptian *Sāqia*: A Computational Approach to Preserving Cultural Heritage and Water Management Systems

Jean-Baptiste Barreau[✉][iD]

Archéologie des Amériques (ArchAm), CNRS, Université Paris 1 Panthéon-Sorbonne, 9 rue Malher, 75004 Paris, France
jean-baptiste.barreau@cnrs.fr
https://archam.cnrs.fr

Abstract. The article explores the impact of transitioning an Egyptian *sāqia*, a traditional water-lifting device, from 2D blueprints to a comprehensive 3D model, offering new insights into historical artifacts. Despite financial challenges hindering the digitization of African archaeological hydraulic structures, the research emphasizes the importance of embracing 3D reconstructions. The 3D model reveals the intricate engineering complexities and cultural significance of ancient hydraulic systems through data collection and processing techniques. Strategic decision-making in data analysis is crucial, with broader implications highlighted. The article advocates for increased support for 3D digitization initiatives in African archaeology, recognizing their transformative potential in preserving cultural heritage. By addressing financial obstacles, 3D reconstructions offer more than mere data acquisition, extending to strategic considerations of paradata. These efforts enrich the global understanding of African history and technological advancements. Investing in 3D digitization is essential for preserving cultural heritage and advancing knowledge of African contributions to human civilization.

Keywords: Egyptian *Sāqia* · 3D Reconstruction · African Archaeology

1 Introduction

The UNESCO published a General History of Africa extensively discussing the history of saqias, an irrigation device [27]. Here are some key points:

- The Kingdom of Kush, located in ancient Nubia, played a significant role in the development of the *sāqia*.
- Nubians perfected this machine during the Meroitic period to enhance irrigation.

M. Ioannides et al. (Eds.): 3D Research Challenges in Cultural Heritage V, LNCS 15190, pp. 164–175, 2025.
https://doi.org/10.1007/978-3-031-78590-0_14

- The *sāqia* revolutionized agriculture by lifting water with less labor and time compared to the previous device, the *shaduf*.
- Unlike the *shaduf*, which relied on human energy, the saqiya was powered by buffaloes or other animals.

India's historical connection with the *sāqia* is noted [37]. Ananda Coomaraswamy suggests its possible invention in India as early as the 3rd century BCE, known as *araghaṭṭa*. Ancient Egypt had water-lifting water wheels as early as the 4th century BCE [42], with the *sāqia* emerging a century later. Archaeological evidence, such as papyri and frescoes, indicates widespread use of the *sāqia* in Ptolemaic and Roman Egypt [30]. Here's what we know:

- The concept of *sāqia* was further developed in the medieval Islamic world.
- Muslim inventors, such as Ismail al-Jazari, crafted intricate *sāqias*, incorporating over 200 components [26].
- Al-Jazari also pioneered the incorporation of the crank in the *sāqia*, along with regulatory devices to enhance irrigation efficiency.

According to Soubira's research [38], differences exist in technology and technical aspects between Andalusian or Moroccan *sāqia* and the Egyptian version. Here's what distinguishes them:

- In the Egyptian version, there's a division into two components, not two wheels but three.
- The gear system involves a horizontal wheel (*ters el-kebir*), a vertical wheel (*ters el-sogir*), and another vertical wheel (*mahalla*) around which the chain of pots (*selh*) is wound.
- The interaction between the two vertical wheels occurs through a shaft beneath the animal's walking path (*madar*).

In 1974, Ménassa and Laferrière conducted a detailed technical analysis of an Egyptian *sāqia*, focusing on one located near Medinet Habou in the Gorna region. Prior to the construction of the *Aswan Dam*, the *sāqia* primarily served as a supplementary irrigation method during low-water periods, particularly in areas not affected by flooding. Its wheels were disassembled during the annual Nile floods and reassembled once the water receded [23].

The *sāqia* is capable of lifting water to a maximum height of 10 to 11 m, which necessitates the construction of a well with a depth of 14 to 15 m. A well with this depth ensures that even if the water level fluctuates due to droughts or dry seasons, there will always be a sufficient reserve of water at a depth where the *sāqia* can access and operate effectively. Additionally, the extra depth can account for the space needed for the lifting mechanism and possible losses due to evaporation or percolation into the well walls.

The technical description includes all elements of the system in great detail, such as the construction of the well and the "anatomy" of the wheels and gears. Particular attention is given to the section dedicated to the operation of the *sāqia*, offering insights into the journey of the water from its extraction to the irrigated plots. Ownership of a *sāqia* involves multiple families due to the high construction, operation, and maintenance costs. Here are some operational details:

– In terms of flow, a *sāqia* can irrigate five *feddans* (one *feddan* is equivalent to 42 ares).
– If it runs continuously for 24 h, it can irrigate almost one *feddan*.
– Regarding yield, one *feddan* can produce ten to twelve or ardab of wheat or corn [23].

The 20th-century saw the *sāqia* endure alongside large hydraulic projects until the 1970s, but nowadays, it is generally replaced by diesel pumps with significantly higher pumping capacity [35]. Detailed technical documents regarding the *sāqia* are presented in Fig. 1, offering insights into its operational mechanisms.

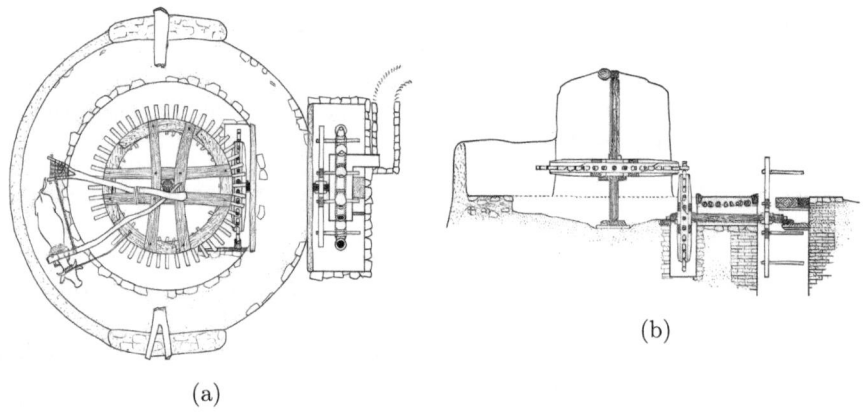

(b)

(a)

Fig. 1. Plan (a) and cross-section (b) of the classic Egyptian three-wheel *sāqia* [23]

3D scans of African sites have been conducted since the advent of associated technologies [5,14,28,36]. In parallel with the inception of 3D graphics [13], 3D reconstructions from 2D documents remain prevalent [7,19]. Due to their significant impact on past communities that relied on them, several 3D reconstructions of European hydraulic systems have been undertaken [11,20,34]. Outside of the numerous 3D reconstructions of Egyptian sites, those involving other sites on the African continent remain relatively scarce today but it emerges [1,3,9,40]. An inventory might be pertinent, but it is not the focus of this article.

Using aLTAG3D [18] for long-term archival of data and metadata related to the 3D model of an Egyptian *sāqia* offers a compelling solution for several reasons. Firstly, it aligns with FAIR principles [32], ensuring that data and metadata are Findable, Accessible, Interoperable, and Reusable, thus promoting longevity and accessibility. Collaboration with CINES, a French national institution for research data infrastructure [8], ensures robustness and reliability through the Open Archival Information System (OAIS) [24]. A custom metadata schema enhances content description for humanities research, promoting inclusivity. The conclusion of the 2017 White Paper by the 3D Consortium [39] presents responses from French researchers to a questionnaire about the use of 3D in the Humanities and Social Sciences. The objective is to determine the metadata required to accompany 3D models to ensure their future understanding and exploitation. This White Paper inspired the development of aLTAG3D, designed to integrate these metadata, including information on the author, the purpose of the acquisition, technical details of the acquisition process, object parameters, and information on the camera, software, and hardware used. Integration with standard vocabularies and mapping to the Europeana Data Model (EDM) [15] enhances interoperability. The adaptability of altag3d's desktop user interface (UI) software to the new metadata schema ensures practicality and efficiency in generating Submission Information Packages (SIPs). In summary, aLTAG3D provides a standardized and user-friendly solution that meets the evolving needs of humanities research, promoting accessibility and preservation of 3D data, metadata and paradata.

2   Methods and Results

Our methodology aims to provide a 100% free and open-source process tailored for research institutions with limited financial resources. It targets 3D reconstructions accompanied by metadata and paradata. In 2018, archaeologists thoroughly reviewed the plans and published data from Ménassa and Laferrière. This material encompasses detailed excavation procedures and data collection techniques. These documents serve as the core paradata for the project, furnishing essential geometric details for 3D reconstruction and outlining the excavation data acquisition process. Moreover, a wealth of drawn representations and various photographic records of similar *sāqia* elements have been amassed, reflecting their widespread use across Africa (cf. Fig. 2). These images are invaluable aids for 3D modeling efforts, enhancing our comprehension.

The 2D images were initially pixelated and then enhanced for improved clarity using the Upscayl software [22] and the real-esrgan algorithm [41]. The 3D modeling was conducted using Blender 3.0.1 software [6] (cf. Fig. 3(a) and (b)). Modeled elements correspond to those depicted in Fig. 1(a) and (b). No measurement scale is provided on the 2D documents, but approximate indications on the diameter of the main wheel and the depth of the well are available. With these, it was possible to scale the model, albeit with less precision than optimal in our case. Figure 1(a) particularly shows the correspondence between the 2D documents and the 3D modeling. Branches were created by modifying existing free models found online, elongated and/or extruded at specific locations. Stones on the ground were initially drawn in 2D, then extruded, beveled, subdivided, and decimated using modifiers. The water buffalo model [25] was also sourced online under a Royalty Free license [29].

Fig. 2. Series of main photos of *sāqias* found on the internet

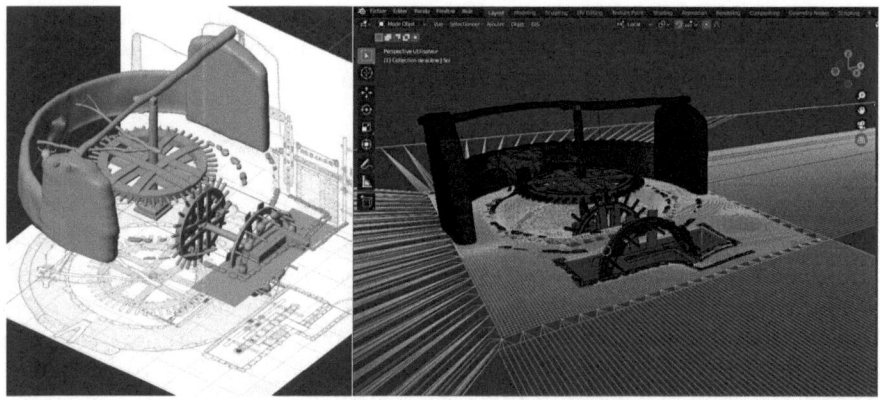

Fig. 3. View of the modeling in the Blender viewport

Regarding materials, our initial goal for this first study was to achieve a "toon" style rendering to strike a balance between quick material creation time and readability akin to technical drawing [21]. For rendering Fig. 4, a sunlight lamp was positioned with an intensity of 5. Concerning rendering parameters, the view transformation was set as standard. Materials were defined as follows: a diffuse BSDF, an RGB shader, a color gradient with constant interpolation, and two colors - one primary and one for shadows.

We also utilized aLTAG3D 1.8.1. Metadata required for generating synthesis information on archival information and archaeological data of the repository included the "site name", "site owner", "object owner", "discovery location", "conservation location", "inventory number", "archaeological description", "archaeological date", "research program", "scientific and technical objectives", "project date", "responsible entity", "sponsor", "keywords" a "paradata file", and the "List of virtual objects". For each virtual object, there are the "title", "creator", "3D date", "virtual object version", "description", a "mesh comprising the virtual object" and a "group of source files" concerning our case, the paradata. For each 3D file, one will find the "file creator", "3D file date", "file format", "orientation axis", "vertical axis", "scene dimensions", "measurement unit", "processing software", "polygon count", "mesh-associated textures", "texture file creator", "texture file date", "texture file format" and "texture type".

Figure 4(a) illustrates a 3D rendering generated using the Eevee rendering engine, Blender's real-time rendering engine. Built on OpenGL, Eevee prioritizes speed and interactivity while maintaining the goal of achieving physically based rendering (PBR) materials [17]. However, some elements are missing in the scene, particularly concerning the position of the user behind the bovine. The human user, their mesh seat, and whip were not modeled as they are inherently tied to a potential project involving virtual avatars and embodiment sensations [33].

Texturing and post-processing can be time-consuming tasks, especially for an individual. To address this issue, we decided to test an AI-based image creation tool, specifically using an existing image. Dzine.ai [2] facilitates design with a layered canvas for precise adjustments. Its features include a drag-and-drop composition interface, unifying elements for a consistent style, conversational prompts, layered cutouts, and high-resolution export. Users can sign up, create a project, import images, apply styles, and export their work. The Fig. 4(b) shows a conversion in a few seconds from a 3D render generated using the Eevee rendering engine to a 'Simplified Scenic' style textured render using Dzine.ai, the online AI design tool. This conversion was done with a Style intensity at 0.7, a Structure match at 0.5, a Color match set to OFF, and a Face match set to OFF. The inferred prompt is quite relevant since it indicates: "The image depicts an ancient stone wheel with a series of spokes radiating from its center, possibly used for grinding or milling. A single figure stands beside the wheel, appearing to be engaged in some form of activity related to it. The setting appears to be outdoors, with natural light casting shadows on the ground. The background is minimalistic and does not provide any additional context about the location or time period". However, there is a crucial element missing in this AI-generated image: water. Moreover, as it stands, textures generated by AI-based image creation tools, while visually enriching 3D reconstruction, cannot be considered paradata in the same sense as 2D plans derived from archaeological excavations. AI-generated textures are artistic and technical interpretations aimed at giving the reconstruction a realistic or aesthetically pleasing appearance, without providing information on the process of collecting the initial archaeological data. They do not document excavation methods or the original archaeological context.

The metadata and paradata entered into the various aLTAG3D forms are consolidated into boxes as depicted in Fig. 5. Regarding paradata for 3D digitization processes, the current information primarily includes descriptions of acquisition protocols, descriptions of applied processing, and the objectives of the project, whether scientific or technical [31]. However, this structure remains adaptable based on the specific needs of the project. An HTML export can be generated, summarizing the archiving information with the archaeological data from the

(a)   (b)

Fig. 4. (a) 3D rendering created using the Eevee rendering engine [17] and (b) conversion to a 'Simplified Scenic' style textured render using Dzine.ai [2], an online AI design tool

repository, the list of virtual objects, the list of 3D files containing the virtual objects, and the list of source groups. Finally, an SIP archive has been created to generate the files required for project archiving and to organize them hierarchically within a folder.

This case study shows that using both metadata and paradata in 3D reconstruction after archaeological digs is a big step forward in preserving and understanding cultural heritage. Metadata helps organize and manage detailed archival and archaeological information. But adding paradata makes this process even better. Paradata describe not only the objects or artifacts but also the context and methods of their discovery and documentation. They explain the decisions made during excavations, providing important background and context. For instance, knowing why and how certain elements were documented can clarify reconstruction choices and lead to a more accurate reconstruction. So, paradata link raw data to its scientific interpretation, offering a detailed and nuanced view. By combining metadata and paradata, researchers and conservators can capture and share the stories and expertise behind the artifacts, enhancing the educational and cultural value of 3D reconstructions.

3 Perspectives

As per the fourth principle of the London Charter [16], it's crucial to develop a method for documenting paradata, thus specifying the correlation between research sources, implicit knowledge, explicit reasoning, and visualization outcomes [4,10]. Implicit knowledge and explicit reasoning surrounding the 3D reconstruction of the Egyptian *sāqia* encompass various aspects within our perspectives. Among them, the first to mention is geographical location, which

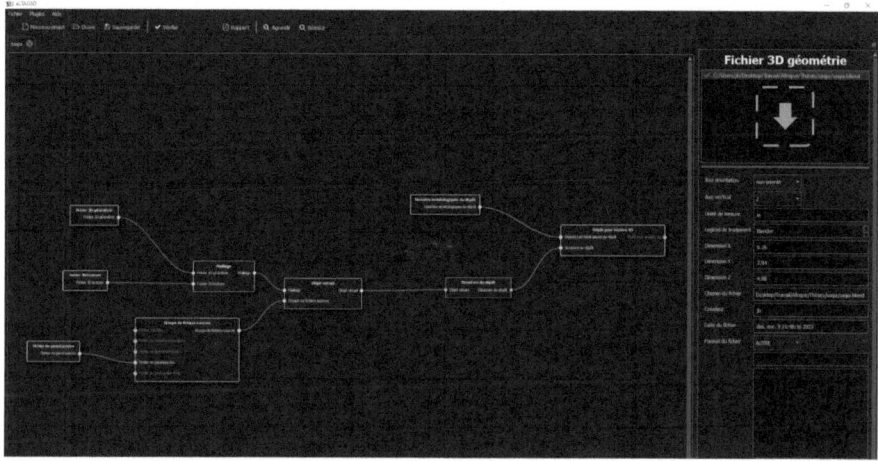

Fig. 5. Screenshot of the Project in Altag3D

would entail meticulous mapping of the surrounding terrain, including rivers and irrigated fields (cf Fig. 6(a)). Understanding the technology and mechanism entails delving into the operational methods (cf Fig. 6(b)) of the *sāqia*, whether mechanical or animal-powered, as well as identifying the type of lifting system utilized, such as rope and bucket (cf Fig. 6(c)) or bucket wheel, alongside precise measurements of water lifting and distribution mechanisms. The historical context would shed light on the dating and presumed use of the *sāqia*, as well as its significance within the region's historical framework, encompassing its societal role and cultural implications. Assessing the environmental and social impacts involves evaluating the *sāqia*'s influence on local water resources, biodiversity, and surrounding ecosystems, as well as its social and economic contributions to the local community. Ethnographic and cultural data, including narratives and testimonies from residents regarding the history and use of the *sāqia*, as well as cultural practices associated with traditional irrigation systems, are also worth considering. For instance, Ménassa and Laferrière (1974) indicate that *sāqia* songs (cf Fig. 6(d)), infused with rhythms and slowness, convey love and imagination, blending tradition and improvisation in the nightly call of the *gāzer*, the child in charge of turning the bovine [23]. On a broader scale, a comparative analysis would further enhance the reconstruction by juxtaposing it with the similar waterwheel or water distribution systems at regional and global levels, offering valuable insights into its technological evolution and cultural context.

From our subject, we aim to contribute to a discourse on facilitating 3D reconstruction efforts in African archaeology, extending beyond well-funded Egyptology. Financial constraints pose a significant challenge to 3D digitization and reconstruction initiatives undertaken by research entities and businesses across the African continent. Particularly in certain African regions, insufficient technological infrastructure, including high-performance computers and reliable internet connectivity, presents obstacles to implementing advanced digitization ini-

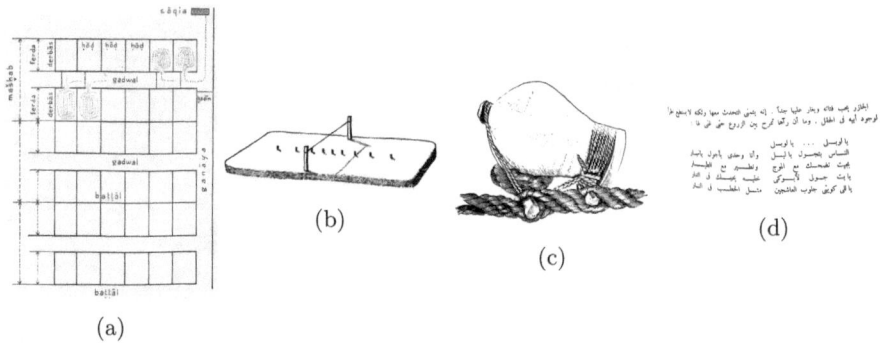

Fig. 6. Example of the organization of an irrigated garden (a), an *'elga* sundial used to calculate irrigation time (b), way of tying a string around a bucket (c) and excerpt from a song (d) evoking the *sāqia* [23]

tiatives. Overcoming these financial barriers requires increased support from governmental and policy entities. Advocating for the importance of digitally preserving African archaeological heritage with policymakers could stimulate larger investments in this field. On the other hand, the use of software such as Blender, aLTAG3D, or any online AI-based image creation tool, available for free, allows African organizations engaged in 3D reconstruction initiatives to circumvent the need for financial resources. Furthermore, access to photographic and graphic documentation of archaeological structures, some of which have recently emerged in Africa, enables viewers of 3D models to draw their own conclusions regarding the accuracy and relevance of reconstruction efforts. Integrating our approach into open-source visualization and online data sharing tools [12], along with accompanying 2D paradata, would enable viewers to assess the relevance of the modeling. Establishing a database of hand-drawn 2D plans/cross-section associations from archaeological excavations would also be valuable for assessing the feasibility of potential reconstructions.

4   Conclusion

In conclusion, this article highlights the crucial importance of paradata in archaeological research, particularly in the 3D reconstruction of historical artifacts such as the Egyptian *sāqia*. Paradata, which document how archaeological data is collected, provide essential context for assessing the relevance of the reconstruction. The study presented here demonstrates how paradata from historical 2D documents were used to guide the 3D reconstruction process of the *sāqia*, offering valuable insights into its functioning and structure. Furthermore, the integration of detailed metadata into a data management framework like aLTAG3D ensures the longevity and accessibility of information associated with the 3D model. By acknowledging the significance of paradata, this research contributes to archaeological methodology by providing a framework for comprehensive documentation of data collection processes. This approach also promotes transparency and reproducibility in research, thereby strengthening the credibility and validity of conclusions drawn from such studies. In the future, it is essential to continue developing and promoting the use of paradata in archaeological research, especially in the realm of 3D reconstruction. By integrating these data into internationally recognized standards and metadata frameworks, we can ensure that attached information is preserved exhaustively and accessible for future generations.

References

1. Abdi, M.T., Osanjo, L.: Cultural heritage and digital era in Kenya. Afr. Des. Rev. J. **1**(2), 143–153 (2022)
2. AI, D.: Dzine.ai - Youtube channel (2024). https://www.youtube.com/@dzine_ai. Accessed 10 July 2024
3. Amokrane, L., Kassab, T., Monjo-Carrio, J.: Ancient restorations: computer-based structural approach for the identification and reinterpretation of the Medracen's constructive sequence. Virtual Archaeol. Rev. **13**(27), 33–48 (2022)
4. Apollonio, F.I., et al.: Classification schemes and model validation of 3D digital reconstruction process. In: Proceedings of the 20th International Conference on Cultural Heritage and New Technologies (2015)
5. Arnaud, B.: Perle du sahel, agadez préserve son patrimoine en 3D (2022). https://www.sciencesetavenir.fr/archeo-paleo/patrimoine/perle-du-sahel-agadez-preserve-son-patrimoine-en-3d_162038
6. Ávila Rodríguez, M., Navarro Catalán, D.M., Cisneros Álvarez, P.: El proyecto arquitectónico del académico josé garcía para sustituir la puerta de los apóstoles de la catedral de valencia: Una propuesta de modelado 3d. Archivo de arte valenciano **103**, 131–147 (2022)
7. Barreau, J.B., Nouviale, F., Gaugne, R., Bernard, Y., Llinares, S., Gouranton, V.: An immersive virtual sailing on the 18th-century ship le boullongne. Presence: Teleoperators Virtual Environ. **24**(3), 201–219 (2015)
8. Béchard, L.: L'archivage électronique dans l'enseignement supérieur et la recherche: problématique et solutions. Gazette des archives **231**(3), 281–291 (2013)
9. Bernard, Y.: Sénégal: Tombes mégalithiques de wanar (2023). https://virtual-archeo.com/senegal-tombes-megalithiques-de-wanar/
10. Börjesson, L., Sköld, O., Huvila, I.: Paradata in documentation standards and recommendations for digital archaeological visualisations. Digit. Cult. Soc. **6**(2), 191–220 (2020)
11. Castro-García, M., Rojas-Sola, J.I., et al.: Technical and functional analysis of Albolafia waterwheel (Cordoba, Spain): 3D modeling, computational-fluid dynamics simulation and finite-element analysis. Energy Convers. Manag. **92**, 207–214 (2015)
12. Champion, E., Rahaman, H.: Survey of 3D digital heritage repositories and platforms. Virtual Archaeol. Rev. **11**(23), 1–15 (2020)
13. Chapman, G.: Do-it-yourself reconstruction modelling. In: Lock, G., Moffett, J. (eds.) Proceedings of the Computer Applications and Quantitative Methods in Archaeology, pp. 213–218. British Archaeological Reports International Series S577, Oxford (1992)

14. Chapoulie, R., et al.: Le rôle paradoxal de l'eau à lalibela (ethiopie): Enjeux et méthodes pour la conservation d'un affleurement naturel anthropisé. Restauro Archeologico **30**(1) (2022)

15. Charles, V., Isaac, A.: Enhancing the europeana data model (edm). EDM WHITE PAPER. Recuperada em **19** (2015)

16. Denard, H.: A new introduction to the London charter. Paradata and transparency in virtual heritage, pp. 57–71 (2012)

17. Dudek, S., Dziedzic, K.: Comparative analysis of the cycles and eevee graphics engines on the example of rendering 3D models of archaeological artifacts. J. Comput. Sci. Inst. **24**, 218–223 (2022)

18. Dutailly, B., Tournon, S., Chayani, M., Grimaud, V., Granier, X.: Altag3D: a user-friendly metadata documentation software. In: DARIAH Annual Event 2023: Cultural Heritage Data as Humanities Research Data? (2023)

19. Galasso, F., Parrinello, S., Picchio, F.: From excavation to drawing and from drawing to the model. The digital reconstruction of twenty-year-long excavations in the archaeological site of bedriacum. J. Archaeol. Sci. Rep. **35**, 102734 (2021)

20. García-León, J., González-García, J.A., Collado-Espejo, P.E.: Documentation and modelling of a hypothetical reconstruction of the first roman watermill in Hispania. Virtual Archaeol. Rev. **12**(25), 114–123 (2021)

21. Hamilton, K.: Wittgenstein and tufte on thinking in 3D: 'escaping flatland'. In: Electronic Visualisation and the Arts (EVA 2012). BCS Learning & Development (2012)

22. Jovanović, I.: Analiza metoda za povećanje slike. Ph.D. thesis, University of Split. Faculty of Science. Department of Informatics (2023)

23. Laferrière, P.: La sāqia: technique et vocabulaire de la roue à eau égyptienne. Institut français d'archéologie orientale (1974)

24. Lee, C.A.: Open archival information system (OAIS) reference model. Encyclopedia Libr. Inf. Sci. **3**, 4020–4030 (2010)

25. Minervino, A.H.H., Zava, M., Vecchio, D., Borghese, A.: Bubalus bubalis: a short story. Front. Vet. Sci. **7**, 570413 (2020)

26. Morelon, R., Rashed, R.: Encyclopedia of the History of Arabic Science. Routledge London (1996)

27. Mukhtār, M., for the Drafting of a General History of Africa, U.I.S.C.: Ancient Civilizations of Africa. General history of Africa, UNESCO (1981). https://books.google.fr/books?id=gB6DcMU94GUC

28. Naeser, C., Kleinitz, C., Bauer, T.: Optische 3d-messungen zur digitalen bestandsdokumentation von dekorierten bauelementen und sekundärbildern der großen anlage von musawwarat es sufra: ein pilotprojekt. Der Antike Sudan. Mitteilungen der Sudanarchäologischen Gesellschaft zu Berlin eV (MittSAG) **20**, 33–48 (2009)

29. Nyinyi, N.: Water Buffalo (Lowpoly)</b> 3D Model—rigmodels.com (2024). https://rigmodels.com/model.php?view=Water_Buffalo_(Lowpoly)-3d-model_4ab07e88abd54c47a8c85b594d12f946. Accessed 04 May 2024

30. Oleson, J.P.: Water-lifting. Handbook of ancient water technology, pp. 217–302 (2000)

31. Quantin, M.: Archivage des modèles 3d (2021). https://hackmd.io/@mquantin/ByIb-3Jhe?print-pdf#, journée d'Études ReUSE - réseau SHN : Vocabulaires, référentiels, standards... méta-modèle !, Amphi S du LS2N, École Centrale, Nantes

32. Quantin, M., Tournon, S., Grimaud, V., Laroche, F., Granier, X.: Combining fair principles and long-term archival of 3D data. In: Proceedings of the 28th International ACM Conference on 3D Web Technology, pp. 1–6 (2023)

33. Richard, G., Pietrzak, T., Argelaguet, F., Lécuyer, A., Casiez, G.: Within or between? Comparing experimental designs for virtual embodiment studies. In: 2022 IEEE Conference on Virtual Reality and 3D User Interfaces (VR), pp. 186–195. IEEE (2022)

34. Rojas-Sola, J.I., García-Gómez, S.: Geometric modeling and digital restitution of a hydraulic press with rotating arm for obtaining olive oil from 1889. In: International conference on the Digital Transformation in the Graphic Engineering, pp. 607–615. Springer (2022)

35. Ruf, T.: La participation des fellahs à l'agriculture irriguée dans l'egypte contemporaine. La Houille Blanche **8**, 66–69 (1996)

36. Rüther, H., Palumbo, G.: 3D laser scanning for site monitoring and conservation in Lalibela world heritage site, Ethiopia. Int. J. Heritage Digit. Era **1**(2), 217–231 (2012)

37. Siddiqui, I.H.: Water works and irrigation system in India during pre-mughal times. J. Econ. Soc. History Orient/Journal de l'histoire economique et sociale de l'Orient 52–77 (1986)

38. Soubira, T.: Hydraulique urbaine, hydraulique oasienne: archéologie d'une ville médiévale des marges sahariennes du Maroc: hydro-histoire de Sidjilmāsa et de la plaine du Tāfilālt. Ph.D. thesis, Université Toulouse le Mirail-Toulouse II (2018)

39. Vergnieux, R., et al.: Livre blanc du consortium 3D SHS. France. hal-01683842v2 (2017)

40. Walmsley, A.P., Lindstaedt, M., Schnelle, M., Kersten, T.P.: Virtual reality for spatial research in archaeology: proto-typing 3D reconstruction tools for the site of Yeha, Ethiopia. In: Proceedings of the Scientific-Technical Annual Meeting of the German Society for Photogrammetry, Remote Sensing and Geoinformation, Munich, pp. 123–133 (2023). https://www.dgpf.de/src/tagung/jt2023/proceedings/paper/05_dgpf2023_Walmsley_et_al.pdf

41. Wang, X., Xie, L., Dong, C., Shan, Y.: Real-esrgan: training real-world blind super-resolution with pure synthetic data. In: Proceedings of the IEEE/CVF International Conference on Computer Vision, pp. 1905–1914 (2021)

42. Wikander, O.: 136 Sources of energy and exploitation of power. In: The Oxford Handbook of Engineering and Technology in the Classical World. Oxford University Press (2009). https://doi.org/10.1093/oxfordhb/9780199734856.013.0007

Usable, Useful, Reviewable and Reusable Metadata
From Metadata and Paradata to UXdata and Back

Erik Champion[(✉)]

University of South Australia, Adelaide, Australia
erik.champion@unisa.edu.au

Abstract. Approaches to both metadata in 3D cultural heritage and strengthening the integration of paradata have been clearly focused on developing new technological solutions. New technologies allow novel and richer communication participation yet metadata in 3D cultural heritage has been decided by a combination of specialized individuals and by frameworks of quantitative standards, but this does not address how to engage and educate the public. As a potential solution, this paper will suggest that metadata and paradata should be linked to UXdata (data recording participant feedback).

Keywords: Paradata · metadata · UXdata

1 Introduction: Who Owns the Metadata Owns the Past?

Arguably, most approaches to both improving metadata and paradata in 3D digital heritage have focused on developing new technological solutions. New technologies allow novel and richer communication participation as well as greater reflection on heritage [1], but metadata in 3D cultural heritage has been decided by a combination of specialized individuals, and by frameworks of quantitative standards. Despite the expertise of GLAM professionals, Seaton et al. [2] have stated that virtual heritage projects typically contain limited possibilities and a limited quantity and quality of data/metadata/paradata.

More controversially, contra to the authority of experts and the predominance of linear and closed digital packages, Iacopini [3] says contextual information is more important than the authority of the source. Hoskins [4] wrote that "…most important is 'what we do with media, rather than what media does' in the shared memory process. While Burkey [5] suggested, "there is a gap in the literature about how cultural heritage communities are using digital heritage initiatives and platforms for collective remembering … digital heritage initiatives deserve more attention as examples for how heritage communities use them for collective remembering."

Further, as pointed out in the doctoral thesis by BrodeFrank [6], "Metadata allows people to perform various operations with data, including searching, managing, structuring, preserving, and authenticating resources" but there are few studies on how and what people search, manage and preserve with these resources. She suggested crowdsourcing can improve and extend metadata. She noted, "… there exists a semantic gap

M. Ioannides et al. (Eds.): 3D Research Challenges in Cultural Heritage V, LNCS 15190, pp. 176–183, 2025.
https://doi.org/10.1007/978-3-031-78590-0_15

in the language and descriptive styles of museum professionals, on the one hand, and the public, on the other, and that crowdsourcing demonstrates promise to help bridge this gap while also providing an opportunity for the public to engage with museums directly."

Such a gap between professionals and the public is at odds with the emphasis of UNESCO [7] definitions of cultural heritage on community-based knowledge and generation-to-generation transfer of knowledge (as opposed to one-way transmission of knowledge from professionals and experts to the public). Given such research [8] and surveys, an argument can be made that the most fundamental and overlooked issue of metadata in 3D cultural heritage documentation and the projects documented has been how it can address and support engagement, understanding, and reuse by the wider public.

2 From Metadata to UXdata

I suggest approaches to improving metadata and integrating paradata are typically technology-focused but due to this focus may miss their importance to the contextual historical organization of knowledge. For example, Börjesson et al. [9] have stressed that metadata, as crucial information, "plays a crucial role in facilitating the discovery, interpretation, and preservation of cultural artefacts, enabling users to search, access, and understand digital heritage resources within digital repositories or collections ... [and that] ... It serves as a vital component in ensuring the long-term accessibility and usability of digital heritage materials."

If the public does not know or understand or can contribute to revising metadata, one might well ask if the metadata of the cultural heritage in question can itself be considered to be cultural heritage. This is perhaps also a semantic issue with paradata. Given digital heritage data can change over time, and thus paradata may change as well, should there be different terms for initial paradata and paradata that have changed over time since its date of inception? While convention might surmise that the previous data should suffice for revisions and alterations, or new paradata can be created for new visualizations, I will suggest a problem may arise with emerging media offering new possibilities for the user experience.

In this new landscape, the Metaverse promises shared experiences across different worlds, platforms and devices. As well, new types of data and sensory devices (haptics, sensors, wearables, biofeedback, and eye tracking may create diverging or converging audiences and experiential platforms. How current and recent paradata will expand or include these new types of data, audience preferences, evaluations and demographics will be an interesting development.

Given that a virtual heritage experience creates, reacts to, or records sensory experiences, can we consider paradata, metadata, and cross-referencing to be UXdata? If metadata can be linked to data that records or in some way measures or relays the user experience (UXdata, conscious and subconscious audience responses, preferences and physiological states), heritage organizations may be able to gain a better understanding of how their models are understood.

3 Paradata

While there are many varying definitions and uses of paradata, it will prove essential in the creation of reviewable and reusable digital heritage and it will need to be able to provide links between static and dynamic sources, for a wide range of individuals and groups. Therefore it is an important consideration but it is also attempting to address two concerns, both description and a scholarly trail of resources for the source material for the final digital heritage project; and a connection to potentially dynamic and revisable linked data sources. I propose that the scholarly community consider bifurcating the term: a term for the source paradata, and a term for the dynamically linked, related data sources.

4 3D Models in Academic Papers

Table 1. Heritage conference papers regarding digital heritage models and assets.

Conference papers	2017	2016	2015	2014	2013	2012	Total
VSMM	55	65	53				173
CAA			117	73	50		240
CIPA	111		82		112		305
EuroMed		105		84		95	284
Digital Heritage			270		211		481
TOTAL	166	170	522	157	373	95	1483

The above table (Table 1), from a 2019 paper by Champion and Rahaman [10], surveyed leading conferences focusing on 3D digital heritage, From a sample of 1483 conference papers (Table 2) from 2012 to 2017, we selected 264 of the total papers published in VSMM, CAA, CIPA, EuroMed, and Digital Heritage Congress. Only 17.9% referred to and contained images of 3D assets or 3D digital models. Only nine papers contained accessible 3D assets or 3D models. 19 articles contained external web links to 3D models but not a single link in any of these papers (Table 3) worked on the final day of our survey (1 September 2018).

A 2020 survey paper by Champion and Rahaman [11] investigated the range of interactive viewing features of commercial and FOSS (Free and Open Software) 3D hosting platforms, repositories, and portals. We concluded that there were very few platforms that provided any useful and meaningful ways of interacting with the models that suited the aims of virtual heritage. Ideally, there will also be tools that can be embedded in the 3D digital model platform or infrastructure that automatically send feedback and other participation data to the system so that it can be continually revised and improved.

Table 2. Total articles containing references to 3D models and heritage assets.

Conference Publications	Total Papers	Mentioning 3D Assets	%
VSMM 2015–2017	173	31	17.9%
CAA 2013–2015	240	38	15.8%
CIPA 2013, 2015, 2017	305	79	25.9%
EuroMed 2012, 2014, 2016	284	61	21.5%
Digital Heritage 2013, 2015	481	55	11.4%
TOTAL	1483	264	17.8%

Table 3. Selected papers included in our study.

Directly Accessible	VSMM	CAA	CIPA	EuroMed	Digital Heritage	Total
3D content	0	1	3	1	4	9
Videos	1	2	1	2	6	12
Other (VR models, photos, images of 3D models, etc.)	1	4	6	5	17	33
3D assets on accessible websites	3	0	5	3	8	19

5   Paradata in 3D Cultural Heritage

Reilly et al. [12] noted the term was: ".. coined in 1998 by Mick Couper to distinguish auxiliary data, describing the processes by which interview survey data were obtained, from the established metadata that describe the collected data themselves." Couper [13] wanted to distinguish auxiliary data from metadata (describing the data).

The contextual information and documentation generated during the process of creating, managing, and disseminating digital cultural heritage resources, provide insights into the creation, usage, and interpretation of digital heritage materials, offering valuable contextual information beyond the content itself. Paradata often includes details such as the creator's intentions, the methods used in digitization or preservation efforts, changes or alterations made to the material, and user interactions or feedback.

It enhances the understanding and interpretation of digital heritage resources, aiding researchers, curators, and users in comprehending digital artefacts' historical, cultural, and technological aspects (see also Rabinowitz, [13, 14]).

Huvila [15] remarked: "The problem [paradata] is wicked in the sense that it is difficult to pin down, there are no clear limits to the amount of information to capture, the correctness of solutions is difficult to establish and situatedness of information needs makes the problem and solutions similarly situated."

Is paradata research and research design data? Then what to call design data and design findings in the making of the digital heritage project or collection? Where does the 3D model sit? Is it a summation of paradata, an abstraction or summary of paradata or a resulting product? Or is it, itself, not so much a model as a framework?

Criteria for improved metadata and more integrated paradata are to ensure metadata is usable (accessible), useful (does what it says and provides what the visitor needs) and can be effectively and measurably reviewed by external parties after the publication of the 3D cultural heritage project and can be effectively reused elsewhere.

I suggest that digital heritage still has unexplored and verified scope to communicate different forms of understanding through filtered interaction and as an open or partially open reflective tool [16] and participative framework.

6   UXdata

Personal preference, cultural understanding, understanding, usefulness, usability, desirability, biofeedback, head-tracking, task performance, comments and observations of the participants. Champion et al. [17] used statistical analysis to link some of the above factors but there are, so far, few studies to advance the potential of this method in digital heritage research.

Transferring physiological data to an understanding of a digital heritage project is hard enough: how to transfer that to an improved ontology and classification of metadata, let alone find, link and provide information on relevant paradata?

One could test how quickly and memorably participants find required heritage projects. One could also link anonymous collated personal data with types of interaction, site/project preferences, and number of successful implementations (how many organizations used this type of interaction, and the feedback they received).

This requires organization beyond corporate standards, this requires agreed metrics in communities, government departments, and scholarly/research organisations.

Heritage organizations do want to know what their audience understands and finds useful and would request the 3D digital heritage models. A survey of the terms they search for and how effective their searches are is incomplete, we will also need to know how it helps them to understand the heritage content.

A more end-user-focused approach has implications for humanities researchers, according to Hansson [18]: "Studies of archival meanings is thus at the core of humanities research, as is the reorganization of these systems to generate new insights." Following Hansson [18], Brodefrank [6] and Ulguim [19], I suggest there is often a knowledge and interpretive skills gap between professionals and the public.

Researchers have noted there is a worrying gap in the level of understanding between professionals and the public on digital heritage, yet UNESCO definitions of culture as community-based knowledge and generation-to-generation transfer of knowledge. Hopefully, as researchers have explained [], data producers and data users can collaborate via data, data linkages, metadata and interaction to not only search and structure but also to rethink how society, technology and the environment can fruitfully combine and preserve cultural heritage. But here I note that these surveys are typically based on Western notions of hierarchy and may not suit indigenous and remote communities [20–22].

7   Recommendations

Internationally there have been various surveys to understand what categories and information are needed for metadata. Generally, these surveys are taken after the project was developed and there is no time to improve the project based on that feedback.

A way forward is to trial different metadata standards and related content, provide information on how they can be used and extended, workshop with a wide range of people and interests exactly how metadata can relate to 3D digital heritage projects and collect data on what engages people, how they interpret and what they modify. In other words, I suggest that to improve the scholarly ecosystem of digital heritage, from the system designer to the community and back to the system designer, we should build creative and evaluative tools and resources into and alongside metadata and paradata that collect UXdata.

I also propose that there are at least six components required for preservation:

1. The dataset (2D, 3D, textures, sounds, scripts, etc.) of the virtual heritage itself.
2. The paradata that helped the research and development of the virtual heritage project.
3. The authorship, institutional links and accreditations, and teamwork.
4. The intentions of the authors.
5. The metadata and system structure and any relevant classification data.
6. Evaluation data (audience tracking, usability studies, audience engagement results, and an attempt to capture usable and useful audience experience and feedback). This may be at a higher, aggregated level due to concerns for privacy, or data storage requirements. With the emergence of biofeedback and haptics for advanced virtual reality systems increasingly accessible to a wider range of audiences, addressing immersive challenges of communicating tangible and intangible heritage, this is an interesting if challenging future research field.

Fig. 1. An example of an editable 3D model in DBpedia with Linked Open Data

As we move from static repositories and platforms to Linked Open Data, AI and machine learning search and content tools, via mixed and augmented reality services capable of integrating real-time data, these features will become more and more important. The above image (Fig. 1) investigates one such potential future development: editable 3D model assets using DBpedia and Linked Open Data have been investigated by Ikrom Nishanbaev et al. [23].

8 Conclusion

Criteria for improved metadata and more integrated paradata help ensure metadata is usable (accessible), useful (does what it says) and provides what the visitor needs and can be effectively and measurably reviewed by external parties after the publication of the 3D cultural heritage project and can be effectively reused elsewhere.

Given that the goal is to collate usable, useful, reviewable and reusable metadata, this paper recommends the incorporation of user experience data in or adjacent to paradata for digital heritage. Referencing metadata with more integrated and dynamic paradata will help ensure metadata is usable (accessible), useful (does what it says and provides what the visitor needs) and can be effectively and measurably reviewed by external parties after the publication of the 3D cultural heritage project and can be effectively reused elsewhere.

References

1. In-uk, K.: The Tripolar UNESCO World Heritage Race (2023). https://koreajoongangda ily.joins.com/news/2023-12-17/opinion/columns/The-tripolar-Unesco-World-Heritage-race/1937775. Accessed 17 Apr 2024
2. Seaton, K.-L., Laužikas, R., McKeague, P., de Almeida, V.M., May, K., Wright, H.: Understanding data reuse and barriers to reuse of archaeological data. A quality-in-use methodological approach. Internet Archaeol. **63**, 1–33 (2023)
3. Iacopini, E.: Digitization of archival data and metadata in archaeology: the case of Ancona. In: Proceedings 2024, vol. 1, p. 9. MDPI (2024)
4. Hoskins, A.: Memory of the multitude: the end of collective memory. In: Andrew, H. (ed.) Digital memory Studies: Media Pasts in Transition, pp. 97–121. Routledge, New York (2017)
5. Burkey, B.: Total recall: how cultural heritage communities use digital initiatives and platforms for collective remembering. J. Creative Commun. **14**(3), 235–253 (2019). https://doi.org/10.1177/0973258619868045
6. BrodeFrank, J.: Strengthening digital engagement to provide intersectional narratives within museums using user-generated metadata: a case study at Chicago's Adler Planetarium and the applications beyond. University of London (2024)
7. UNESCO: Supporting museums: UNESCO report points to options for the future (2023). https://www.unesco.org/en/articles/supporting-museums-unesco-report-points-options-fut ure?hub=417. Accessed 17 Apr 2024
8. Lombardi, M.: Sustainability of 3D heritage data: life cycle and impact. Archeologia e Calcolatori **34**(2), 339–356 (2023). https://doi.org/10.19282/ac.34.2.2023.18
9. Börjesson, L., Sköld, O., Huvila, I.: Paradata in documentation standards and recommendations for digital archaeological visualisations. Digit. Cult. Soc. **6**(2), 191–220 (2020)
10. Champion, E., Rahaman, H.: 3D digital heritage models as sustainable scholarly resources. Sustainability **11**(8), 1–8 (2019)

11. Champion, E., Rahaman, H.: Survey of 3D digital heritage repositories and platforms. Virtual Archaeol. Rev. (VAR) (2020). https://doi.org/10.4995/var.2020.13226
12. Reilly, P., Callery, S., Dawson, I., Gant, S.: Provenance illusions and elusive paradata: when archaeology and art/archaeological practice meets the phygital. Open Archaeol. 7(1), 454–481 (2021)
13. Couper, M.P.: Usability evaluation of computer-assisted survey instruments. Soc. Sci. Comput. Rev. 18(4), 384–396 (2000). https://doi.org/10.1177/089443930001800402
14. Rabinowitz, A.: Communicating in three dimensions: questions of audience and reuse in 3D excavation documentation practice. Stud. Digit. Heritage 3(1), 100–116 (2019)
15. Huvila, I.: Improving the usefulness of research data with better paradata. Open Inf. Sci. 6(1), 28–48 (2022)
16. Opgenhaffen, L., Lami, M.R., Mickleburgh, H.: Art, creativity and automation. from charters to shared 3D visualization practices. Open Archaeol. 7(1), 1648–1659 (2021). https://doi.org/10.1515/opar-2020-0162
17. Champion, E., Bishop, I., Dave, B.: The Palenque project: evaluating interaction in an online virtual archaeology site. Virtual Reality 16(2), 121–139 (2012). https://doi.org/10.1007/s10055-011-0191-0
18. Hansson, K.: Metadata as imaginary demands: exploring metadata markets in digital heritage with speculative design. J. Assoc. Inf. Sci. Technol. (2023). https://doi.org/10.1002/asi.24806
19. Ulguim, P.: Models and metadata: the ethics of sharing bioarchaeological 3D models online. Archaeologies 14(2), 189–228 (2018)
20. Verran, H., Christie, M., Anbins-King, B., Van Weeren, T., Yunupingu, W.: Designing digital knowledge management tools with Aboriginal Australians. Digit. Creativity 18(3), 129–142 (2007). https://doi.org/10.1080/14626260701531944
21. Parke, E.: Australia's digital divide means 2.8 million people remain 'highly excluded' from internet access. In: Australia's Digital Divide Means 2.8 Million People Remain 'Highly Excluded' from Internet Access, vol. 2023, vol. 1 Online, ABC (2022)
22. Rennie, E., Yunkaporta, T.: Aboriginal communities embrace technology, but they have unique cyber safety challenges. In: The Conversation (Australia), vol. 2023. vol. 1. The Conversation, Online (2016)
23. Nishanbaev, I., Champion, E., McMeekin, D.A.: A comparative evaluation of geospatial semantic web frameworks for cultural heritage. Heritage 3(3), 875–890 (2020). https://doi.org/10.3390/heritage3030048

Digitising the National Collection

Anthony Cassar(⊠)

Technology and Experience Development Unit, Heritage Malta, Villa Bighi, Kalkara, Malta
digitisation@gov.mt

Abstract. The digitisation of cultural heritage, particularly within national collections such as those of Heritage Malta, presents a blend of opportunities and challenges. The establishment of the Digitisation Unit has been pivotal in adopting 3D digitisation technology, which enhances the preservation and accessibility of the National Collection. However, the lack of common international standardised methodologies and procedures has led to inconsistencies in the quality and interoperability of 3D models.

This paper explores the critical differences between 2D and 3D digitisation, highlighting the advanced equipment and methodological complexities involved in 3D processes. It discusses the experiences faced during the digitisation of the National Collection, with a focus on item prioritisation and the need for robust strategies and standards. The importance of metadata and paradata, along with equipment and methodological challenges, are examined to illustrate the multifaceted nature of 3D digitisation. Despite these challenges, strategic actions such as developing internal guidelines, investing in storage solutions, and participating in initiatives like TwinIt! are identified as crucial for overcoming current barriers. The paper concludes that while the field of 3D digitisation is still evolving, the concerted efforts of institutions like Heritage Malta, coupled with ongoing innovations and standardisation efforts, hold promise for preserving and sharing cultural heritage with future generations, ensuring its accessibility and integrity in the digital age.

Keywords: Digitisation · 3D · Metadata · Paradata

1 Challenges of 3D Digitisation of Cultural Heritage in the Context of National Collections

1.1 Heritage Malta and the National Collection

Heritage Malta is the Maltese national agency responsible for managing, conserving and promoting Malta's cultural heritage. It was established as part of the Cultural Heritage Act of 2002, a legislative framework aimed at preserving and promoting Malta's rich historical and cultural assets. This act was a pivotal step in safeguarding the nation's heritage, recognizing the need for a dedicated body to oversee the conservation and management of Malta's national cultural and natural sites, museums and collections.

M. Ioannides et al. (Eds.): 3D Research Challenges in Cultural Heritage V, LNCS 15190, pp. 184–195, 2025.
https://doi.org/10.1007/978-3-031-78590-0_16

The Cultural Heritage Act of 2002 marked a significant milestone in the preservation of Maltese cultural heritage. Prior to its enactment, all aspects of the management and regulation of cultural heritage were centralised in the Museums Department, which became overstretched. The Act set up several institutions with specific duties. The primary purpose of this establishment was to ensure a coherent and effective strategy for the preservation, conservation, and promotion of Malta's cultural patrimony.

As the national agency, Heritage Malta's broad remit encompasses several key areas:

1. Museum Management: Heritage Malta oversees a network of 90 museums and historical/natural sites across Malta and Gozo, including public monuments, underwater sites, and prominent national and UNESCO-listed sites. These include the Prehistoric/Neolithic complexes including Hagar Qim, Ġgantija and the Hypogeum of Ħal Saflieni, the Grand Master's Palace, the National Museum of Archaeology, the National Art Museum, and the Malta Maritime Museum.
2. Conservation and Restoration: Heritage Malta is tasked with the conservation and restoration of Malta's historical sites and collections. This involves meticulous work to preserve buildings, monuments, and objects within the national collection ensuring they are preserved for future generations.
3. Research and Documentation: An essential aspect of Heritage Malta's work is conducting research and documenting historical artefacts and sites.
4. Public Engagement and Education: Heritage Malta prioritises public engagement and education with a visitor-centred vision, offering dynamic exhibitions, educational programs, and outreach activities to foster appreciation of Malta's cultural heritage. By making museums fun and interactive, the agency ensures cultural heritage is accessible and enjoyable, enhancing public knowledge and creating meaningful connections with Malta's rich history and traditions.

Heritage Malta is responsible for stewarding the national collection, which spans prehistoric artefacts to modern historical items and natural specimens. The agency ensures these treasures are conserved, documented, and made accessible to the public. Recently, Heritage Malta has also embraced intangible cultural heritage, incorporating diverse types of audiovisual content into its collection. By doing so, and by developing digital resources and collaborating with international institutions to share Malta's heritage with a global audience, Heritage Malta not only preserves the past but also ensures that the cultural heritage of Malta remains a vibrant and integral part of contemporary life.

1.2   The Setting Up of the Digitisation Unit

Heritage Malta's Digitisation Unit was set up in 2019 at the Malta Maritime Museum, funded by the Norway Grants. This represented a significant leap in preserving Malta's rich maritime heritage through modern technology. The Norway Grants provided approximately two million euros, with half allocated to civil works and the other half to setting up the digitisation studios. This initiative was crucial for digitising thousands of artefacts housed within the museum, which includes a diverse range of items such as paintings, navigational instruments, ship models, and intangible cultural heritage like oral histories (Norway Grants EEA, 2021).

Further investment from national funds expanded the digitisation unit's services to encompass the entire national collection, not just that of the Maritime Museum. Equipped with state-of-the-art technology, including high-resolution scanners, 3D laser scanning, photogrammetry, and videography, the unit aimed to create highly accurate digital representations of the cultural treasures entrusted to Heritage Malta. The setting up of the Digitisation Unit was underscored by its comprehensive approach to preservation, not only safeguarding physical artefacts but also enhancing accessibility and engagement through digital formats. This effort ensured that Malta's rich history is preserved and accessible to a global audience, fostering educational and cultural exchange (Heritage Malta, 2024; Norway Grants EEA, 2021).

A pivotal aspect of this project is the development of a Collections Management System (CMS), enabling Heritage Malta to meticulously catalogue and manage the national collection. The CMS facilitates detailed documentation and inventory control, enhancing the accessibility of digitised assets for both research and public use. This system ensures that digital archives are well-organised, easily searchable, and available for diverse applications, from academic research to public exhibitions. (Heritage Malta, 2024).

The newly established Digitisation Unit faces significant challenges in digitising millions of artefacts from the national collection. The vast array of items, including paintings, navigational instruments, ship models, and oral histories, require substantial time and resources (Heritage Malta, 2024). Additionally, the unit had to be created from scratch, necessitating the recruitment and training of a new team. This process was further complicated by the nascent stage of digital heritage studies as a career path in Malta, where digital heritage studies were just emerging.

The steep learning curve involved in mastering advanced digitisation technologies such as high-resolution scanning, 3D laser scanning, and photogrammetry further compounded the difficulties. The unit's staff had to quickly gain proficiency in these areas to ensure high-quality digital representations of the artefacts. This combination of high expectations, vast project scope, and the novelty of the field created a challenging environment that required substantial effort and perseverance to overcome (Norway Grants EEA, 2021).

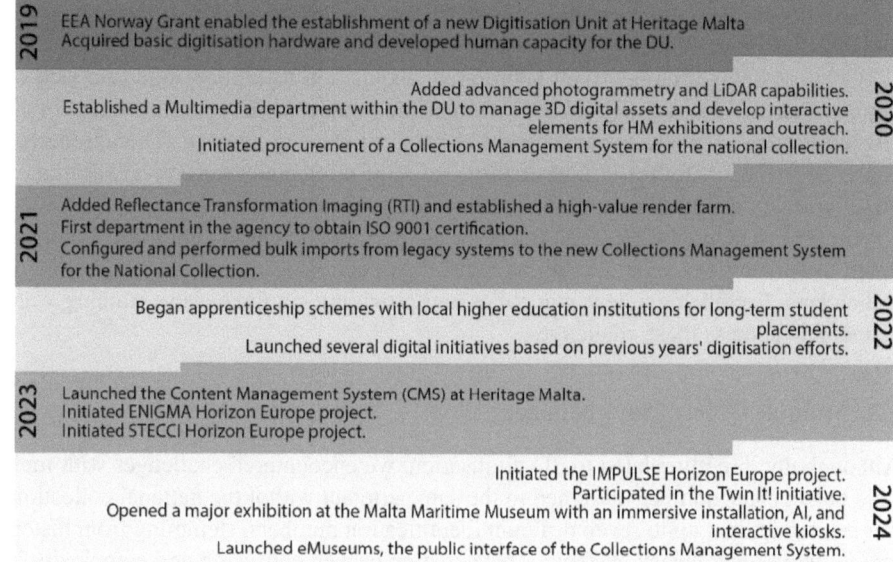

2 Experiences Faced When Digitising the National Collection

Digitising items from the national collection presented complex challenges necessitating strategic planning and collaboration among various stakeholders. The process required addressing technical and logistical considerations, prioritising items carefully, and adhering to standards and methodologies that were often underdeveloped.

2.1 Prioritisation of Items for Digitisation

A primary challenge was determining which items to digitise first. The extensive nature of the collections made prioritisation overwhelming, with curators and departments holding differing opinions on which items were most important. Selection criteria were crucial and multifaceted, involving historical significance, physical condition, demand for access, and relevance to ongoing projects. A coordinated approach was essential for a balanced digitisation effort.

Digitisation requests came from multiple sources, such as project-linked requests, curators' needs for exhibitions or research, and external requests. Managing these conflicting demands required a robust system to evaluate and prioritise requests, aligning digitisation efforts with the institution's strategic goals.

2.2 Challenges Due to Lack of Standardised Methodologies and Procedures

A significant challenge in the digitisation process was the lack of standardised methodologies for metadata, paradata, and acquisition techniques. Metadata and paradata ensure the usability and authenticity of digital assets, but inconsistencies and inefficiencies arose without clear procedures.

Curators often struggled with appropriate acquisition techniques due to a lack of digital expertise. This sometimes led to unrealistic or unsuitable requests, such as high-resolution scans of delicate manuscripts that risked causing damage. The absence of consistent standards for resolution, quality, and acquisition methods further exacerbated these issues, resulting in a haphazard digitisation process.

Uniform standards are crucial for ensuring the reliability of digital assets. Without them, the process varied in quality and usability, depending on individual curators or technicians. Establishing clear guidelines and providing comprehensive training were essential to address these challenges.

2.3 Multiple Object Entry Numbers

Although not directly related to 3D digitisation, we encountered challenges with multiple object entry numbers assigned to the same artefact within the national collection. Some artefacts had up to seven different identification numbers, stemming from historical initiatives and legacy systems. This situation caused confusion and complexity in managing and retrieving digital assets. Addressing this issue required a comprehensive review and consolidation of entry numbers to streamline the digitisation process and ensure accurate documentation.

2.4 Storage Space Challenges

Managing digital storage space posed a practical challenge, particularly with the growing number of 3D objects. The exponential growth of digital assets required substantial storage capacity, often exceeding the capabilities of existing server setups. Continuous requests for additional storage space were common, highlighting the need for a scalable and robust storage solution that could accommodate the growing digital collection.

2.5 Strategic Actions to Address Challenges

To address the need for a structured digitisation approach, the institution implemented several strategic actions. The institution adopted the European *Study on Quality in 3D Digitisation of Tangible Cultural Heritage*, providing a comprehensive framework for 3D digitisation and ensuring high-quality and consistent digital assets. Using standards like Spectrum and Dublin Core ensured systematic metadata and documentation management. This alignment facilitated aggregation certification with Europeana, improving accessibility and integration with European digital heritage initiatives. Significant investments in advanced storage setups ensured the necessary capacity, security, resilience, and safety for the growing 3D assets, acknowledging their increasing value and importance.

3   Moving from 2D to 3D Digitisation

Cultural heritage digitisation has evolved from 2D to 3D, offering enhanced detail and accuracy but posing challenges such as the need for specialised equipment, methodological changes, standards development, demanding post-processing, and storage and accessibility issues. Europe's perspective emphasises the importance of 3D digitisation for preserving cultural heritage, supported by initiatives like Europeana's *TwinIt* campaign. These endeavours highlight a commitment to addressing challenges and harnessing 3D technology to protect and disseminate Europe's diverse cultural heritage.

3.1   Equipment Challenges

Transitioning to 3D digitisation requires specialised equipment, unlike the more affordable and straightforward 2D scanners or cameras. Tools such as laser scanners, structured light scanners, and photogrammetry setups are expensive and require specialised training for proficient operation (Remondino, 2011). Moreover, maintaining and calibrating this equipment also demands higher technical expertise and additional resources, posing a significant barrier for smaller institutions.

3.2   Methodological Challenges

Transitioning from 2D to 3D digitisation requires a fundamental shift in methodologies. Unlike capturing a flat image, 3D digitisation records an object's geometric and surface properties, adding complexity. This complexity is heightened when scanning glossy, reflective, or transparent surfaces (Fig. 1). Techniques like photogrammetry and structured light scanning require meticulous planning and execution. Photogrammetry, for example, involves taking numerous overlapping photographs from various angles and processing them to create a 3D model, a time-consuming and precision-dependent process (Kersten & Lindstaedt, 2012).

4   The *TwinIt!* Experience

The European Commission's *TwinIT!* initiative aimed to use 3D digitisation to capture intricate details of cultural artefacts and heritage sites, creating a comprehensive digital repository for immersive experiences. It sought to standardise 3D digitisation practices across Europe, fostering collaboration and providing a framework for preserving and accessing cultural heritage. The initiative highlighted 3D digitisation's potential to revolutionise the documentation, sharing, and experience of cultural heritage, aiming to create a unified digital archive supporting education, research, and public engagement. (Europeana, 2023).

Heritage Malta's submission of the 3D model of the Ċittadella (Citadel) (Fig. 2) marked a significant milestone in the *TwinIT!* initiative. The Ċittadella, a historic fortified city in Gozo, served as a case study for 3D digitisation, showing how advanced digital technologies can capture intricate cultural heritage details. This initiative aligns with Europeana's objectives and demonstrates the practical benefits of 3D digitisation.

Fig. 1. HMS Hibernia Figurehead: Captured using photogrammetry with a Sony A6000 camera. Date: August 2021. Courtesy of Heritage Malta, Digitisation Department, Technology and Experience Development Unit.

Fig. 2. Drone photogrammetry using Autel Evo of the *Ċittadella*. Date: June 2023. Courtesy of Heritage Malta, Digitisation Department, Technology and Experience Development Unit.

Heritage Malta's proactive approach underscores its commitment to innovation in cultural heritage preservation. By being the first to contribute a 3D model, Malta sets a benchmark for other nations, showcasing the feasibility and value of 3D digitisation projects (Heritage Malta, 2023).

The *TwinIT!* initiative, though visionary, revealed several challenges related to 3D digitisation of cultural heritage. A key concern was the technical complexity in producing precise and high-fidelity 3D models. This endeavour necessitated advanced equipment, specialised expertise, and substantial resources, which were not universally accessible to all cultural heritage institutions (European Commission, 2023). Moreover, the standardisation of methodologies was crucial. Without consistent standards for resolution, quality, and metadata, the effectiveness of a unified digital archive could be compromised. The *TwinIT!* initiative addressed this by advocating for common practices, but the implementation of these standards across diverse cultural institutions remained a challenge (Europeana, 2023).

Heritage Malta's contribution to the *TwinIT!* initiative embodied the European vision for 3D digitising cultural heritage, which included preserving cultural artefacts and enhancing their accessibility and engagement potential. By creating immersive 3D models, Europeana aimed to make cultural heritage more engaging and educational (European Commission, 2023). The *TwinIT!* initiative reflected a forward-thinking approach to cultural heritage preservation, leveraging modern technology to safeguard the past for future generations. Heritage Malta's pioneering effort exemplified the collaborative spirit and innovation that Europeana aimed to inspire across Europe.

5 The Importance of Metadata and Paradata in 3D Digitisation

Metadata and paradata are crucial in digitising cultural heritage, ensuring the preservation, accessibility, and usability of digital assets. Metadata is structured information that describes, explains, locates, or facilitates the retrieval, use, or management of a resource. In cultural heritage digitisation, metadata includes the title, creator, date, format, and keywords, which are essential for cataloguing and retrieving digital assets. Paradata documents the processes and methodologies involved in creating, transforming, and preserving digital objects, particularly 3D models. It includes technical specifications, software used, digitisation decisions, and alterations. Paradata ensures transparency and reproducibility, allowing future users to understand the context and methods behind a digital asset's creation, which is vital as the fidelity of digital representations increases.

Documenting both metadata and paradata is essential in digitising of cultural heritage. Metadata ensures digital assets are searchable and identifiable within databases and repositories. Without comprehensive metadata, digital collections risk becoming inaccessible or difficult to navigate. Paradata is vital for 3D digitised cultural heritage assets, documenting the complex processes and decisions involved in creating 3D models through methods like photogrammetry, RTI, and multispectral imaging. It is not simply a case of documenting the hardware and software used, the settings and parameters chosen, but also documenting the rationale behind these choices and how multiple image sets have been compiled to form one model, as is increasingly the case today. Such detailed documentation ensures long-term preservation and potential re-creation of these assets from raw data captures, maintaining their relevance as technology evolves.

Metadata and paradata together enhance the usability, integrity, and longevity of digital cultural heritage collections. The Digitisation Unit, with its resources and expertise, manages its own 3D models in-house, controlling the entire workflow and advising curators on acquisition methods. This involvement allows detailed process documentation, stored and retrieved using Digital Lab Notebook software. This meticulous documentation and streamlined workflow contribute to advancing research and preservation efforts.

6 Current State and Limitations in Existing Standards of 3D Digitisation of Cultural Heritage

The 3D digitisation of cultural heritage has advanced, with many institutions adopting this technology to preserve and highlight historical artefacts. However, standardising 3D digitisation practices is still evolving. A significant challenge is the lack of standardised methodologies and protocols. Unlike 2D digitisation, which has established guidelines, 3D digitisation lacks universally accepted standards, leading to variations in quality and interoperability of 3D models (Guidi, Russo, & Beraldin, 2014). Without standardised procedures, it becomes difficult to compare, share, and integrate 3D data across different projects and institutions, hindering collaborative efforts and the broader usability of digitised assets.

6.1 Differences Between 2D and 3D Digitisation

The primary difference between 2D and 3D digitisation is the dimensionality of the captured data. 2D digitisation, such as scanning photographs or documents, captures flat images that are easier and cheaper to produce. In contrast, 3D digitisation captures an object's geometry, texture, and colour, providing a more comprehensive representation. (Balletti & Ballarin, 2019). It requires sophisticated equipment, software, greater storage capacity, and processing power. The resulting 3D models offer enhanced visualisation and interactive capabilities, making them particularly valuable for educational and preservation purposes.

6.2 Current Standards and Techniques

Various standards and guidelines ensure the quality and consistency of 3D digitisation. For example, the Europeana platform provides detailed guidelines for 3D documentation of cultural heritage, including metadata, file formats, and technical specifications to ensure interoperability and long-term preservation. (Guidi & Frischer, 2020). Techniques employed including photogrammetry, laser scanning, and structured light scanning have their advantages and limitations (Adamopoulos et al., 2020). Laser scanning is highly accurate but expensive, whereas photogrammetry is more cost-effective but less precise. Understanding the strengths and weaknesses of each method is crucial for selecting the appropriate technique and ensuring the highest quality digital preservation of cultural heritage.

6.3 Limitations and Challenges

Challenges in 3D digitisation include the absence of universally accepted standards, leading to variability in techniques and equipment that affects the quality and usability of 3D models (Cieslik, 2020). Additionally, the excessive cost of high-resolution scanning equipment and the technical expertise required for effective 3D digitisation pose significant barriers (Tausch et al., 2020). Moreover, integrating 3D digitised data into existing digital repositories and databases is complicated by differing file formats and metadata standards (Oruc, 2020). This lack of standardisation hinders the global sharing and dissemination of 3D cultural heritage data, limiting its accessibility and potential impact.

6.4 Post-processing Challenges

Post-processing in 3D digitisation is another area fraught with challenges. Converting raw data into a usable 3D model involves alignment, merging, cleaning, and texturing, all of which require specialised software and skills. Errors in post-processing can result in inaccurate or incomplete models, undermining the digitisation effort. Additionally, the process is time-intensive and often lacks automation, making human expertise crucial (Gomes et al., 2014).

6.5 Storage and Accessibility

The transition to 3D digitisation poses significant challenges in data storage and accessibility. 3D data files are larger than 2D images, necessitating more storage capacity and robust management solutions (Champion, 2015). Institutions like Heritage Malta must invest in high-capacity storage systems and establish strong backup and disaster recovery plans. Additionally, providing public access to 3D data is challenging, as it often requires specialized software or platforms, which may limit accessibility. Balancing accessibility with the integrity and usability of 3D models is a complex task.

7 Conclusion

The digitisation of cultural heritage, as demonstrated by Heritage Malta's initiatives, is crucial for preserving and promoting our collective heritage. By establishing a standardisation digitisation process and adapting to new technologies, institutions can greatly enhance the accessibility and preservation of cultural artefacts. Heritage Malta's dedication to emerging technologies and new techniques upholds high standards in digital acquisition, vital for the long-term integrity of these cultural treasures.

Moving forward, it is essential for cultural heritage institutions to collaborate on developing universal standards and guidelines for 3D digitisation. Such collaboration will ensure consistency in quality, interoperability, and long-term accessibility of digitised assets. Investing in technology infrastructure and ongoing training will help institutions overcome current challenges and fully leverage 3D digitisation. By embracing and leveraging technological innovations and international cooperation, the field of 3D digitisation can continue to evolve, preserving cultural heritage for future generations and expanding global access to these valuable resources.

Disclosure of Interests.   The authors have no competing interests to declare that are relevant to the content of this article.

References

Adamopoulos, E., Rinaudo, F., Ardissono, L.: A critical comparison of 3D digitisation techniques for heritage objects. ISPRS Int. J. Geo-Inf. **2**(5), 99–110 (2020). https://www.mdpi.com/2220-9964/10/1/10

Balletti, C., Ballarin, M.: An application of integrated 3D technologies for replicas in cultural heritage. ISPRS Int. J. Geo-Inf. **2**(5), 111–120 (2019). https://www.mdpi.com/2220-9964/8/6/285

Best Practices for Digital Heritage. https://www.unesco.org/new/en/culture/themes/digital-heritage/digital-heritage-best-practices/. Accessed 25 June 2024

Champion, E.: Critical Gaming: Interactive History and Virtual Heritage, 2nd edn. Routledge, Milton Park (2015)

Cieslik, E.: 3D digitisation in cultural heritage institutions guidebook. University of Maryland, USA (2020). https://www.academia.edu/download/79212093/3D-Digitisation-Guidebook.pdf

European Commission: TwinIT! Initiative. https://ec.europa.eu. Accessed 28 June 2024

Europeana: Europeana and cultural heritage. https://www.europeana.eu. Accessed 15 July 2024

Gomes, L., Bellon, O.R.P., Silva, L., Araujo, B.D.: 3D reconstruction methods for digital preservation of cultural heritage: a survey. Pattern Recogn. Lett. **50**, 3–14 (2014)

Guidi, G., Frischer, B.D.: 3D digitisation of cultural heritage. In: 3D Imaging, Analysis and Applications, Springer, Heidelberg (2020). https://doi.org/10.1007/978-3-030-44070-1_13

Guidi, G., Russo, M., Beraldin, J.A.: Acquiring 3D models with active sensors. In: 3D Recording, Documentation, and Management of Cultural Heritage, pp. 57–81. Whittles Publishing, Dunbeath (2014)

Heritage Malta: Ċittadella 3D model submission. https://www.heritagemalta.org. Accessed 15 July 2024

Kersten, T.P., Lindstaedt, M.: Image-based low-cost systems for automatic 3D recording and modelling of archaeological finds and objects. In: Ioannides, M., Fritsch, D., Leissner, J., Davies, R., Remondino, F., Caffo, R. (eds.) Progress in Cultural Heritage Preservation. LNCS, pp. 1–10. Springer, Heidelberg (2012). https://doi.org/10.1007/978-3-642-34234-9_1

Metadata and Cultural Heritage. https://www.dlib.org/dlib/january97/01weibel.html. Accessed 10 July 2024

Metadata Importance. https://www.ncbi.nlm.nih.gov/pmc/articles/PMC5980777/. Accessed 15 July 2024

Oruc, P.: 3D digitisation of cultural heritage copyright implications. J. Intell. Prop. Info. Tech. Elec. Com. L. **11**(1), 25–30 (2020)

Paradata in 3D Digitisation. https://www.culturalheritageimaging.org/What_We_Offer/Publications/paradata.html. Accessed 25 Oct 2023

Remondino, F.: Heritage recording and 3D modelling with photogrammetry and 3D scanning. Remote Sens. **3**(6), 1104–1138 (2011). https://doi.org/10.3390/rs3061104

Tausch, R., Domajnko, M., Ritz, M., Knuth, M.: Towards 3D digitisation in the GLAM sector: lessons learned and future outlook. IPSI Trans. Internet Res. **20**(1), 12–24 (2020)

Understanding Paradata. https://www.sciencedirect.com/science/article/pii/S1877050919312365. Accessed 12 July 2024

Author Index

A
Akhlaq, Sara 89
Alkemade, Henk 63
Ammirati, Luisa 36
Apollonio, Fabrizio Ivan 115
Argasiński, Karol 115
Attico, Dario 151

B
Bachi, Valentina 63
Bajena, Igor Piotr 115
Baker, Drew 12, 24
Barreau, Jean-Baptiste 164
Beck, Daniel 103
Brumana, Raffaella 151
Bruschke, Jonas 103

C
Cassar, Anthony 184
Champion, Erik 176
Charles, Valentine 63
Chayani, Mehdi 75
Chenaux, Alain 127
Codina, David Vivó 139

D
de Gruchy, Michelle 36
Depraetere, Marin 89
DezenKempter, Eloisa 127
Díaz, Verónica Díez 89
Dionizio, Rafael Fernandes 127

F
Fallavollita, Federico 115
Fernie, Kate 63
Foschi, Riccardo 115
Franczuk, Jakub 115
Ftaita, Amira 36

G
Genzano, Nicola 151
Gerganova, Maria Radoslavova 151

Granier, Xavier 75
Grellert, Marc 103

H
Heslinga, Lianne 63
Heumann, Ina 89
Huvila, Isto 1

I
Ioannides, Marinos 24
Isaac, Antoine 63

J
Jover, Agustí Costa 139

K
Karittevli, Elena 24
Keenaghan, Garrett 127
Koszewski, Krzysztof 115
Krajacic, Petra 127
Kuroczyński, Piotr 115

L
Laroche, Florent 75
Luengo, Pedro 139
Lutteroth, Jan 115

M
Medici, Marco 63
Meegan, Eimear 127
Mudge, Mark 52
Münster, Sander 63
Murphy, Maurice 127

P
Panayiotou, Panayiotis 24
Pla, Sergio Coll 139

Q
Quantin, Matthieu 75

M. Ioannides et al. (Eds.): *3D Research Challenges in Cultural Heritage V*, LNCS 15190, pp. 197–198, 2025.
https://doi.org/10.1007/978-3-031-78590-0

R

Reilly, Rebecca O.   127
Rigauts, Thomas   36
Roascio, Stefano   151

S

Schroer, Carla   52
Schwarz, Daniela   89
Sosa, Albert Samper   139
Stille, Wolfgang   103

T

Tournon, Sarah   75
Tsoupra, Eleftheria   63

V

Varela, Gerardo Boto   139

W

Wacker, Markus   103
Watrous, Bethany   36